THE BOYS IN GREEN

THE BOYS IN GREEN

The FAI International Story

SEAN RYAN

MAINSTREAM
PUBLISHING

EDINBURGH AND LONDON

DEDICATION

To all those footballers who wore the green jersey,
with honour, for Ireland – at any level

First published in Great Britain in 1997 by
MAINSTREAM PUBLISHING COMPANY (EDINBURGH) LTD
7 Albany Street
Edinburgh EH1 3UG

ISBN 1 85158 939 2

A catalogue record for this book is available from the British Library

Typeset in 11pt Berkeley
Printed and bound in Great Britain by Butler & Tanner Ltd, Frome

CONTENTS

Prologue

Jack Answers the Call

In the summer of 1985, Jack Charlton took stock of his lifestyle – and did not like what he saw. He had been in full-time football since May 1952, when he had signed for Leeds United as a teenager, but for the past 12 years he had been stuck on the managerial merry-go-round, the glory days of playing long gone.

Managing has always been a poor substitute for playing but, when you are 'football daft' as Charlton is, it is something you are glad to do, just to be involved. It had all started so well, guiding Middlesbrough to promotion as champions of division two in 1974 and picking up the Manager of the Year award in the process. He had also guided Sheffield Wednesday to promotion from division three, but he soon learned that the price you have to pay as a manager takes a toll, even if you are football daft.

He had now come to the conclusion, after a relatively short time in the job (he became manager of Newcastle in 1984), that there was too much work and too much travel involved in managing Newcastle United. His initial enthusiasm had waned and, pursuing his philosophy that life is too short to be stuck doing things you are not enjoying, he was ready to get out. All he needed was an excuse.

The excuse was handed to him on 10 August in a surprising way. Newcastle were playing Sheffield United in a pre-season friendly and, with his team winning 1–0, Charlton decided to bring on some of his untried players. As he did so, a section of the crowd started shouting, abusing him for his refusal to bid for Eric Gates, who had just been signed by north-east rivals Sunderland.

Newcastle fans always tend to think that their manager should spend big money to install a new legend at St James's Park, but Charlton thought differently. He had always been careful about money and he wasn't prepared to bid for every 'name' player who came on the market.

Annoyed by the fans' abuse, Charlton stormed out of the ground after the game, announcing his resignation. Stan Seymour, the Newcastle Chairman, told him not to be 'such a great big baby', but three days later Charlton confirmed his decision, the cooling-off period apparently reinforcing his conviction that it was time to get out.

A phone call to his home asking him to contact Robert Maxwell was ignored. Maxwell was looking for a manager for Oxford United, but Charlton showed no interest. He had had his fill of club management. He would not be idle, or short of money, but as far as football was concerned he was taking a much-needed break. It would require a very special job to entice him back.

A month later, on 11 September, in Berne, the Republic of Ireland had to settle for a 0–0 draw with Switzerland, which left their World Cup hopes depending on wins over the Soviet Union (away) and Denmark (home). Manager Eoin Hand's job was on the line.

When the Soviet Union duly won 2–0 in Moscow on 15 October, it was the end of the '86 World Cup trail for the Irish. Quizzed about Hand's position during a press conference on the flight home from Moscow, FAI President Des Casey was on the defensive and gave nothing away. Privately, he decided it was time to give an airing to his belief that a UK-based manager was needed.

The response to Casey's promptings proved positive. There was a feeling among the majority of the members of the FAI executive that, as they were relying on UK-based players, the time had come to appoint someone of the calibre and experience that those players would respect.

A disastrous 4–1 home defeat to Denmark on 13 November gave added impetus to Casey's suggestion and the die was cast at an executive meeting on 22 November when the decision to headhunt was taken. Casey and Dr Tony O'Neill were instructed to contact as many suitable candidates as possible, and arrange a weekend in England to interview them. They would report back to the executive on their findings, putting in order of preference those they felt best suited the job.

This was a move tinged with desperation by the FAI whose finances were in a bad way. Dependent as they were on international match receipts for the bulk of their funds, the team's lack of success had caused attendances to plummet. A loss of £20,164 had been returned at the AGM and an even bigger loss was on the cards now that the team had been eliminated from the World Cup.

This explains the near crazy schedule which Casey and O'Neill undertook, cramming as many interviews as possible into one weekend. They concentrated on managers with a recent track record, an exception being the former Manchester United and Scotland wing-half Pat Crerand.

On Friday, 6 December, the FAI headhunters flew into Manchester Airport and conducted their first interview at the Excelsior Hotel. The person they interviewed was Jack Charlton, who explained how he had become disenchanted with management at club level but, if the Irish wanted him, he would do the job. The pragmatic Charlton spoke about what was required; the way he would approach the job if appointed; and how he would prepare the team.

In his opinion the Irish talent had not been fully exploited, and his appraisal of the squad impressed both Casey and O'Neill. The question of salary was not a problem as far as Charlton was concerned. This job was an ideal challenge – and would not interfere with his other pursuits.

The headhunters moved on to Manchester's city centre where they interviewed Pat Crerand before heading down the M6 for a meeting with Gordon Lee in the Knutsford Service Station. In pouring rain, visibility was so bad that a wrong turn was inevitable but the interview finally took place among the truckers and other M6 transients who frequent motorway cafés.

A more civilised venue, the Crest Hotel in North London, was arranged for Terry Neill's interview at 11p.m. that night. An attempt was also made to contact Brian Clough but Nottingham Forest were not keen.

On Saturday morning the headhunters, their cover blown, suffered the worst jibes the English tabloid press could throw at them. Casey and O'Neill were portrayed as knocking on people's doors and offering a £60,000 salary.

Fortunately, those interviewed treated the job in a more responsible manner. All showed a lot of respect for the Republic of Ireland, and pinpointed matters which could help the FAI's relations with the clubs.

After taking in the QPR–West Ham game, where they sat next to England manager Bobby Robson, the FAI duo's next appointment was with Theo Foley at his home in Blackheath. Foley had been in Hull with the Millwall team so the interview was scheduled for midnight. Casey, who was driving, took another wrong turn on to the Dover Road, prompting the droll O'Neill to surmise about a ferry crossing and an approach to French manager Michel Hidalgo, who was available at the time!

Sunday morning saw the intrepid pair in Peterborough to see Noel Cantwell, and then it was on to hotels in the Birmingham area for separate meetings with Billy McNeill and Johnny Giles.

Later that week, Casey was in touch with the Nottingham Forest Chairman who made it clear that his board were not in favour of an approach to Clough as they felt the Irish job would conflict with his position at Forest.

On 13 December, an advertisement was placed in the Irish newspapers inviting applications. A token gesture to the home-based hopefuls, it nevertheless produced applications from the likes of Alan Mullery, John Bond and Tommy Docherty.

The home-based applicants – Liam Tuohy, Jim McLaughlin, Ray Treacy and Paddy Mulligan – were interviewed by either Casey or O'Neill and on 20 December they presented the FAI executive with a comprehensive report. The three most favoured candidates were Charlton, McNeill and Giles, with Tuohy the leading home contender. A decision was made to defer consideration of the matter because McNeill's position was unclear.

At this stage, maintaining confidentiality was a big problem. At one stage, Casey and O'Neill felt they could not report to the executive committee any more as the information was bound to appear in the newspapers the following day. Giles was a victim of the leaks. Unhappy at being part of a highly publicised managerial rat-race, he announced his withdrawal.

The council were expected to vote on the position of team manager at their meeting on 10 January, 1986, but Casey announced afterwards that 'the Executive recommended that the appointment be deferred', explaining that clarification was still sought in regard to some of the candidates. Questioned by the media, he conceded that there was a short list of three – McNeill, Tuohy and Charlton.

The previous day he had flown to Manchester for a meeting with Peter Swales, Chairman of Manchester City, and Freddie Pye, another director, to discuss an arrangement by which McNeill would be made available to take over the Irish team.

The clarification which the FAI sought was in relation to the financial compensation which City would require when McNeill had to absent himself from Maine Road on Irish team business. While Casey and O'Neill were not asked to make a recommendation, it appears that McNeill was their number one choice and, by definition, the number one choice of the FAI.

However, the terms of compensation suggested by City proved to be prohibitive: their conditions for McNeill to become Irish manager were not considered practical or feasible by the FAI. McNeill himself was not convinced by the FAI offer. 'They were offering me a part-time job and, when I thought about it, I felt it wouldn't be on. I wanted the day-to-day involvement with the club and, with two jobs, I would have fallen between two stools.'

Shortly after, McNeill fell out with a number of the City directors and moved on to Aston Villa – 'the biggest mistake of my life'. However, he made it clear that his move had nothing to do with City's demands which thwarted the FAI's bid to land him as manager.

With McNeill a non-runner, Casey and O'Neill arranged another interview with Charlton. This took place in a Manchester hotel on 20 January, and, as a result, they decided to push for his appointment. However, convincing their colleagues on the executive committee was another matter.

Prior to the crucial vote at the executive meeting on 7 February, there were two further developments: Giles was persuaded to re-enter the race by friends on the council and Casey learned that Bob Paisley, the former Liverpool manager who had earlier indicated that he was not interested, had changed his mind and was back in the running.

When Giles, on the eve of the meeting, was tipped in some of the papers as the new manager and was reported to be coming over to Dublin, Casey endeavoured unsuccessfully to get in touch with him to let him know that he was by no means home and dry. Giles travelled and was in Dublin when the executive voted on Hand's successor.

In a highly charged atmosphere, 18 men sat down in the council room in 80 Merrion Square: Des Casey, Pat O'Brien, Liam Rapple, Charlie Walsh, Joe Delaney, Milo Corcoran, Tony Byrne, Noel Heavey, Pat Grace, Dr Tony O'Neill, Fran Fields, John Farrell, Michael Hyland, Charlie Cahill, John Sullivan, Pat McFadden, Pat Quigley and Jack Smith.

Casey, as President, first put forward the motion that Giles be allowed back in the running, and this was agreed. He then sought the acceptance of Paisley as a candidate, a motion which came as a surprise to many of those present but which was also passed, even though Paisley had not been interviewed.

A secret vote was taken: nine were for Paisley, just one short of the majority he needed, and three for each of the other candidates, Giles, Charlton and Tuohy. This clearly showed a preference for a UK-based manager.

After a complex series of five secret votes, during which Giles and Tuohy were eliminated, Casey and O'Neill finally got their way when Charlton was appointed on a 10–8 vote to acclamation from all the council members present, with the exception of Grace and Byrne, who had been pressing Giles's case. The closeness of the voting suggests that, had he declared his interest earlier and been available for interview, Paisley might well have got the nod over Charlton.

In the week before the vote, Charlton had said of the Irish squad: 'A lot of them have gone past their best. They should have qualified over the last few World Cups when the draw was not particularly hard on them. They lacked a couple of players and that was probably their downfall. One or two of your best players have maybe four or five years left and then it will be a matter of finding someone to replace them.'

When asked what attributes he saw himself bringing to the job, he replied with no false modesty: 'I know the game inside out. I've been involved with football all my life and I've been a staff coach with the FA since I was 26. Every club I was with has prospered.' He saw the Irish job as a new challenge and asserted: 'I wouldn't take it unless I thought I could produce something.'

To the disappointment of the FAI and the media, Charlton was not contactable when Casey telephoned to tell him of his appointment. But the new manager wasted no time in getting to grips with the job, taking in the Liverpool–Manchester United league game on 9 February. Six of his squad were in action: Mark Lawrenson, Ronnie Whelan and Jim Beglin (Liverpool) and Paul McGrath, Kevin Moran and Frank Stapleton (Manchester United).

His first press conference in Dublin on 12 February was marked by a degree of euphoria hitherto unheard of in Irish soccer. Expectations had been raised to new heights by his appointment and he made it clear that qualification for World Cup or European Championship finals was his target.

He hinted that the Republic might have to adopt a new style of play, more akin to that of Northern Ireland, and he also felt that the squad was short of talent up-front and on the right side of midfield.

A tip-off from Dave Langan that Oxford United's prolific striker John Aldridge was eligible for Ireland, sent Charlton to the Manor Ground where Aldridge informed him that Ray Houghton was also eligible. Charlton promptly persuaded the two of them to throw in their lot with Ireland.

The pieces of the jigsaw were coming together nicely. Now, if only he could get some time with the squad, Charlton felt he could almost guarantee qualification for the final stages of a major competition. Once again he was in luck. An invitation arrived at Merrion Square for the international team to take part in a tournament in Iceland at the end of May.

1

With Foreign Office Approval

When the Republic of Ireland departed for the World Cup finals in Italy in June 1990, the official party of over 40 included 22 highly paid, full-time professional footballers, a manager, assistant manager, coach, physio, kitman, interpreter and assorted other officials. In addition, they were followed the length and breadth of Italy by up to 20,000 green-and-white bedecked followers. Meanwhile, their achievements gave rise to deserted streets at home as the nation lent its support through the medium of television. It was quite a contrast to that St Patrick's Day 64 years earlier when an FAI squad departed from Dublin for Italy to take part in the country's first international.

Instead of the flight from Dublin Airport and a month-long preparation in Turkey and Malta which the Italia '90 stars enjoyed, the boys of '26 departed from Westland Row railway station *en route* for Dun Laoghaire and a sea crossing to Holyhead. They stopped the following night (Thursday) in Paris before resuming their journey by train to Lausanne, where they stayed on Friday night, arriving at their destination, Turin, about six o'clock on Saturday evening, less than 24 hours before a game that was so vital to the infant Association.

There was no big complement of officials accompanying the players while, of the latter, five had been in action on the day of departure in the FAI Cup final in which Fordsons surprised Shamrock Rovers 3–2. The Fordsons representative, James 'Sally' Connolly, carried a vivid memento in the shape of an ugly looking black eye. After a five-year-long wait for this first international, the players' lack of preparation, plus the fact that all were part-timers, did not augur well for their chances against the Italians.

The split with the Belfast-based Irish Football Association in 1921 had been triggered by many things, one of which was dissatisfaction with the selection of international teams. Four 'Southern' players was the maximum allowed on any IFA team. However, by setting up their own association, the FAI did not automatically qualify for international status.

Despite opposition from the English FA, orchestrated by the IFA and supported by the Spanish FA, the FAI was accepted as a member of FIFA in September 1923, but only after an emergency committee had consulted with

13

the British Foreign Office on the Free State's status. A direct result of this was that the FAI changed its name to FA of the Irish Free State (FAIFS).

In October, a conference of the international board in Liverpool decided to accept the FAIFS as an Association 'with Dominion status', and gave permission for British clubs to play in the Free State. This led to visits from the Welsh League and Celtic, and a team was also sent to the 1924 Olympic Games in Paris.

The dream of an all-Ireland team had not been lost, and a conference on 8 March, 1924, came very close to agreement – the IFA's insistence on a permanent Northern Ireland chairman of the international selection committee proving the stumbling block.

Despite encouraging results at the Olympics (a defeat of Bulgaria and an extra-time loss to Holland), there was no indication of full international action until the Italian offer was made in September 1925. The FAIFS did play the USA Olympic team in Dublin on the latter's way home from Paris for a guarantee of £200 but the lack of interest in this out-of-season fixture can be measured by the receipts (£257) compared to those secured by the visit of Celtic (£1,232), who were paid £480 and were obviously worth every penny of it. The Celtic match went a long way towards paying the cost (£837) of sending the 16 players, trainer and five Olympic Committee officials to Paris.

By the time the FAIFS annual report for 1925 came out on 29 July, the IFA position regarding internationals had hardened. While they were prepared to allocate games alternately to Dublin and Belfast, they would do so only on condition that the FAIFS waived any claim to a share of the receipts from the Dublin games, a suggestion which was promptly rejected.

After the Belgian FA indicated that, through lack of finance, they could not make a trip to Dublin, the breakthrough came at a Council meeting on 30 September 1925, when a letter was read from the Italian FA offering a game in Italy the following March. A letter of acceptance was sent even before terms were discussed and when the Italian terms finally arrived in December they were omitted for some reason from the minutes.

It was fitting that Italy should be the first opponents for, as FAI Vice-President Robert Murphy recalled, it was the determined efforts made by the Italian representatives that secured the election of the Free State at the FIFA Congress in 1923.

'At a moment when a letter had been read from the English FA threatening to disturb international friendly relations if our claims were conceded, the representatives of Italy and Switzerland, placing right before might and justice in front of expediency, paved the way for the recognition of our claims,' he wrote in *Football Sports Weekly*.

Selecting a team was not easy. There were very few Free State-born players in the UK leagues and no club would be willing to release a player for over a week in mid-season. It was, therefore, left to the League of Ireland to provide the talent to take on Italy.

Of the Free State-born players who were with English clubs, most, like Jimmy Dunne at Sheffield United, Harry Duggan at Leeds United and Tommy Muldoon at Aston Villa, were confined to the reserves. Of the obstacles facing Irish players, one was psychological, as described by Charlie Dowdall, a talented inside-forward who had been on the books of Swindon Town and Barnsley.

'It was very difficult for me to believe that I could be as good as the English players and that's why I never did myself justice in England,' he recalled. When he played against Sheffield United reserves this feeling of inferiority was compounded by the sight of the great Jimmy Dunne languishing in the same league. While Dunne stuck it out and eventually made the breakthrough to first division football, a disillusioned Dowdall quickly returned to Ireland.

The main talking point when the team was announced was the absence of Shamrock Rovers' prolific goalscorer Billy 'Juicy' Farrell, who had dominated the charts for the previous two seasons. He had disappointed in an interprovincial game during which he was hindered by a hip injury suffered the previous day in a 6–1 Shield win over Brideville to which he contributed a hat-trick.

Farrell played that day against advice and his own better judgement and effectively lost his place on the Irish team through his loyalty to his province. Fate was not kind to him – later that summer, he was involved in a motorbike accident which ended his career.

The centre-forward spot went instead to Athlone Town's Ned Brooks, who had scored a hat-trick against the United States in 1924 and who had, as a Shelbourne player, been capped by the IFA against Scotland in 1920. However, Brooks, who had a short spell as a professional with Stockport County, was denied his international cap in tragic circumstances. A week before the team was due to depart for Italy his seven-year-old son Harold was knocked down by a car and died in hospital. This let in reserve centre-forward Fran Watters (Shelbourne), whose selection ahead of Farrell was just as controversial.

Another controversial choice was right-back Frank Brady (Fordsons), a grand-uncle of Liam Brady. Brady was in dispute with his club, having been dropped for a Cup replay against Shelbourne on 16 January. He took no further part in his club's successful Cup campaign and did not regain his place until after his return from Italy. However, during the time he was out of favour at Fordsons, he played for the League of Ireland in a 3–1 defeat of the Irish League, a performance that obviously influenced the selectors.

Two football 'legends' travelled to Italy – right-half Mick 'Boxer' Foley (Shelbourne), who was captain, and Shamrock Rovers' inside-left Bob 'Give It To Bob' Fullam. Both were at the veteran stage, Foley, 34, having made his English league debut in September 1910 for Leeds City. He played over 100 games in a six-year spell with Leeds before returning to his first club, Shelbourne.

Fullam, 29, made his name with Rovers, spending only one season abroad at Leeds United. While not very pacy, he was renowned for the accuracy of his passing with his left foot, and the power of his shooting; also for his great understanding with John 'Kruger' Fagan and his leadership – he hated losing so much that a bad result could move him to tears.

The team that finally stepped out at the Stadio Communale in Turin on 21 March 1926, consisted of three civil servants, three casual dockers, two employees of Henry Ford, a bookmaker, an Army officer and one member of the unemployed. Goalkeeper Captain Harry Cannon and left-winger Fagan were also veterans of the Free State's War of Independence.

Amateurs Cannon, left-back Jack McCarthy, Dowdall and reserve Paddy 'Dirty' Duncan received inscribed gold medals to the value of three guineas to mark the occasion and the professionals were paid a fee of £5.

The Italians advertised the game on cinema screens, at railway stations and hotels and cafés up and down the country. They were banking on a record attendance after victories over Czechoslovakia and France but were sorely disappointed when heavy rain limited the crowd to 12,000. In fact, the first paragraph of the match report in *Corriere della Sera* was devoted to berating the untimely arrival of the rain.

Italy scored through inside-right Baloncieri after just 13 minutes, the second goal was delayed until the 36th minute, when inside-left Magnozzi was on target and centre-half Bernardini completed the scoring a minute before half-time.

While the Irish camp suggested that the Italians could not add to their tally due to the good work of Cannon and Brady in particular, the writer in *Corriere della Sera* was not so complimentary. 'A huge difference in class divided the two teams,' he reported, adding that 'our goal was never seriously in danger through the merits of the Irish.'

The financial side of the tour was not a success either, according to *Football Sports Weekly*, because 'Free State football is not recognised as first class'. The writer also made the point that, in future when teams go on tour, matches should not be played until at least two days after arrival.

The players were not given much respite, stopping on the return journey to play Cercle Athletique de Paris under the name Irish Nomads on Wednesday, 24 March. The game finished in an honourable draw, with Fullam opening the scoring for the Nomads in the first half and French international Langellier equalising with four minutes left.

When the Irish captain, Foley, applied on behalf of the players for extra pay in respect of this game, the request was turned down at a council meeting on 22 May. However, the meeting decided to give each of the 14 players an international cap.

The accounts show that the trip to Italy cost £683 and was principally responsible for a loss of £53 for the season. The Italian FA contributed very little – £100 at most – but there was the promise of a return game in Dublin in 1927.

Unlike the army of media people who accompanied the Republic to Italia '90, there was not a single reporter on that trip in 1926. The *Irish Independent* depended on a telegram from FAI official Bob Murphy for its report which was naturally brief and was included on a news page. The preview of the game, while acknowledging that it was 'the most momentous event in the short history of Free State soccer', was limited to about 250 words.

At a meeting on 26 October, it was decided to accept 23 April 1927 as the date for the return game 'notwithstanding that Italy had also an international with France on 24 April'. It was clear what the Italians thought of Free State football. Their B team made the trip to Dublin while their A team played a 2–2 draw with France in Paris.

The game has always been regarded as a full international by the FAI, but while the visitors' team contained only three players new to international football – Juventus forwards Munerati, Vojak and Pastore – it included only one member of the squad that was chosen to play Ireland in Turin, Padova defender Barzan, and on each occasion he was only a reserve.

The FAIFS approached the Irish Rugby Football Union to hire Lansdowne Road for this first international in Dublin in 14 years. Terms were agreed at a minimum guarantee of £150 and 10 per cent of receipts over £1,500. Prices of admission were set at five and four shillings for the stands, three shillings for the touchline and uncovered stand and one shilling on the terraces. Admission was by ticket only.

For the first time the selectors called on players based in Britain and straightaway ran into the problems that were to plague successive selectors and managers: players defecting. The first defection occurred when goalkeeper Tom Farquharson had to cry off as he was playing in the FA Cup final for Cardiff City the same day.

Two other players were forced to withdraw – the legendary Patsy Gallagher (who had only recently left Celtic for Falkirk) and Tony Hunston (Chelsea). They were replaced by one of the greats of Irish soccer, the veteran Billy Lacey, who had returned to Shelbourne after an honours-laden career with Liverpool, and Christy Martin, who had come to prominence helping Bo'ness win promotion to Scotland's first division and had scored a hat-trick against Clydebank the previous Saturday.

Lacey, 37, had helped Liverpool to successive League titles in 1921–22 and 1922–23, and had a remarkable record at international level. He was first capped by the IFA in 1909 and gained his last cap from the FAI in 1930. A native of Enniscorthy, Co Wexford, he filled practically all eleven positions for the IFA in 23 internationals, including three in one famous game against Scotland in Belfast in 1914 when the British Championship was won for the first time. In his three appearances for the FAI, Lacey lined up at outside-right, inside-right and right-back.

Frank Brady captained the side from left-back but most interest centred on centre-half Mick O'Brien, who had been transferred from Hull City to Derby

County for £3,000 a few months previously. A native of Kilcock, Co Kildare, O'Brien played no soccer until he was 18 when his family moved to South Shields. He then became something of a wanderer, accumulating 17 clubs in a 22-year career which was interrupted by a spell in the Navy and Royal Flying Corps during the First World War. He was with a different club on each of the four occasions he was capped by the FAI.

A well-built six-footer, he was a highly regarded centre-half and was capped on 10 occasions by the IFA. He had also lined up at inside-left for a Football League XI against the Army in 1921, scoring twice, indicating that, like Lacey, he was another good all-rounder.

The attendance was reported as a disappointing 20,000 by the papers, although the FAIFS report recorded it as approximately 28,000. To Fullam fell the honour of scoring the home team's first goal at this level, crashing the ball into the net after a Martin shot had rebounded to him in the sixth minute.

The Irish led until early in the second half when the Italians were helped by the use of a substitute and the home side's refusal to do so. When a Fullam piledriver from a free-kick laid out full-back Zanello just before half-time he was replaced by Barzan, but when wing-half Muldoon was injured, the Irish selectors simply rejigged the team, with Fullam going to left-half and Muldoon finishing the game a limping passenger on the left-wing.

Another factor in Italy's victory was their willingness to 'soften up' the opposition with short-arm jabs on the referee's blind side. Martin, who was small in stature, became a little cautious when he saw what he was up against, but the fiercely competitive Fullam was not as submissive.

Italy's right-winger Munerati proved the matchwinner with goals in the 52nd and 81st minutes, both from passes by club colleague Pastore, but the second was of the 'soft' variety, goalkeeper Frank Collins allowing a poorly hit shot from 20 yards to slip under his body.

Ernie Mackay, who had played with Collins in the first IFA junior international side to win in Scotland in 1921, said that a war wound which rendered Collins slow to get down on his right side may have been responsible for the Italian winner.

The disappointment of the Irish supporters at losing was alleviated to some extent, by a masterly display from O'Brien, who had shaken off a bout of flu to play.

'O'Brien is one of those players who can be labelled great,' enthused the writer in *Sport*. 'What magnificent grace and ease he introduces into his football. His display was a treat and still one got the impression that he held something in reserve.'

For the council of the FAIFS there was also the good news that international matches could be profitable. Receipts amounted to £1,660 and, while expenses ate up £1,409 of this, the balance of £251 was a nice profit. The main expenses were monies due to Italy and included a guarantee of £208 and the cost of their travel, £265. Ground rent to the IRFU amounted to £302, while the Irish team's travel expenses and wages came to only £109.

After their Italian experience, the FAI turned to Belgium, playing them in three successive years, twice away, and winning each time. Belgian football was not of a very high standard, being mainly amateur, but the games offered worthwhile experience for the FAI's small pool of players.

The game in Dublin on 20 April 1929, marked the FAI's first international at Dalymount Park, the ground which was to become synonymous with the big-match scene until its position was usurped by the more commodious Lansdowne Road in the 1980s.

It also marked the first international appearance in his native city of goalkeeper Tom Farquharson, who had been forced to leave Dublin because of his Republican sympathies during the War of Independence. A student at the time, he had been arrested, along with his friend Sean Lemass, later to become Taoiseach, for pulling down British Army posters in St Stephen's Green. This proved embarrassing for his father, who did a lot of business with the British so, after Tom had been released on bail, he was packed off to work in Blackwood in the Welsh valleys.

Although he had won a Leinster Minor Cup medal with Annally, Tom first took up rugby, until Welsh League side Oakdale were short of a goalkeeper one day and he offered his services. From there he moved to Abertillery for season 1921–22 but finished the season at Cardiff City, playing in the final game of what was their first season in division one.

He went on to make a record 445 league appearances and helped win the FA Cup in 1927. He was capped seven times by the IFA before winning a further four caps for the FAI and also represented the Welsh League against the League of Ireland.

During his career, Farquharson became known as the 'Penalty King' for his many fine saves of spot kicks. He liked to move about his line to unsettle the taker. It was the success of this ploy, adopted by many keepers through the years, which ultimately led to a change in the laws of the game with the goalkeeper no longer permitted to move until the kick had been taken.

Jimmy 'Snowy' Dunne, so called because of his blond hair, made his long awaited debut for the FAI – he had already been capped by the IFA – the following year on 11 May in Brussels when, with two goals and a brilliant all round display, he tantalised the Belgian defence and led Ireland to a 3–1 win.

Dunne, 25, had just completed his first season as a regular with Sheffield United – having waited patiently since his transfer from New Brighton in 1926 – and had scored 36 goals in 39 games, hitting four goals in successive games in January, a feat which put him on a par with the big names of the day such as George Camsell, Dixie Dean and Hughie Gallacher. His goals helped Sheffield avoid relegation from division one on goal average.

As the first Irishman to figure so prominently in the English scoring charts, he was idolised by football fans in Ireland. In the 1930–31 season he scored 41 goals for Sheffield United, which is still a club record.

The Irish team in Brussels was probably the strongest yet fielded. There were no defections and it included four England-based players – Dunne, Farquharson, O'Brien (then with Norwich City) and Harry Duggan (Leeds United).

This game marked the last international appearance of the great Billy Lacey, just four months short of his 41st birthday, the oldest player ever capped by the FAI. He travelled as reserve with the Irish team to Spain the following year and his final involvement was as coach.

After their fine win, the professionals requested a bonus, pointing out that it was the custom to give spending money to teams playing on the Continent. Their request was turned down on the grounds that the gate did not ensure more than the guarantee and, therefore, the trip was a financial loss.

The good news was that Spain had applied for a game the following season. This was the jackpot in more ways than one as the Spanish FA agreed to a home and away series, the first game to take place in Barcelona on 26 April 1931, with the return in Dublin the following 13 December.

The terms for the trip to Spain of half receipts (after all taxes) with a guaranteed minimum of £650 were attractive – for the first time the Association could look forward to making a profit on an away game – but there was a slight doubt about the game. A revolution was threatening to interfere.

However, even revolutionaries like their diversions and the game went ahead, the Irish team departing from Dublin on Monday, 20 April. Travelling by boat and train, they did not arrive at their destination until the following Friday and at one stop along the way – Bordeaux railway station – the players amused themselves by kicking a paper football around the platform while waiting for their connection.

The team contained only two cross-channel players – goalkeeper Farquharson, who captained the team, and left-winger Peter Kavanagh (Celtic), who had turned down a second cap from the IFA in order to travel. Of more significance was the inclusion of Shamrock Rovers' 21-year-old centre-forward Paddy Moore.

Moore was a happy-go-lucky type of fellow whose brilliance as a schoolboy was such that, wherever he played, he attracted a crowd. He had carried this crowd appeal into senior football, first with Richmond Rovers, then Shamrock Rovers, before signing for Cardiff. At 19, he was probably too immature for that scene but he took up the challenge of re-establishing himself when he returned to Rovers, and his first cap was a fair indication that he had succeeded.

Before the game, Farquharson asked, on behalf of the players, if any bonus could be paid. He was informed by the officers present that they had no power to pay anything outside the agreed wages but promised that the matter would be placed before council on their return.

A wildly enthusiastic Catalan crowd packed the stadium and the Irish faced a team full of confidence following a recent 0–0 draw with Italy. Adding to the fervour of the home crowd was the presence of eight Catalans in the Spanish team, including goalkeeper Zamora, said to be one of the highest-paid players (£50 a week) in the world.

So it was a major surprise when Moore gave the visitors the lead after 35 minutes with a cool exhibition of finishing. Receiving from John Joe Flood, he was in a one-to-one situation with Zamora and coolly lobbed the ball over the keeper's head into the net. So disgusted was Zamora that he tore off his jersey and threw it into the back of the net, suffering the derision of his own fans.

Ireland's lead did not last long, Spain equalising following a goalmouth mêlée before half-time. Rain made the conditions greasy for the second half which was a more even affair but, with minutes to go, the Portuguese referee took a hand.

Farquharson, having made a save, braced himself for a challenge from an incoming forward who bounced off the goalkeeper. The referee immediately awarded a penalty to the disgust of the Irish who protested en masse. The Spanish fans sympathised with the Irish to the extent that, when Farquharson made a great save from the penalty, they cheered him lustily for several minutes.

From the clearance, Kavanagh made a break down the wing and, as Zamora advanced, his shot hit the post and went behind. As soon as the goalkick was taken, the final whistle was blown.

It was a tremendous result and the fixture also proved to be a money-spinner for the FAI, who received £1,243 as their share of the receipts. This, as much as anything, was responsible for the FAIFS granting the players their request for a bonus.

A total of £122 was paid out in wages and bonuses to the players and trainer who travelled to Spain, with £39 or £3 a head accounting for the bonus. There was no chance of similar largesse from the return game at Dalymount Park, even though it attracted a record crowd of over 30,000, thanks largely to the FAI experimenting for the first time with a Sunday kick-off. The receipts were less than for the initial foray into the international scene in 1927 and left a profit of only £182.

Sunday had its drawbacks as a match day. Jimmy Dunne and Derry City's Ballybofey-born outside-left Jimmy Kelly were not released, owing to their clubs' scruples about Sunday play. Harry Duggan was also refused permission to travel, while Paddy Moore was injured. Sunday internationals also meant that cross-channel players could be in action on Saturday and then face an all-night boat journey before lining up in Dublin. Farquharson had to travel overnight from Cardiff after assisting his team to victory over Clapton Orient in an FA Cup tie.

Most interest centred on former Celtic legend, Patsy Gallagher, playing out his career with Falkirk who released him at the end of the season. A thin, wisp of a player, he was under 5ft 6ins and barely over seven stone when he played his first trial for Celtic in 1911.

Patsy – he hated the name, preferring to be called Paddy – spent 15 years with Celtic, winning four Cup and seven league medals and 15 IFA caps and earning the nickname 'The Mighty Atom' for his energetic displays. His dribbling skills were legendary but he was undoubtedly chosen on this occasion as a crowd puller for he no longer had the pace or stamina required of an inside-forward. It was a sad end to a glorious career.

Lacey had been appointed coach but he had little chance to leave his imprint as he was unable to get in touch with all of the players until the morning of the game. The subsequent 5–0 defeat prompted one commentator to suggest that team selection be left to the coach and that he be given time to get the players together and have a few practice matches. Little did the writer know that it would take 40 years of failure to convince the selectors to relinquish control and that it would take a UEFA initiative – scheduled international dates – to swing the pendulum further in favour of Ireland.

As Spain had been beaten 7–1 by a rampant England at Highbury the previous Wednesday, the outlook for the Irish was not promising, and the glow which had emanated from the 1–1 draw in Barcelona evaporated, leaving the FAI contemplating a start-all-over-again policy.

2

A Push too Far

'Football Unity At Last', read the headline in the *Irish Independent* on the morning of Thursday, 3 March 1932. 'IFA Agree to FS Proposals', read a secondary heading. A special meeting of the IFA in Belfast the previous night had 'unanimously approved' the requests of the FAI for 'a Joint Committee of equal representation from the IFA and the FAIFS, with alternate chairmen to control international matches and the net profits or losses in each year to be divided equally'.

The background to this sensational development began at the international board meeting in Gleneagles on 13 June 1931, when a motion to change International qualification was defeated. Had it been passed, the motion would have limited the IFA to selecting only players born in Northern Ireland. The debate was enhanced when Tom Farquharson decided to make a stand by declining the IFA's invitation to play against Scotland on 19 September.

This development, plus the suggestion made by the English FA of a conference between the Scottish, Welsh, Irish and English Associations with the FAIFS, helped to concentrate minds north of the border.

In November the IFA wrote requesting permission to select Free State-born players for the amateur international against England on 7 November. Council refused permission. The previous year, three Free State players – Fred Horlacher, Jimmy Bermingham and Alec Morton (all Bohemians) – had been selected and had contributed handsomely to a 3–1 win, the first in 18 years. However, they did so at some cost, as they were subsequently suspended for three months by the FAI, who had instructed them not to play.

The FAI's hard line was having some effect, and the English FA felt the ground was secure enough for it to opt out of the conference, leaving it to the two Irish Associations to get together, but promising to be available to help out later if needed.

Saturday, 13 February 1932 was the date chosen for the first meeting, with Dublin the venue. Nine delegates were chosen to represent the FAIFS: T.J. Murray, J.L. Brennan, M. Murphy, L.C. Sheridan, J.I. Wickham, A. Byrne, J. Younger, E.J. MacDonnell and S.R. Prole. At the IFA's insistence, the meeting was not open to the press.

It was a major achievement on the part of the delegates to secure agreement on the two issues which had, as recently as 1924, been thrown out by the IFA. No wonder that, as the *Independent* reported,'elation showed on the faces of members of the Council of the FAI' when the IFA decision was telephoned to their meeting in Mary Street on Wednesday, 2 March.

Little wonder, too, that columnists like NAT in the *Evening Herald* wrote: 'So Ireland, for the purpose of international soccer, is to be one and undivided again . . . The IFA delegates were obviously impressed by the arguments and inducements elaborated on behalf of the Free State; that their Council were convinced there would be a financial gain is demonstrated by the readiness with which the proposals were unanimously accepted.'

'Ralph the Rover' in the *Belfast Telegraph* accorded the new move a guarded welcome: 'Probably what weighed more than anything was the fact that there are something like 600 clubs in membership of the Free State whereas the IFA doesn't reach the 200 mark. Representation, therefore, on an All-Ireland Council would be more than two to one in favour of the South and everybody knows exactly what that would mean.

'Perhaps the pact arrived at is the best move possible so far as the North is concerned. We must all accept it and do our bit in making the arrangement work as smoothly as possible.'

Alas, it proved a false dawn, for when the Conference resumed in Belfast on 12 March to finalise arrangements, it broke up in disagreement and relations between the two bodies which, nine days earlier, had been positively fraternal, were reduced to outright animosity, with football once again the loser.

The cause of the split was the FAI's bid for a place on the international board on which the IFA had two representatives. Having given in on so much, there was no way the IFA were going to give in on this issue as well and they were backed up by the Scottish FA who responded to an appeal from the FAI by pointing out that they, the FAI, could not expect to have double representation on the Board as they were already represented on it by FIFA.

The FAI's contention was that, in view of its willingness to accept an equal share in the finance and administration of international fixtures, it should be entitled to one of the IFA seats on the board. In hindsight, the FAI were like children who, having been given a sweet, persist in asking for more. The door to unity was ajar but, in pushing, they pushed too far and it swung back in their faces.

'Ralph the Rover' outlined the concessions the IFA had made: 1) to let the FAI have half the gate receipts; 2) alternate chairmen from north and south; 3) equal representation on the Committee to govern Internationals; 4) internationals to be played alternately in north and south. 'But having got what they wanted in 1924 they now start looking for something else. It was the same in 1924'.

It is easy to sympathise with the IFA view, but the great progress which they had made since 1924, especially on the international front, plus the fact that football was attracting better support in Dublin than in Belfast, probably prompted the FAI to adopt an aggressive attitude to the talks, when a diplomatic approach may have borne more fruit.

At their AGM in June, they proceeded to exacerbate the situation by banning all matches between teams under their jurisdiction and teams under the IFA's jurisdiction. One of the principal casualties was the inter-league series which had proved an ideal test for future international players. As the series was not resumed until 1938, a vital source of supply was cut off at a time – encompassing their first two World Cup campaigns – when the FAI selectors had most need of it.

The two bodies never again came as close to achieving a unity which is the desire of all true Irish soccer followers. The men who sat around the table in Belfast on 12 March 1932 were tantalisingly close to making history, but they rejected the opportunity and the fall-out is still being felt.

Meanwhile, with a guarantee of £500, the FAI set off for Amsterdam to play Holland on 8 May 1932. Their travel expenses amounted to just over £437, while the wages of the players and trainer, Val Harris, came to £76. Apart from the amateurs, the players were paid £8 for the honour of representing their country.

A junior international played against Scotland at Falkirk the previous October had a bearing on the selection, for two of the junior team's stars moved into League of Ireland football. Corkman Mick McCarthy, 22, lined out in goal for Shamrock Rovers and inside-forward Alec Stevenson for Dolphin. Shortly before their international call-up, they were on opposite sides in the FAI Cup final, with McCarthy coming out on top.

For the skilful Stevenson, 19, there was adequate compensation ahead. On his return from Holland, he was snapped up by Glasgow Rangers where he enjoyed a successful spell before being transferred to Everton where he won an English league medal in an outstanding career.

Surprisingly, while he was always made available for the IFA during his time at Everton, he had to wait until he was at the veteran stage after the Second World War before he lined up again for the FAI. Puzzled by this, Stevenson approached both Everton secretary–manager Theo Kelly and FAI secretary Joe Wickham for an explanation but neither was prepared to offer one. Stevenson, who was a Protestant, was accused in some quarters of refusing to play for the FAI on religious grounds, but he was adamant that religion had nothing to do with it – on his side, at any rate.

Right-winger Billy Kennedy, who kept a comprehensive diary, wrote before the game: 'Our team is very young and on the light side. The rumour has gone round Amsterdam that we are a soft thing for Holland. Looks are deceptive.' How right he was.

Trainer Val Harris put the players in the right frame of mind with what passed for a team talk. 'Pat O'Callaghan put the tricolour flying high here in the 1928 Olympics,' he said, 'and it's up to you lads to see that it's still flying high this evening.' They proved inspirational words from the old international.

The Irish opened the scoring after 20 minutes, Moore touching in a long drive from Joe O'Reilly. With Mick O'Brien playing a commanding role at centre-half, there was no further score until the 51st minute when Moore, from a centre by Kennedy, shot from 20 yards, a goal that brought the 30,000 crowd to its feet.

After that, the brilliance of keeper McCarthy ensured there was no comeback for the Dutch. But, for all his heroics, he was never capped again, getting into the frame only once more – as travelling reserve in 1939 to Hungary and Germany.

This win by a young team was a welcome boost to the morale of all concerned. On their return to Dublin, three of the team were signed by Aberdeen, who paid less than £1,000 for Moore, O'Reilly and full-back Jimmy Daly. With Stevenson going to Rangers, Jimmy Dunne firmly ensconced as a leading light in the English first division and Harry Duggan finally making the breakthrough at Leeds United, the FAI had never had such a strong hand.

Unfortunately, the flow of continental matches stopped and, with games against England, Scotland and Wales not yet an option, the international arena was closed to the FAI at a critical period.

The council meeting in January 1933 considered an invitation from FIFA to participate in the 1934 World Cup competition. The matter was referred to the finance committee which recommended acceptance.

The only international football the Free State's players experienced after the Holland game, and prior to the World Cup, was under the auspices of the IFA. Stevenson, Duggan, Moore, Dunne and Kelly were all capped and, on one occasion (against England at Blackpool on 17 October 1932) the latter four all played in the forward line.

Although England won 1–0, the IFA selectors retained the team *en bloc* for the next game against Wales on 7 December. However, injury prevented Moore and Duggan taking their places so the Blackpool game remains the only time the great Dunne and Moore played together at this level.

When the draw was made for the World Cup, the FAI was paired with Belgium and Holland, with two to qualify for the finals in Italy. In view of earlier results, Ireland seemed sure to take its place in the finals – and that was the view of the three countries involved. A council meeting in September 1933 was told that Holland and Belgium objected to being grouped with Ireland. It appeared they considered the Free State too strong.

Later the Dutch and the Belgians offered £1,250 and £500 respectively to the FAI to play the games in Amsterdam and Brussels. The FAI held out for one home game and at a conference in London on 7 January 1934 terms were agreed, with the FAI paying Belgium £500 to play in Dublin and Holland paying the FAI £650 to play in Amsterdam. It was also agreed that, before half-time, the goalkeeper and two players could be substituted in the event of serious injury and, after half-time, only the goalkeeper could be replaced.

Council put their Cup competition first when, in January, they turned down the offer of a game against Czechoslovakian club Sparta on 24 January because of the League of Ireland clubs' involvement in the FAI Cup. Instead, a trial game was arranged for 14 February – 11 days before what should have been regarded as the most important game in the FAI's history.

Joe O'Reilly, who played in 20 of Ireland's 30 pre-war internationals, including all four World Cup ties, recalled: 'The World Cup at that time meant nothing to me. It was just another international.' Joe's carefree approach reflected the official attitude.

Meanwhile, England's ongoing dispute with FIFA and their annoyance at the FAI's failure to clamp down on Irish clubs signing disaffected English league players without compensation (a practice which became known as the 'Open Door'), put the cat among the pigeons as far as the FAI were concerned.

Co-operation suddenly became non-existent as the *Evening Echo* reported: 'The attitude which the English FA has taken in regard to sanctioning release of players is no great tribute to them – they have refused permission to several clubs to release players although the clubs were quite willing.'

When the FAI wrote to the English League, the League replied that clubs under its jurisdiction had been instructed not to release any of their players who might be wanted by the Free State FA for the World Cup.

Fortunately, this sanction did not extend to Scotland where Aberdeen manager Paddy Travers not only released O'Reilly and Moore for the Belgian game but also accompanied them on the overnight trip to Dublin as he was aware that Moore, who scored for Aberdeen that afternoon in the 2–2 draw with Celtic at Parkhead, had developed a drink problem that would eventually end his career prematurely.

The FAI's cause was further undermined by a lack of co-operation from within their own ranks. Shamrock Rovers were the culprits, including two of the World Cup team – right-back Peadar Gaskins and right-half William 'Sacky' Glen – in their side for a league tie against Drumcondra, 24 hours before the biggest game in the Association's history. This resulted in a crisis at noon on the day of the match when Glen, who had pulled a leg muscle in training on Tuesday and made little impression in Rovers' game on Saturday, failed a fitness test.

The selectors had two reserves: Cork Bohemians' left-back Jeremiah Lynch and Shelbourne inside-forward Johnny Squires. With time running out, they opted for a defensive re-shuffle which saw Gaskins switched to right-half and Lynch promoted to right-back. This resulted in the defenders being at sixes and sevens for the first half, with a notable improvement in the second half when Gaskins switched with centre-back Joe O'Reilly.

By that time they had been further hit by injury, with inside-left Tim O'Keeffe reduced to passenger status on the wing. Why the selectors did not replace him as the rules allowed is a mystery, especially as the Belgians replaced left-winger S. van Eynde when he broke his leg.

The matter of Gaskins and Glen playing on the eve of a World Cup tie was dropped after a discussion at council on 7 March – with no censure or penalties applied to either the club or individuals concerned. This again indicates that the importance of the competition had not yet registered.

Rovers, by way of explanation, stated that they had expected a postponement but, when the League decreed that the game must go ahead, they were faced with having to give a walkover or play the two players due to lack of substitutes. That club and players should have been put in such an invidious position suggests a strange lack of co-operation between the League and its parent body, the FAI.

The game against Belgium will always be remembered as Paddy Moore's match, but it did not start well. Belgium shot into a 2–0 lead after 26 minutes before Moore got his first chance a minute later. Then, receiving from O'Reilly, he feinted to create the space before shooting to the net.

The mood in the dressing-room was sombre at half-time, for the speedy Belgians had given the Irish a chasing, but Moore, in his own cheeky way, cheered up his team-mates with a 'Don't worry, lads, I'll fix things up in the second half.'

However, the Belgians increased their lead two minutes after the break. Within a minute Moore responded with a dazzling run from the centre circle for his second goal and, 11 minutes later, a conversion of a Jimmy Kelly cross to level the scores. Another quick Belgian raid gave them a 4–3 lead in the 66th minute, substitute F. van Eynde notching his second goal.

Nine minutes later, with the crowd in a fever of excitement, Ireland forced a corner. Kelly's kick was cleared but only as far as Joe Kendrick who lobbed it back for Moore to jump in ahead of the defenders for a dramatic equaliser – and a place in the record books as the first player to score four goals in a World Cup tie.

When Holland thrashed Belgium 9–3 on 11 March in an annual friendly fixture, the signs were ominous for Ireland's visit to Amsterdam on 8 April. The Dutch team to play Ireland contained only one change from that side and had a wealth of experience, their players boasting a total of 123 caps, while the Irish could only muster 26 caps between them.

Once again the English League's ban played havoc with the selectors' plans. Farquharson was the original choice in goal but he had to be replaced by Jim 'Fox' Foley of Cork, while Willie Fallon also fell victim to the ban when he was called up to replace the unavailable Jimmy Kelly. Paddy 'Woodener' Meehan (Drumcondra) took Fallon's place, being effectively third choice outside-left.

Cork's Tim O'Keeffe, who had played against Belgium and who was the winger in form, was not considered because of a misdemeanour after the Dublin game. One of the Belgian players reported that his wallet had been stolen and it was eventually found in the possession of O'Keeffe. As a result, the FAI had no option but to ban the Corkman from international football. While this ban was subsequently lifted in 1938, his eventual tally of three caps was not a true indication of his ability.

Aberdeen once again came to the rescue, releasing Moore and O'Reilly, but there were three newcomers to international football on the team – Meehan and inside-forwards Johnny Squires (Shelbourne) and Billy Jordan (Bohemians).

The FAI received a fee of £650 and, with expenses of £497 and players' wages of £78, they recorded a tidy profit. However, had they held out for a percentage of the receipts they would have done far better as the game aroused unprecedented interest.

The attendance of 38,000 was 7,000 more than the previous record, with the receipts being a massive £13,010. The Olympic Stadium's capacity of 33,000 was sold out, with temporary stands erected to accommodate another 5,000 fans. Tickets which had cost three and four guilders changed hands for 25 and 30 guilders on the morning of the match.

It took the home side 42 minutes to open the scoring through Smits and, two minutes later, Squires equalised when Moore created the opening. Moore gave the Irish the lead 12 minutes after the re-start when he forced goalkeeper van Male over the line following a Billy Kennedy cross.

Then, in the 68th minute, Bakhuys equalised with a disputed goal. Foley pushed out a Dutch shot for what the Irish defenders thought was a corner but Bakhuys, playing to the whistle, got the ball at the back line and shot in to the roof of the net. Then came a late surge of Dutch goals, with Bakhuys (79 minutes), Vente (83 minutes) and Smit (87 minutes) on the mark.

Billy Kennedy recorded in his diary: 'I don't know how it happened and I am trying yet. What a beating and I thought we had the game well in hand when we were winning 2-1.'

Fred Horlacher (Bohemians) became Ireland's first substitute just before the interval when he replaced club colleague Jordan who was taken off after wrenching his ankle in a tussle with Vente. While Jordan felt he was fit enough to continue, his plea to remain on the field was ignored by the selectors, who were probably mindful of the criticism they had received for not replacing O'Keeffe against Belgium.

Ireland's hopes now depended on Holland repeating their 11 March six-goal defeat of Belgium when they met on 29 April. But that hope proved illusory as Holland could only manage a 4–2 win in Antwerp, allowing Belgium to qualify, along with their Dutch neighbours, on goal difference.

Thus Ireland's first World Cup venture, hindered from start to finish, ended on a losing note. Neither Holland nor Belgium made any impression at the finals in Italy, both going out in the first round: Belgium lost 5–2 to Germany, while Holland were beaten 3–2 by Switzerland, results which only seemed to confirm that the wrong teams had gone through.

With four years to prepare for the next World Cup finals, the FAI had plenty of time to get their house in order but, apart from a more regular supply of internationals – thanks to FIFA's intervention – there was little evidence of a sustained plan. In fact, the FAI became increasingly bogged down in a war of point-scoring with the IFA which ultimately proved fatal to their hopes of a World Cup breakthrough.

Hungary visited Dublin on 16 December 1934, and the following May the FAI undertook their first continental tour, with games against Switzerland and Germany, but the problems concerning the release of players from English clubs persisted.

Hungary aroused a lot of interest as they had beaten England 2–1 in Budapest in May. The FAI paid a fee of £700 to entice them but, even with a crowd of 25,000, made a profit of less than £200.

Wholesale changes saw Ireland field a team which included only four previously capped players – Foley, Moore, Gaskins and Horlacher. Despite that, they gave a very good account of themselves, being beaten by two goals scored in the last six minutes at a time when they had only 10 men and a full-back whose mobility and enterprise had been restricted through injury. In addition, the Irish team's preparation was confined to 'a cup of tea and a chat in the Gresham Hotel before the game' as centre-half Charlie Lennon recalled.

New cap, Dundalk's Joey Donnelly, very nearly did not get into Dalymount Park, being refused entry by the Bohemian club commissionaire. His player's pass had not arrived before he left home.

'I insisted I was going in whether he liked it or not because I was not going to lose my £8 match fee – that was a lot of money in those days,' recalled Donnelly.

The selectors retained six of the team that played Hungary to go on tour the following May. That number was increased to seven when Donnelly was called up to replace the injured Paddy Farrell (Bohemians). Only one English club was represented – Manchester City, who released reserve full-back Leo Dunne.

Instead of choosing a squad, the selectors named a team and three travelling reserves. One of the latter, Jimmy Daly (Shamrock Rovers), got a surprise call-up for the first game in Basle on 5 May when Moore, having imbibed too freely on the journey from London, was declared unfit. Daly, a right-back, slotted in at outside-right in the subsequent re-shuffle. In the circumstances, a one-goal defeat was no disgrace.

A back-in-favour Moore was recalled to action three days later against Germany in Dortmund and, although he was unlucky not to score when he hit the post with a header, he was not at his best. Goalkeeper Foley was once again Ireland's hero, keeping the eager German forwards at bay for long periods.

Ireland opened the scoring in the 19th minute when captain Peadar Gaskins shot in to the net but 13 minutes later Damminger equalised and the same player sent the 35,000 crowd wild when he scored again in the 47th minute. Lehner added a third for Germany two minutes from time.

German magazine *Kicker* noted that the Irish attack was 'very dangerous' and had plenty of chances during the 90 minutes, but was inclined to spoil a lot of its good work with 'uncontrolled high balls into the German penalty area'.

Ireland were playing only their 13th international when they met the

Germans, for whom it was number 111, with 53 of those played in the years it had taken the FAI to play 13. The tour, undertaken for a fee of almost £600, most of which was paid by the Swiss FA, resulted in a loss of £129. On the plus side was the promise of return games the following year.

The selectors decided to institute a home-based international panel under coach Billy Lacey for the game against Holland on 8 December 1935. They intended the panel to form the nucleus of future international teams but found it difficult to agree on a team from the 27 panellists, eventually going outside for centre-half Paddy Andrews (Bohemians), outside-left Joe Kendrick (Dolphin) and centre-forward Moore, who hadn't been fit enough to play in the final trial.

In terms of preparation, the team did better than usual, with Lacey putting them through their paces at Dalymount on Monday and Wednesday, and giving a tactical talk on Friday. However, Holland's superior speed, passing, shooting and stamina won the day 5–3, although Ireland contributed to their own defeat by missing a penalty when the scores were level at 3–3 shortly after half-time. In addition, the Dutch team's use of obstruction, which would have resulted in free-kicks in Ireland or England, was allowed by the German referee as the practice was permitted on the Continent.

With five games lined up for 1936, the FAI were entitled to think that they had at last found their niche in international football. This may explain their decision to mark the game against Switzerland at Dalymount Park on St Patrick's Day with a statement aimed at the IFA which did nothing for the cause of reconciliation. For the first time, the FAI used the term Ireland instead of Irish Free State, stating that this was done to stop misrepresentation by the IFA, who still claimed the right to select players from any part of the country.

The game also marked the first international appearance in Dublin of the great Jimmy Dunne. His presence undoubtedly added thousands to the attendance which, at 32,300 (receipts £1,967), beat the previous record and earned the FAI a handsome profit after they had paid the Swiss their guarantee of £530.

Also contributing to the big attendance was the date, the national holiday. When the FAI applied to reserve the same date for 1937 they were refused by the League of Ireland on the grounds that it would be required for an inter-league game. Once again, the tail was wagging the dog, with the FAI, the senior body, being put in its place by the League.

The crowd got the result they wanted and it was secured by the man they had come to see, Jimmy Dunne. For Dunne, who had been interned for his Republican activities by the Free State authorities during the civil war, it was a triumphant return to his native city where he had suffered rejection in the past.

As a young player with Shamrock Rovers he had been confined to the reserves by the form of the prolific Billy 'Juicy' Farrell, but his scoring feats prompted one scout to recommend him to New Brighton, claiming that he was sending over 'a future Ireland centre-forward'. That was in November 1925, and while

31

he made an instant impact at New Brighton, when he was transferred to first division Sheffield United the following February, it was the start of another apprenticeship in the reserves.

He had to wait three years for his chance in the first team – at one stage Sheffield put him on their transfer list – but when it finally arrived he took the first division by storm, setting a club record before moving to Arsenal in September 1933 for a fee of £8,250. Sheffield United were relegated the season Dunne left for Highbury.

Derry City left-winger Jimmy Kelly had the unique experience of playing for two victorious Ireland teams within a week, having lined out for the IFA in a 3–2 defeat of Wales in Belfast the previous Wednesday.

When the selectors named their team to play Hungary and Luxembourg on their second continental tour in May, Kelly was first choice left-winger but he had to be left out against Hungary because of the IFA's ban on Sunday football. Willie Fallon deputised.

Once again the players faced a long and difficult overland trip, leaving Dublin on Tuesday and arriving in Budapest on Friday. On these tedious train journeys, the usual form of relaxation was a game of cards and a sing-song led by Jimmy Dunne who always brought his button accordion.

A party of 16 players travelled under the care of trainer Jerry McCourt (Dundalk). Injury problems suffered on the first tour had alerted the FAI to the need for reserves, and they had reason to be grateful for that lesson when Owen Madden picked up an injury against Hungary and took no further part in the tour, returning to Norwich City for treatment.

Madden was immediately plunged into controversy when it was revealed that he had signed for Norwich along with Jackie O'Reilly, before playing in the Cup final for Cork on 19 April. When Cork protested over the players' moves, for which they had received no fees, the FAI suspended the players and they were omitted from international consideration for three years, being reinstated to play against Hungary in Cork in 1939, when Madden declined and O'Reilly was not selected. Madden, who did win one cap from the IFA, never got another chance, but O'Reilly was capped after the war.

The 3–3 draw with Hungary on 3 May was a contrast in styles: Hungary's short passing against the Irish team's use of long passes out to the wings. Hungary took an early lead but two goals by a very in-form Dunne and Donnelly put the visitors in front at half-time.

Sarosi, who had opened the scoring, levelled matters two minutes after the break from the penalty spot after Con Moulson handled. Dunne restored Ireland's lead in the 68th minute, only for Sas to equalise five minutes later.

On Wednesday, 6 May, the Irish took on a Rhineland XI in Cologne before an attendance of over 10,000. With three changes, they went under 4–1, with Dunne again on target and Donnelly being presented with a Man of the Match trophy.

The final game, on Saturday, 9 May, was in Luxembourg and, with Dunne and

Kelly each netting twice and Donnelly also on target, the Irish recorded a 5–1 win. This was a record score which was to stand for almost 50 years.

For captain William 'Sacky' Glen, the tour marked the end of his international career. He linked his sudden loss of favour to a difference of opinion with new Shamrock Rovers' owner Joe Cunningham.

'When the Cunninghams took over Rovers that year I got out,' he recalled, 'and after I left Rovers I never got another cap so maybe I sacrificed my international career for my principles.'

Cunningham went on to become an important power-broker within FAI circles and if he used his muscle to end Glen's international career it would not be the last time that a club owner influenced selection.

Scoring five goals against Luxembourg was one thing, but to score five against Germany was something else. Yet that is what a depleted Irish side managed at Dalymount on 17 October.

The only new cap was centre-forward Tom Davis, then in the process of setting a club record of 33 goals at Oldham Athletic and reputed to possess the hardest shot in the north of England.

The row with the IFA intensified when the FAI let it be known that they were now claiming the right to select players from any part of Ireland. The selectors backed up the claim by selecting Derry-born Hugh Connolly (Cork) at left-half. He thus became the first player born outside the 26 counties to be capped by the FAI. An attempt was also made to secure Wolves' Belfast-born right-winger Jackie Brown but he was injured. The IFA resolved to raise the matter with the international board, a move which was to cause difficulties later on for the FAI.

The team was in the charge of Billy Lacey, and he managed to have most of the squad for training at Dalymount on Thursday evening.

The Germans, meanwhile, although beaten by Scotland on Wednesday, had turned in a dazzling display orchestrated by inside-left and captain Szepan, quickly nicknamed Saucepan by the Irish fans. They made history by arriving at Baldonnel aerodrome by Junkers airliner – the first international team to arrive by air – while 400 supporters arrived in a 20,000-ton cruise liner replete with Nazi flags and favours. The Nazi presence was also evident on match day when the Germans stood to attention giving the Nazi salute while the Army band played their national anthem.

The 5–2 Irish victory was undoubtedly the most glorious in the brief history of the FAI, with Paddy Moore, playing possibly his greatest game, the home side's mastermind. He had a direct influence on four of the goals and he provided the generalship which Szepan had been expected to provide for the Germans.

Dr Otto Nertz, the German manager, said afterwards: 'The German government has been sending me to Highbury to study football technique but they should have sent me to Dublin to watch Paddy Moore'. The following day Moore lined up for Shamrock Rovers against Cork and turned in another brilliant display, scoring twice in a 6–1 win. Sadly, there were not to be too many more of these vintage displays from the Ballybough genius.

The selectors were so keen to keep the same team for the game against Hungary on 6 December, that they chose to overlook the fact that Moore had not played for some weeks due to injury. The only changes were at left-half – where Connolly was replaced by Con Moulson – and at outside-left where the injured Mattie Geoghegan gave way to Willie Fallon. An attempt was made to secure IFA international wing-half Billy Mitchell (Chelsea) but the IFA's appeal to the international board bore fruit and Chelsea refused to release the player.

In order to stage the game on a Sunday, the FAI had to have the approval of the League of Ireland, and offered a sum of £160 as compensation. The League held out for £170.

Five of the six cross-channel players were in action on the Saturday and had to endure a trip to Dublin by boat that night. It was a stormy passage and all except Fallon complained of sickness when the boat arrived two hours after its scheduled time. Left-back Bill Gorman had reported to Dublin on the Thursday.

Hungary, who had lost 6–2 to England at Wembley on the Wednesday, made six changes, and included six of the team which was to reach the 1938 World Cup final. A crowd of 27,000 were treated to what was probably the most exciting international seen in Dublin since 1927.

The selectors' gamble in playing Moore did not pay off in what proved to be his last international appearance. He was not helped by an incident in the 28th minute when he came into contact with O'Reilly's boot. He was off the field for five minutes getting treatment for a cut over his eye and, during the interval, he became drowsy and had to be shaken up to resume, probably suffering from a mild form of concussion. He never fully shook off its effects in the second half, while his eye wound was still giving trouble two days later.

Referee Nattrass from England said after the game: 'Ireland might have got a second penalty in the second half when your inside-left (Moore) was fouled, but he was in a scoring position and I played the advantage rule and he failed to use his chance.' Even when not fully fit, Moore was still a danger, but his injury pointed up once again the FAI's unwillingness to use substitutes.

Fallon, who opened the scoring, was one of the home team's successes, with Donnelly and O'Reilly also to the fore. The Irish made a great contest of this game, coming from 3-1 down after 48 minutes to bombard the Hungarian goal. But they had only a penalty converted by Tom Davis to show for their efforts thanks to the heroics of the visitors' two goalkeepers, Palinkas, who had to retire hurt, and Szabo, his replacement.

This spirited display augured well for the future – if the selectors were able, or willing, to keep the team together in the run-up to the World Cup qualifiers.

3

The Tommy Breen Affair

Although it was a year in which Ireland played two World Cup qualifying ties, 1937 will always be remembered as the year of the Tommy Breen affair. Breen started his senior career with Newry Town before taking his goalkeeping skills to Belfast Celtic and, from there, in November 1936, to Manchester United.

He was rated as one of the best goalkeepers Ireland had ever produced by renowned scout Billy Behan, one of his Old Trafford predecessors. However, the 1936–37 season was not a happy one as United, who had been promoted as champions from division two the previous season, went straight back down again despite his best efforts.

Breen was already an established IFA international, but he was chosen by the FAI for their continental tour in May only when first choice Jim 'Fox' Foley was ruled out with a leg injury.

For a guarantee of 60,000 francs (£600), the FAI had agreed to travel to Paris for a game on 23 May and had also arranged a game with Switzerland six days earlier. With the World Cup games in the autumn, the tour offered an excellent opportunity to prepare a squad. However, the selectors preferred to prove a point to the IFA.

Three players born north of the border – John Feenan (Sunderland), Jackie Brown (Coventry City) and David Jordan (Wolverhampton Wanderers) – were selected, causing apoplexy in IFA circles. The IFA view was that the selection of the three players by the FAI was a breach of the agreement reached at the 1923 Liverpool conference.

With Eamon de Valera's new Constitution – which claimed the whole island as one country – shortly to be ratified by the people of the Free State, the FAI felt justified in their action. Not all were happy at this move. The wisdom of selecting the players merely for the purpose of asserting a claim to their services was questioned, when the criterion for selection should have been ability.

While Brown became a regular IFA international and was the subject of a move to first division Birmingham City, neither Feenan nor Jordan was ever capped by the IFA and they made little impression at league level.

Paul Denis, writing in the *Irish Times*, made an interesting point: 'It is surprising to see only two home men in the team. Certainly the side is strong, but is it encouraging the game here to regard only two players as worthy of selection? It is doubtful if Free State football followers will take much interest in the performance of the team and who could blame them?'

However, the selectors had good reason to feel justified in view of the results they achieved. Against Switzerland, Jimmy Dunne gave Ireland the lead after half an hour with a splendid shot from 20 yards, and fine defensive work frustrated the best efforts of the Swiss attack after that.

Immediately after the post-match banquet, the Irish team were whisked away to the Alpine resort of Interlaken where they spent the next four days before moving on to Paris. For Joe O'Reilly, those days in Interlaken proved to be the nearest he ever came to collective training with Ireland.

Breen saved a penalty just 12 minutes into the game as the French started off at a cracking pace and hit the woodwork twice in the first half. After the break it was Ireland's turn to take up the running and, in the 50th minute, Jordan converted a nice pass from Dunne to open the scoring. Seven minutes later, with France pressing, a long ball from O'Reilly was collected by Brown who gave goalkeeper Di Lorto no chance to clinch the win.

The on-field success was matched off the field, as the FAI were able to report a profit of £361. However, from the point of view of World Cup preparation it was not much help as only four of the squad played any part in the qualifying games.

The timing of the World Cup ties with Norway did Ireland no favours, with both games on Sundays (10 October and 7 November) and during a period when it was difficult to secure the release of players from cross-channel clubs.

Only three cross-channel players were made available for the trip to Norway – George Mackenzie (Southend United), John Burke (Norwich City), both new caps, and Charlie Turner (Southend United) – prompting one commentator to speculate that there must be some significance in the fact that their clubs could do without them. Injury prevented Burke lining out and he was never called up again.

Two significant new caps were left-back Mick Hoy (Dundalk) and right-winger Tommy Donnelly (Drumcondra), who both benefited from the FAI's keenness to establish their all-Ireland influence, Hoy being from Tandragee and Donnelly from Enniskillen.

The players were given a rousing send-off on the Tuesday night at the start of their marathon journey. They were guests at the Sunderland-Celtic clash of English and Scottish Cup winners the following day before departing that night on a long North Sea crossing followed by a 12 hour train trek to Oslo, arriving on Friday night, less than two days before kick-off. Apart from some exercises on board the North Sea steamer, the players had no opportunity to train until Saturday.

Norway were playing their 110th international as against the FAI's meagre total of 22, and they had reached the semi-finals of the Olympic Games in

Berlin the previous year. They had a 17-year-old messenger boy, Tom Blohm, in goal, but their star player was inside-right Reidar Kvammen, a policeman, in whom Arsenal had shown an interest.

Kvammen opened the scoring after 30 minutes following a corner. Mattie Geoghegan equalised seven minutes later, but it was only thanks to goalkeeper Mackenzie's brilliance and a missed penalty by Holmberg, whose shot hit the post, that Ireland were level at half-time.

Although the Irish defenders were finding the going tough against the speedy Norwegians, Jimmy Dunne, who had been getting no change out of Eriksen, secured the lead when he converted a pass from Billy Jordan four minutes after the break. However, Kvammen crashed winger Brustad's centre in to the net to equalise after 64 minutes.

Ireland had three good chances after that but it was left to Martinsen to decide the issue in the 78th minute when he atoned for earlier misses by converting Isaksen's pass from close range.

Norway felt a 5–1 or 6–1 result would have been a more accurate reflection of the play, with sports paper *Sportsmanden* offering the following headline: '37 chances gave 3 Norwegian goals'. This may account for Norway's willingness to go along with a sensational protest against the inclusion of Dunne in the Irish line-up.

The protest was made by FIFA observer, Anton Johanson of Sweden, on the grounds that Dunne, having played for the IFA, who were not members of FIFA, was ineligible. The Norwegian secretary was so sure the protest would be successful that he stated the return leg would rank only as a friendly.

FAI Secretary Joe Wickham made overtures to FIFA and the selectors went ahead and chose Dunne for the game in Dublin before word came through that Norway had decided to take no action on the protest that 'had been suggested to them'.

The selection of two 18-year-olds, Jackie Carey (Manchester United) and Kevin O'Flanagan (Bohemians) was a bold move, but the selectors did not put all their faith in youth as left-half Tom Arrigan (Waterford) was winning his one and only cap at the age of 33 and inside-right Harry Duggan (Newport County) was 34.

Carey had been signed by United from St James's Gate for a fee of £200 the previous November. He had made his first-team debut in September against Southampton and one writer noted that he was 'the cleverest forward in the match, the only one with real constructive ability.'

O'Flanagan, who had played at famous schoolboy club Home Farm with Carey – something which cost him, but not Carey, his place on the Dublin Gaelic football minor team – was a schools sprint champion who was putting his pace and strength to good effect with the Dalymount club.

Only six months earlier, he had made a sensational junior international debut, scoring twice in a 4–3 win over the Birmingham FA at West Brom. As a result, he had received offers from Liverpool, Manchester United and Aston

Villa, but his parents insisted that he complete his education and he had only just begun his medical studies when he was called up for the World Cup tie.

The selectors also called up Tommy Breen in a team which showed eight changes from that so narrowly beaten in Oslo. Although Mackenzie had been the star on that occasion, the feeling was that the taller, more experienced Breen would strengthen the Irish defence.

Manchester United released Breen and Carey on Thursday so that they could prepare properly for the game. It was a splendid gesture by the Old Trafford club, but the news which broke later that day caused a sensation: Breen had cried off the team in order to play for the IFA against Scotland the following Wednesday in Aberdeen.

Why would a Drogheda-born player turn his back on his parent association and an important World Cup tie in favour of lining out with the rival Belfast-based IFA? Part of the answer lies in Breen's own good nature and part in the good nature of FAI Secretary Joe Wickham.

The IFA, selecting their team to play Scotland, found themselves in a quandary. The goalkeeper they wanted was Breen but their rules stated that a player must not play for three days before an international fixture. Thus, Breen, if he lined up with the FAI on the Sunday, would be ineligible for the game against Scotland.

When they rang him offering him his place on the team, they did so with the proviso that he would cry off the FAI team. When Breen said that he had already accepted the FAI invitation to play, the IFA stood their ground. Even United's suggestion that they would arrange for Breen to travel directly from Dublin to Aberdeen after the game, cut no ice. The IFA indicated that the FAI had two goalkeepers at their disposal, while they had only one.

Faced with this ultimatum – and almost certainly not appreciating the importance of a World Cup tie compared to the then highly rated British Championship – Breen phoned Joe Wickham and, after informing him of his predicament, asked for his release. Wickham, being one of football's gentlemen, decided not to hold the player against his wishes and granted his request, although he felt that the request should have come from the IFA rather than from the player.

This sensational development caused a lot of comment, with the opposing viewpoints neatly summarised in the rival Belfast newspapers. In the unionist *Belfast Telegraph*, 'Ralph the Rover' said: 'The football community will applaud him for this decision. It took pluck to phone the secretary of the FAI to say he was not playing for them and that was what Breen did. I salute him for being so plucky.'

The nationalist *Irish News* commented: 'The IFA selectors practically held the pistol to Breen's head and the Manchester United goalkeeper thus lost what would have been the unique distinction of playing for the Free State and the IFA in two international games.'

Breen's decision proved an embarrassment to Manchester United. Secretary-manager Louis Rocca wrote to the Irish papers explaining how the club had given Breen and Carey four days' leave to prepare for the game with Norway.

'They were both to leave on the Thursday before the game. Carey did so but through the action which the Northern Association took in the matter, Breen decided to turn out for them. Manchester United had no call whatever on which team Breen would play for. The matter was left to the player himself.'

By all accounts, Breen had a fine game against Scotland, some early saves giving his team-mates confidence. The game ended in a 1–1 draw – the only time he was not on a losing side in nine appearances for the IFA.

The decision meant that Breen was not popular in FAI circles and, at their December meeting, a resolution was passed which struck the name of 'Thomas Breen, Windmill Road, Drogheda, at present playing with Manchester United Football Club, off the records of the FAI' and added: 'that he be not invited to play for his country on any future occasion'.

When war broke out, Breen returned to Belfast and played at first for Celtic and then Linfield, at the time one of the few Catholics to line out for that famous old club. He won IFA Cup medals with Celtic in 1941 and with Linfield in 1945 and 1946. He moved to Shamrock Rovers for the 1946–47 season and was capped three times, but his final tally of five caps for the FAI was a poor return for a goalkeeper of his talent and more a reflection of the selectors' disapproval of his fateful decision in November 1937.

The selectors had another scare when Breen's replacement, Mackenzie, was hurt playing for Southend United. Although not completely fit, he was persuaded to turn out. He was one of four players – Gorman, Turner and Duggan were the others – who played for their clubs in England 24 hours before this vital game and then endured long train rides and the night boat across the Irish Sea.

Roared on by a vociferous 27,000 crowd, Ireland took the game to Norway from the kick-off, but 15 minutes of non-stop attacking only produced one goal – headed by Jimmy Dunne after 10 minutes when new cap Tommy Foy's cross was headed on by Duggan.

The levelling of the aggregate scores so soon led to a false confidence in the Irish ranks, with even the full-backs pushing up to join in the attacks. This proved costly, a mistake by Gorman after 16 minutes paving the way for Holmberg to pass to Kvammen who equalised.

Kvammen scored again after 33 minutes, dribbling through from midfield and when Martinsen made it 3–1 four minutes after the break, Ireland's hopes of World Cup glory vanished. O'Flanagan reduced the arrears in the 62nd minute when he finished a Dunne backheader, and two minutes from time Duggan shot the equaliser from Carey's cross.

Eliminated 6–5 on aggregate, it was another case of what might have been. Post-game analysis which suggested Mackenzie was at fault for two of Norway's goals added fuel to the fire generated by Breen's controversial defection.

New cap O'Flanagan found it all a great experience, but did not notice much gloom among the players over their elimination from the World Cup.

'Sure, I had never even heard of FIFA in those days,' he recalled.

Norway were considered one of the better teams seen in Dublin, and this was borne out by their performance in the World Cup finals. They went out to eventual winners Italy 2–1 after extra-time in a game in which they hit the woodwork three times and had a goal disallowed. It proved to be Italy's hardest match.

Paddy Bradshaw played in only five internationals – all in the 1938–39 season – yet he made such an indelible impression that he dominated the last pre-war season.

Everything about Bradshaw's football career reads more like fiction than fact. Born in a poor part of Dublin in 1912, he left school at an early age to supplement the family income and worked mainly on the docks. His football talents soon brought him to prominence and proved a help in securing employment. A hard, tenacious striker with a tricky bodyswerve and great pace, he could beat defenders on a sixpence. He scored prolifically with head and either foot.

He had chances to move into League of Ireland football but turned them down. He also had an offer from Manchester City and had his bags packed ready to travel when he succumbed to personal doubts over his lack of education and he stayed at home.

At the end of the 1937–38 season, he was 26 and at his peak. Selected for the FAI Juniors to play the Birmingham FA in Dublin, he hit a hat-trick in a 3–4 defeat and, six days later, he was on target for the Leinster FA in a 2–2 draw with Motherwell. The interest in him increased, with St James's Gate scooping their rivals by persuading him to sign – and then balancing the books somewhat by selling their top scorer Willie 'Wagger' Byrne to Dundalk. Bradshaw was set to become the new King of the Iveagh Grounds.

Meanwhile, Ireland were in demand as warm-up opposition by several World Cup finalists. Czechoslovakia requested an Irish visit to Prague, and this was combined with an invitation from Poland, breaking new ground in each case.

The selectors once again opted for an all-Ireland team, naming northerners Jackie Brown (Coventry City), Walter McMillen (Chesterfield) and Harry Baird (Manchester United). They probably felt there would be no repercussions as the inter-League series with the Irish league had been resumed on St Patrick's Day, evidence that the FAI's ban on matches with teams under the IFA's jurisdiction had ended.

However, as far as the IFA were concerned, they were the only football body entitled to represent the whole island. Apparently at their behest, Brown, McMillen and Baird received telegrams from the English FA ordering them not to play on the grounds that they were not born in the Free State.

Baird, who had just helped Manchester United win promotion to the first division, was bitterly disappointed, and readily gave the players' point of view: 'I hope the FAI realise that I have not let them down. I was anxious to play, especially as the IFA have never honoured me, and this would have been my first international match.

'It means a financial loss to me, and I am not in the game merely for the good of my health. It looks to me as if this development will widen the gap between the North and South, and following the resumption of the games between the League of Ireland and the Irish League, this is a great pity.

'Of course, I have no option but to obey the FA, otherwise I might be suspended, and football is my livelihood. I do not want to let anybody down, either the North or South, but I think it strange that the IFA can pick anybody they like, and the FAI cannot do the same.'

Local heroes O'Reilly, O'Flanagan and Dunne, surprisingly dropped in the first place, were recalled to fill the vacancies and contributed handsomely to the best spell the Irish team enjoyed before the war.

Con Moulson (Notts County) was also forced to withdraw and the selectors brought Matt O'Mahony (Bristol Rovers) in at centre-half for his first cap. This tour also marked the return of O'Keeffe after his four years in the wilderness.

Czechoslovakia, who had lost only 5–4 to England the previous December, were quickly into their stride and after three minutes were awarded a penalty when Gorman handled. Left-winger Nejedly scored from the spot. In the 42nd minute, O'Keeffe worked the ball down the left and sent in a cross which Tom Davis converted from close range.

The Czechs went ahead again straight from the second half kick-off. It was a splendid individual effort by Nejedly, who beat several defenders in a thrilling run before shooting. Injuries to Nejedly and centre-half Boucek, who came off second best in a collision with O'Reilly, weakened the home side, but they kept the Irish out until the very last minute when O'Flanagan placed a corner for Dunne to volley a magnificent equaliser.

Czechoslovakia made their mark in the World Cup finals, but not in a way they would like to remember. They met fancied Brazil in the quarter-final and held them to a 1–1 draw in one of the most savage encounters in the history of the tournament. Nejedly had his leg broken, goalkeeper Planicka suffered a fractured arm and two Brazilians and a Czech were sent off. The referee was 'rested' for the replay which Brazil, with nine changes, won only 2–1.

After their exhilarating display in Prague, Ireland's performance four days later in Warsaw was a bitter disappointment. Poland scored three times in the first half and not even the half-time change to a new football at the request of the Irish made any change in the pattern of play.

The Irish forwards had plenty of chances but contrived to miss them all, with Carey, Davis and Dunne the main offenders. Poland, on the other hand, added a further three goals and their players, all amateurs, were carried shoulder high from the pitch by their jubilant supporters.

41

The game was notable for a rare use of the substitution rule with Billy Harrington (Cork) replacing Mackenzie in goal in the 60th minute when the score was 5–0. Mackenzie was taken off ostensibly because he was injured, but Harrington later claimed that it was a 'diplomatic' injury as the Southend goalkeeper did not want to be the only keeper involved in what was then a record defeat.

The tour was the most successful financially for the FAI, showing a profit of £483. The Polish and Czechoslovakian FAs each contributed £700, while the players' wages amounted to only £150. As an amateur, O'Flanagan received a gold medal for each season he was on international duty.

Poland, like Czechoslovakia, went out to Brazil in the World Cup finals. The score was 4–4 after 90 minutes but Brazil squeaked through 6–5 after extra-time.

The climate was changing in Britain. When the FAI sought six cross-channel players for the 18 September visit of Switzerland they secured five – a significant improvement on previous seasons. The one refusal came from Huddersfield Town, who were unable to release full-back Billy Hayes as they not only had a game on the day before the international but also on the day after.

The Swiss came with a big reputation, having beaten England 2–1 in May and then accounted for Germany in the World Cup finals before going out to beaten finalists Hungary. But as soon as they arrived in Dublin their officials made it clear that the game would only go ahead if their defenders were allowed to obstruct opposing forwards in defence of their goalkeeper.

This rule had been set aside since the previous season but, despite lengthy argument by English referee, R.A. Mortimer, the Swiss refused to budge.

'I went on the field practically without a pea in my whistle,' said a disgusted Mr Mortimer. A big home crowd of 31,000 was treated to a fine display by what *Irish Independent* writer Bill Murphy described as 'the best team Ireland has placed in the field for a long time'. Yet it was a team which the selectors had difficulty in choosing.

It included two new caps – Dundalk left-half Dickie Lunn and St James's Gate's new centre-forward Paddy Bradshaw, who had played his first senior game only a month previously. On that occasion, against Limerick, he had scored five goals in a 10–2 win and he kept on scoring to complete a meteoric rise from junior to senior international within the space of five months.

On his last junior international appearance, Bradshaw had scored a hat-trick and, on his return to the scene of that triumph, he made a brave bid to emulate that feat. He opened the scoring after 20 seconds, the quickest goal ever scored by Ireland, when he blocked goalkeeper Huber's attempted clearance: After eight minutes, Dunne made it 2–0 when he headed in Fallon's corner and Bradshaw made it 3–0 after 20 minutes when he headed in Dunne's cross.

It was a sensational start for Bradshaw, who became the target for some rough treatment from the Swiss who used their bodies, but principally their elbows, to minimise his effectiveness. However, this was an aspect of the game for which he was well able, and it took some fine saves from Huber to deny him his hat-trick. He also had the satisfaction of initiating the move, midway through the second half, which led to Tommy Donnelly scoring Ireland's fourth goal.

Centre-half Matt O'Mahony became the first cross-channel player to fly in for an international. He arrived from Bristol only an hour before kick-off, but proceeded to play superbly, giving a performance which must have impressed the IFA as he was their only new cap the following month when they played Scotland.

Switzerland's below-par performance can partly be explained by the disturbed political situation in Europe at the time. With British Prime Minister Neville Chamberlain visiting Germany's Adolf Hitler, the Swiss made arrangements to complete their journey in the shortest time possible in case of the declaration of war. They arrived in Dublin on Saturday evening, thus taking away the advantage most visiting teams enjoyed against Irish players who had to travel from England and perform on consecutive days.

Interest in international football peaked on 13 November 1938, when Poland visited Dalymount, attracting a record attendance of 35,000 and record receipts of £2,023 at prices ranging from one shilling (5p) and two shillings (10p) on the terraces to three shillings (15p) or four shillings (20p) in the stand.

This heightened interest was reflected in the presence for the first time of the twin Heads of State, President Dr Douglas Hyde and Taoiseach Eamon de Valera. While their presence was a great boost to the FAI's prestige, it resulted in a storm of controversy raging over the President, who was introduced to the teams before kick-off. Dr Hyde was removed from the list of patrons of the Gaelic Athletic Association (GAA), which had little room to manoeuvre because of its ban on members playing soccer or attending soccer matches.

The selectors were happy to retain all but two of the side which had beaten Switzerland so handsomely, calling up right-back Billy Hayes (Huddersfield Town) for his first cap, with Mick Hoy dropping out, and recalling Kevin O'Flanagan in place of Tommy Donnelly, one of the goalscorers against the Swiss, who had since been released by Shamrock Rovers.

Hayes found himself in the same predicament as Tommy Breen a year earlier when he was selected by the IFA to play against England three days after the Poland game. Like Breen, he chose to withdraw from the FAI selection – and found himself on the wrong end of a 7–0 defeat in Manchester. He was not selected again by the FAI until after the war. His defection let Hoy back into the side.

Seven of the players humiliated in Warsaw started the match and Ireland quickly took the game to Poland. After several near misses, Fallon shot the opening goal in the 10th minute. Bradshaw, putting himself about as usual, clashed with the goalkeeper and the ball ran loose to Carey whose shot was blocked but only as far as Fallon, who promptly netted.

Three minutes later it was 2–0, with Carey heading in Fallon's corner. The Polish goalkeeper Madejski then had to be replaced by reserve Mrugala following a clash with O'Flanagan, but they got back into the game in the 16th minute when Mackenzie could only palm down a terrific drive from Wostal and Willimowski was on hand to reduce the arrears.

With the Poles coming more into the game, O'Reilly did well to take the ball off the toe of dangerman Willimowski but, in the 67th minute, the siege was lifted when O'Flanagan forced a corner and placed his kick accurately for Dunne to head home.

The Poles continued to attack and were rewarded in the 74th minute when Piatek was on target after Willimowski's drive rebounded off Mackenzie's chest. Willimowski twice came close to securing an equaliser but the Irish, with a little luck, held out for an exciting victory. It was fitting that Dunne scored the winner for he was the outstanding player on the pitch, his clever dribbling, hard shooting and accurate passing posing endless problems for the visitors' defence.

Considered at the time as the greatest day in the history of the FAI, the victory enhanced the country's prestige on the Continent, resulting in an invitation from Germany to play there the following May. However, the FAI's request to the English FA for a match was turned down on the grounds that they could not consider the proposition until the 'domestic differences between North and South are cleared up'.

The massive inferiority complex which Irish soccer had towards Britain was illustrated by the importance the FAI placed on gaining acceptance from that quarter. This was clearly illustrated when the international against Hungary on Sunday, 19 March was totally overshadowed by the visit to Dublin of the Scottish League two days earlier.

For a start, failure to agree on a free date in Dublin with the League of Ireland resulted in the Hungarian match being played in the Mardyke, Cork, the first international fixture to be located outside Dublin. It attracted a crowd of 18,000, who paid £1,100, but it suffered from the hyping up of the Scottish league tie.

The inter-league game was regarded as 'the most attractive and far-reaching fixture that has been secured and staged by the South since they set out to fend for themselves in 1921–22', according to one commentator, who added, 'for 20 years various and futile efforts have been made to gain recognition and equal status with the big countries at home. Equality is admitted by the visit of the Scottish League.'

The Scots proved a tremendous draw, attracting another 35,000 crowd to Dalymount. They were playing for a guarantee of £500 or 50 per cent of the receipts if they were over £1,000, and they returned to their base with over £900. The League of Ireland, which had beaten the Irish League 2–1 in Belfast six days earlier, defeated the highly rated Scots by the same margin, with Bradshaw on the mark in both games. He was one of five players who shared in those exciting victories – Hoy, O'Reilly, O'Flanagan and Dunne were the others – and who were also named to play Hungary.

The only new cap was left-half Ned Weir (Clyde), who had been brought to the notice of the FAI and the IFA by a Dublin fan, Matt Murtagh, who had spotted him playing for Scottish second division side St Bernard's the previous season. Transferred to Clyde, his rise to stardom was crowned by a five-star matchwinning display against Rangers in the Cup, and this led to him lining out for the IFA against Wales only four days before he made his FAI debut.

Hungary travelled against an unsettled domestic background when their troops invaded Czechoslovakia. They stopped off in Paris on the Thursday and drew 2–2 with France, arriving in Dublin on Friday before travelling to Cork on Saturday.

Ireland got the start they wanted after 14 minutes thanks to the irrepressible Bradshaw, who got in ahead of the defence to head home Foy's corner kick. However, the Hungarians then took over and had several near misses before Kollath equalised in the 35th minute. Five minutes after the break, Hungary went in front, Szengeller shooting past the advancing Mackenzie. Tempers became frayed at this point, with kicks being freely exchanged between some Hungarian defenders and a couple of Irish forwards.

The Irish put in a fine rally and Carey, three minutes from time, got on the end of a move involving himself, Dunne, Foy and Bradshaw to fire in a great shot for the equaliser.

Matt O'Mahony was recalled when the selectors, naming their side for the continental tour in May, gave a vote of confidence to the players who had gone through the season unbeaten at home.

In order to ensure the players were at their best on arrival in Budapest on Tuesday evening, night travel was avoided *en route*. An interesting development was the organising, by German FA Secretary Dr Xandry, of a stadium in Vienna for training on Tuesday afternoon. The players had a further day to acclimatise before the game on Thursday, 18 May.

When Kollath put Hungary in front after 39 minutes, it seemed Ireland were set for another defeat by the Magyars, but speedy winger O'Flanagan turned the game around in the second half when he hit two magnificent goals in the 52nd and 77th minutes, the first with his left foot from about 25 yards and the second with his right from the same distance. Put through by Carey, O'Flanagan used his speed to race away and crack in the lead goal which was a real crowd-pleaser, with the fans applauding for fully a minute.

When full-back Billy O'Neill collapsed with time running out, O'Reilly told him to stay down to give the team time for a breather but a Hungarian player, anxious to get on with the game, grabbed hold of O'Neill's legs and started hauling him off the pitch. O'Reilly reacted by shouldering the Hungarian practically into the crowd. However, Hungary's strong pressure was finally rewarded with an equaliser one minute from time by Kollath.

Nemzeti Sport praised the Irish as 'a skilful side which could play quickly', while lamenting their own team's missed chances. The Dundalk full-back pairing of Hoy and O'Neill and wing-half O'Reilly earned kudos for their excellent defending.

There were no official interpreters with the FAI party in those days and, as a result, the players developed the habit of speaking pidgin English to the locals. At the banquet after the game, Bradshaw ate something which disagreed with him and lay down in agony, his eyes closed. Reserve 'Sonny' Molloy bent over him saying, 'Me go . . . get taxi . . . bring doctor,' whereupon Bradshaw, his eyes still closed, responded: 'Who do you think I am? A f***ing Red Indian?'

Arriving in Bremen on Sunday, they lined out against Germany on Tuesday, 23 May, in front of a crowd of 35,000, a record for the Weser Stadium which was hosting its first international. An interesting sidelight to this game is revealed ingenuously in the following extract from the official report to council:

> 'In Bremen our flags were flown though, of course, well outnumbered by the Swastika. We also, as a compliment, gave the German salute to their Anthem, standing to attention for our own. We were informed this would be much appreciated by their public which it undoubtedly was.
> 'The German Sports Minister at the Banquet paid special tribute to our playing the match as arranged despite what he described as untrue press reports regarding the position in Germany and their intentions.'

This was Ireland's 12th game since the sides had met in Dublin in October 1936, but Germany had managed to play 26 internationals in the interim. In addition, thanks to Hitler's expansionist policies, the Germans were now able to call on players from Austria, one of whom, Wilhelm Hahnemann from Admira Vienna, was included in their line-up.

In a fast and exciting first half, misfortune struck when Dunne collided with Rohde and had to be carried off in the 35th minute. Four minutes later Germany took the lead, with Helmut Schoen, later to become one of the all-time great managers, scoring.

Hopes were raised when Dunne returned to play on the wing in the 54th minute, with Bradshaw moving to inside-right and O'Flanagan to centre-forward, a switch which the young winger often made with great success during games with Bohemians. The Irish began to play with more zest, and the equaliser came 20 minutes into the second half when Fallon crossed and Bradshaw, with a splendid header, put the ball into the net.

German magazine *Kicker* had high praise for goalkeeper Mackenzie and centre-forward Bradshaw 'who posed many problems for the German defence' and stated that, 'from a competitive point of view, there was no weak point in the Irish team, their only deficiency being a lack of precision in passing.'

On the journey home the team sailed from Hamburg to Southampton where, although it was 18 months since he had left the town, the dockers gave a rousing salute to Jimmy Dunne – a heart-warming tribute to one of football's gentlemen and an acknowledgement of the debt they owed the man whose goals had saved Southampton from relegation to the third division in the 1936–37 season.

The FAI's fifth continental tour, which crowned their best season so far, was their last for seven years – thanks to Hitler. Those pre-war years saw Ireland gradually come to terms with the requirements of the international game. The increasing respect which the continental countries had for the Irish promised more regular international fare and, after two close calls, it seemed only a matter of time before Ireland qualified for the World Cup finals.

4

War and Peace

While international football remained a viable proposition within the German sphere of influence up to the end of 1942, for Ireland and the rest of Europe the beginning of hostilities in Poland in September 1939 signalled the end of an era.

For Irish football, the war was a mixed blessing. Most of the English-based players returned home, unhappy with the prospect of conscription and the British Government's restriction of football wages to £1. This, together with the temporary end to the drain of up-and-coming players wooed by full-time football across the Irish Sea, led to a strong domestic League which fuel shortages restricted to Dublin, Cork, Limerick and Dundalk.

When the selectors got back to business in 1946, only two of the players who had lined out in the last pre-war game in Bremen were available for selection – Manchester United's Jackie Carey and the former Bohemian winger Kevin O'Flanagan, now a doctor working in London and playing for Arsenal.

However, the strong domestic situation had seen a host of promising players come to the fore, many of whom later moved to England. Among the most prominent were Drumcondra centre-half Con Martin, Shamrock Rovers' duo Peter Farrell and Tommy Eglington, Waterford-born centre-forward David Walsh, Jackie O'Driscoll and Tommy Moroney (Cork United), Limerick-born full-back Tom 'Bud' Aherne and Eddie Gannon (Shelbourne).

While it is possible they would have been snapped up by English clubs anyway, the devastation caused by the war to the ranks of Britain's professional footballers helped them establish themselves more quickly than might have been the case.

Martin, Aherne, Farrell, Eglington and Walsh formed the backbone of the international team in the immediate post-war years, along with pre-war favourite Carey, while Moroney and Gannon were also called to the colours regularly.

Filling the gaps was a problem for the selection committee, which continued to rule the roost until 1970, long after most other nations had handed over the task of team selection to managers and/or coaches.

From the start the selection committee was dominated by League of Ireland club representatives and, in the post-war period, the two most prominent members were Shamrock Rovers' Captain Tom Scully and Sam Prole of Dundalk (and later Drumcondra). The other three berths on the committee rotated to some degree, but Scully and Prole were practically ever-presents.

It was inevitable that the selectors, in seeking talent, would look to their own clubs first and so it is no great surprise that Shamrock Rovers and Drumcondra provided more players for Irish squads than other League of Ireland clubs during this period. While caps were in most cases deserved as both clubs were to the fore in Irish football, by the same token Rovers and Drums benefited from their association with the selection committee when it came to signing the best local talent.

During the war, relations with the authorities in Northern Ireland had improved. As a result, when the FAI resumed its international travels with a tour to Portugal and Spain in June 1946, the emergency committee of the IFA, meeting in Belfast on 9 May, decided they would offer no objection 'to players of Northern Ireland clubs being selected by the FAI for inclusion in the team to visit Portugal and Spain.'

The selectors responded by interpreting this message in its widest possible sense, not only including Free State-born players with Northern clubs but also four Northern Ireland-born players with northern and English clubs – Walter McMillen (Belfast Celtic), Jackie Vernon (Belfast Celtic), Josiah 'Paddy' Sloan (Arsenal) and Jimmy McAlinden (Portsmouth).

It was hardly what the IFA's emergency committee had in mind but the tour went ahead without undue controversy, possibly because the English FA had in April recommended rejoining FIFA, and Scotland, Wales and Northern Ireland were expected to follow suit. In such circumstances, there was no point in spoiling the ship for a ha'porth of tar, despite the IFA's deep-rooted objections to its players playing on Sunday, the day for which both games in the Iberian peninsula were scheduled.

The tour was made on the strength of a £2,000 guarantee from Portugal plus a return game. The FAI paid all expenses from Lisbon to Madrid, for the game against Spain, and back to Lisbon. Spain were to be paid a similar amount of expenses when they played a return game in Dublin. It meant incurring a substantial loss but it was considered worth it.

Travel, for the first time, was by air, an Aer Lingus DC3 transporting the party to Lisbon, with a refuelling stop at Bordeaux. Placed as it is on the western extremity of Europe, Ireland has more reason than most European countries to be grateful for air travel.

Arsenal's Sloan proved to be the star attraction for the locals, presumably because of his association with the world-famous Highbury club, but on the pitch he was overshadowed by the exploits of Glentoran centre-back Con Martin.

Martin, a sports all-rounder who won a Leinster Gaelic football championship medal with Dublin in 1942 (he was not presented with it until

1972 because of the GAA's ban), was introduced to soccer while in the Air Corps and signed for Drumcondra. After an inter-league game in March 1946 he was signed by Glentoran who bought him out of the Air Corps. He was chosen as reserve for the tour, most likely because of his versatility, having played in most defensive positions with Drums.

After half an hour of the first game against Portugal, with Ireland already trailing 3–0, goalkeeper Ned Courtney was injured and the selectors put Martin in goal. He kept a clean sheet, Ireland going down 3–1, and so retained his place the following Sunday against Spain in Madrid. Labelled the 'Yellow Canary' by the Spanish media because of the colour of his jersey, Martin gave an outstanding display as Ireland, with a goal by Sloan, earned a surprise victory.

Shortly afterwards, when Manchester United were searching for a goalkeeper, Carey recommended Martin to Matt Busby but even Busby could not persuade Martin to sign.

'I preferred to go to Leeds as a centre-half and on reflection that was probably a mistake,' he recalled. Later, when he moved to Aston Villa and the club ran into a goalkeeping crisis, Martin found himself between the posts for the best part of a season. However, he was never asked to play in goal again for Ireland, being considered too valuable in the centre-back role.

The game which the FAI craved finally came their way. A letter arrived on 29 August from the English FA accepting the FAI's invitation to play in Dublin on 30 September, two days after England's game with Northern Ireland in Belfast. For FAI stalwarts who had experienced the bad days of the 1930s when the English made life awkward, this was the final recognition of the status they wanted so much.

There was no question of playing Northern Ireland-born players on this occasion. A team of Free Staters, including the long-awaited return of Alec Stevenson after a lapse of over 14 years, took on an English team of All-Stars who had destroyed the IFA selection 7–2 in Belfast. Another who returned from oblivion for this game was goalkeeper Tommy Breen, banned by the FAI from international football in 1937, but restored perhaps by his association with Shamrock Rovers.

The haphazard nature of the FAI's selection and preparation was illustrated by the selection of a honeymooning Paddy Coad and the late call-up of centre-forward Mick O'Flanagan for the injured David Walsh.

'I had a pub in town and was working from 10 in the morning,' recalled Mick. 'Around ten to two I got a phone call from Tommy Hutchinson, the Bohemian member of the selection committee, telling me that I was playing against England at Dalymount at 5.30.

'I went home to Terenure for a bite to eat, had a short rest and then headed off to Dalymount. It was not really sufficient notice as only the previous evening I had brought a party of English journalists to Templeogue tennis club and hadn't got home until nearly two in the morning.'

Two of the FAI team, captain Carey and full-back Bill Gorman, had been on the wrong end of the 7–2 scoreline in Belfast but they proved to be the kingpins of the Irish defence, especially when the other full-back Billy Hayes was reduced to a limping passenger on the wing and Carey moved from wing-half to full-back for the second half.

England were unchanged from their triumph in Belfast where each of the five forwards had scored, with Wilf Mannion claiming three. Tom Finney, Raich Carter, Tommy Lawton and Bobby Langton completed a formidable attack, but it met its match in a game which prompted L.V. Manning of the *Daily Sketch* to write: 'Never has there been such a rip-roaring, thrilling football match in my time as this amazing game in Dublin. It was won by a goal from Finney 10 minutes from the end, and England were lucky to survive the most storming assault any England team can have been subjected to.'

Henry Rose in the *Daily Express* went further: 'If ever a team deserved to win Eire did. They out-played, out-fought, out-tackled, out-starred generally the cream of English talent, reduced the brilliant English team of Saturday to an ordinary looking side that never got on top of the job. What spirit these Irishmen showed. It was something with which our fellows could not cope.'

Stevenson showed what Ireland had been missing all those years in the 1930s when Everton refused to release him. In a great tradition of Dublin-born inside-lefts, he varied the play with clever passes and gave the home fans the thrill of the game in the 60th minute when he fired in a shot which crashed off the crossbar, with Frank Swift beaten. Swift, one of football's great characters who sadly lost his life in the Munich air disaster in 1958, turned and blew a kiss to the crossbar.

The effect on the IFA of this fine performance was dramatic. Where before they had studiously avoided selecting any more than four players from the Free State, for their next match, away to Scotland on 27 November, they included seven!

Gorman, Martin, Farrell, Carey, David Walsh, Stevenson and Eglington were the magnificent seven who all justified their inclusion in a 0–0 draw. From then until the 1949–50 season, the IFA regularly selected five to seven Free State players – and were rewarded with some creditable results, including a 2–2 draw against England at Goodison Park, which proved to be a foretaste of things to come.

Despite the FAI's good displays in 1946, they had to be content with the return games against Spain and Portugal for their international fare in 1947.

The game against Spain on 2 March provided a further shot in the arm for the Free State.

'We looked like world-beaters that day,' recalled centre-half Con Martin. Two goals from David Walsh, who was making a big impression at West Bromwich Albion after his transfer from Linfield, and another from Paddy Coad, earned the Irish a thrilling 3–2 win.

The game attracted a record crowd of over 42,000 and record receipts of almost £5,000 but Dalymount Park proved incapable of hosting such a crowd comfortably.

Portugal, with a 2–0 win in Dublin on 4 May, brought the home side back to earth. Although the Irish had most of the play, they could not score and even contrived to miss a penalty, full-back Billy Hayes shooting yards wide just a minute after the interval.

At the end of a long, hard season, the exhausting travel on the boat after playing on Saturday afternoon caught up with most of the players but, for team captain Carey, it was the start of the most exciting week of his distinguished career. He travelled to Amsterdam the following day for the Rest of Europe trials, played a game against a Dutch team on Tuesday, flew to Scotland on Wednesday for a team briefing, rested on Thursday and Friday and on Saturday captained the Rest of Europe against Great Britain before a crowd of 134,000 at Hampden Park. Playing at right-half – his fourth different position that season – he did extremely well in what was billed at the time as the Match of the Century. Unfortunately, mismatch would have been more accurate as Great Britain strolled home 6–1.

Carey evidently benefited from the move to defence from his pre-war inside-forward position as he grew in stature in the game and showed leadership qualities which were appreciated both at club and international level. In the 1948–49 season he had the distinction of captaining both the FAI and the IFA teams, while in 1948 he captained Manchester United to a popular FA Cup triumph.

'In those years just after the war, Carey was very special to the rest of us, because we were very raw and he was established in the first division,' recalled Con Martin. 'He had the experience and the ability to organise us and we all admired him.'

After their defeat by Portugal, the FAI had to wait for over a year before their next international, which was a return game in Lisbon. For this game and the one against Spain the following week, they introduced a new goalkeeper, George Moulson (Lincoln City), a brother of pre-war centre-half Con Moulson. Because of his complexion, which appeared to have more affinity with the Middle East than Ireland, the goalie was nicknamed 'Mohammed'.

The way the selection committee operated is illustrated in the story Paddy Coad recalled about Moulson.

'Captain Tom Scully went over to watch him and when he came back I asked him how did Moulson play. Scully replied that he did not get much to do – Lincoln had won 5–0 or something – but he had a great kick.'

Defeat was Ireland's lot in the three games Moulson played – against Portugal and Spain (away) and Switzerland (home) but it was his blunder in the last game which caused the selectors to look elsewhere. Played before the smallest attendance for over 20 years, 25,563, Ireland should never have lost to a Swiss team that was rated one of the worst ever to visit Dublin. The Irish were more or less constantly on the attack but their old failing in front of goal let them down.

Eight of the players had played the previous day and had then suffered a very rough crossing on the night boat. The worst affected was Moulson who was a bad sailor. He duly had a nightmare game, dropping shots, missing crosses and letting in a harmless looking 30 yard free-kick by Bickel for the only goal of the match.

Goalkeeper was proving a problem position – perhaps the selectors should have persuaded Con Martin to stay between the posts – for Moulson and his predecessor Tommy Breen each lasted three games, followed by Limerick's Billy Hayes, who lasted only one.

Hayes was only 21 when he was capped against Belgium at Dalymount Park on 24 April 1949, but of more interest is the fact that he was only 5ft 5ins in height. His claim to be the smallest-ever international goalkeeper is being researched for the *Guinness Book of Records*. He left Limerick the following season and went on to enjoy a career in English football with Wrexham and Torquay United.

Unfortunately, Hayes's lack of inches told against him when, with Ireland's forwards once again showing their lack of firepower despite most of the possession, a 40 yard lob from Mees cleared Con Martin and bounced over the advancing Hayes for Belgium's first goal. Mermans added a second six minutes from the end to record Belgium's first win over Ireland, who had now put together a run of five defeats.

Against the Belgians, the selectors had experimented, including six League of Ireland players, four of them in the forward line. That experiment was deemed a failure as only Paddy Coad of Shamrock Rovers – rated the best Irish player never to have moved to England – was retained for the following game against Portugal at Dalymount Park on 22 May. Coad, from the penalty spot, clinched Ireland's first victory in six games. The goal was Ireland's second in those six games.

It was a timely end to the run of defeats for, in January, the FAI had been drawn to play Finland and Sweden in the World Cup, a grouping with which they were not in the least pleased, principally from a financial viewpoint.

The game against Portugal was in the nature of a final trial for the World Cup ties, which began in Sweden on 2 June. The team to play Sweden was to be selected the day after the game. Emphasising its importance, the selectors arranged for collective training – with Carey in charge of coaching – at Milltown in the week before the game.

Apart from the honour of representing their country, those immediate post-war games had an added attraction for the UK-based players.

'It was our chance to eat something substantial for a change,' recalled Con Martin. 'With rationing still in force in England, you could find that the local chip shop would open only once a week, so a trip home, where food was plentiful, had great appeal.'

Financially, the international scene was not proving as lucrative for the FAI as it had before the war. Portugal and Spain drove hard bargains, as a result of which, when the receipts from the tour to Iberia in 1948 and the subsequent return games in Dublin in 1949 were totted up they showed a net loss of almost £500, a colossal sum at that time.

One of the reasons was the increase in travel costs, while another factor was the players' wages. Pre-war the wages never amounted to anywhere near £100, but now players were receiving £20 a game, which meant a bill of £220 for the FAI plus whatever they paid the reserves. This latter figure varied from £5 upwards, depending on the selectors' whim. On foreign trips, all players were paid the match fee.

Typical of the selection committee's pre-match arrangements are the following instructions recorded in their minutes after they had selected the team to play Switzerland in Dublin on 5 December 1948: 'Secretary to arrange for information from English clubs regarding players playing the previous day immediately by phone after their matches on the Saturday and the Committee to meet if necessary on Saturday evening'.

As Coad recalled: 'We used to turn up at the Gresham Hotel at 12.00 on Sunday not knowing who would arrive over from England. League of Ireland players would then be called in if there were any vacancies.'

As regards switches which might be made in the course of the game, the same minutes record: 'T. Scully and S. Prole with Team Captain (J. Carey) to make changes at half-time if considered necessary.' On occasions where Ireland was trailing with time running out, Carey himself moved into the attack but this switch never had a bearing on the result.

At least the selectors had learned a few lessons from their pre-war schedule. Against Portugal on 22 May 1949, Peter Farrell was brought on as a substitute, the first time a sub was used in a home game. Even then, it was peculiarly done, with Farrell replacing centre-forward David Walsh when he went off for treatment in the 35th minute and then going off again four minutes later when Walsh was fit to resume.

The main problems were the lack of scoring forwards and a general lack of pace throughout the team. David Walsh was the only genuine goalscorer in the attack and he came in for the heavy obstructionist treatment which the continentals were so good and so cute at dishing out. Lacking support, his record of five goals in 20 internationals may seem paltry but it was merely indicative of a greater malaise.

A pattern was also emerging in relation to the pool of players from which the selectors chose their teams. With more Irish players based in England and Scotland playing full-time football, the part-time League of Ireland player, who had been a mainstay before the war, was being phased out. The team should have been stronger for that, but the results were, if anything, poorer. Something was wrong with the set-up, but it would take many years of hard lessons before the correct answer would be forthcoming.

5

The Parting of the Players

Season 1949–50 was one of the most memorable in FAI history, encompassing the first World Cup campaign in 12 years, an historic game against England and a contretemps with the IFA which ended with the Republic's players parting company irrevocably with the Belfast-based body.

There was evidence that the collective training undertaken before the game against Portugal on 22 May – and which was repeated before the trip to Stockholm on 2 June – had a beneficial effect for, although beaten 3–1 by Sweden, the Irish were by no means disgraced in the country's first World Cup tie since November 1937. A month previously, Sweden had beaten England by the same score.

Defenders Carey, Rory Keane and Con Martin were again outstanding but the forward line disappointed, despite the boost of an early goal. David Walsh took advantage of a slip by centre-half Nordahl to open the scoring after 10 minutes.

The selectors made only two changes for a friendly against Spain in Dublin 10 days later. The minutes of their meeting state: 'Players to report at Gresham on Sunday at 12.45 for lunch. Steamed fish to be ordered. Hotel accommodation to be reserved for Keane, Moroney, Walsh and Corr.' The four mentioned were the non-Dubliners.

A combination of tropical heat on 12 June and a brilliant display by the speedy Spaniards proved too much for Ireland, even the masterly Carey catching a tartar in winger Gainza, whose 'fairy feet danced a fandango to the amazement of Carey', according to Bill Murphy in the *Irish Independent*.

Once again the Irish took the lead, this time from a Con Martin penalty after 14 minutes, but, between the 30th and 37th minutes, Spain scored three goals to demonstrate their superiority and completed the scoring four minutes from time. In Gainza, Zarra and Basora, Spain had top-class forwards who were to prove their worth in the World Cup finals the following summer, when Spain finished fourth.

The selectors picked an entirely new attack for the World Cup tie against Finland in Dublin on Thursday, 8 September. Johnny Gavin (Norwich City), Arthur Fitzsimons (Middlesbrough), Jim Higgins (Dundalk), Peter Desmond

(Middlesbrough) and Tommy O'Connor (Shamrock Rovers) were all new caps and, when Higgins was forced to cry off, he was replaced by another new cap, Shelbourne's Brendan Carroll.

That seems to have exhausted the stock of forward talent for in naming the subs, the selectors opted for goalkeeper Billy Hayes (Limerick) and centre-half Paddy Daly (Shamrock Rovers). As it turned out, they were in need of a forward after only 25 minutes when the unfortunate Carroll had to be replaced. Daly came on at centre-forward but moved back to centre-half, with Con Martin leading the attack.

The attendance was 22,479, the lowest for a World Cup tie, and the lowest in Dublin since 1929. For a change, the faithful fans were rewarded with a home win and some goals. However, it was not very convincing, with two of the goals coming from free-kicks – the first direct from a corner by Gavin, and the second from the penalty spot by Martin, after Desmond had been brought down.

The third goal was also scored by Martin, when he headed in a corner in the 68th minute. The conclusion he drew from the game was that regular centre-forward David Walsh was sure to score a hat-trick in the return game 'as the Finns were so poor'.

The game against England at Goodison Park 13 days later was part of both teams' preparations for World Cup ties. England dropped right-wing pair Stanley Matthews and Stan Mortensen, while the Irish followed suit by introducing the Everton pair Peter Corr and Peter Farrell on the right and recalling the unrelated Walshs, Willie at right-half and David at centre-forward.

England had a formidable team, all from the first division with the exception of the legendary Tom Finney. Ireland could only muster seven players from first division clubs, the other four being divided equally between the League of Ireland and the second division. An English victory was regarded as a foregone conclusion. The bookmakers offered 10/1 against an Irish win but got few takers.

The Irish team were booked into a hotel in Southport the night before the game and Con Martin recalled: 'There was a magicians' convention on in the hotel and I remember thinking that we would need a magician to beat England.' It was probably a view shared by the rest of the Irish players, although Peter Farrell was suitably patriotic and took bets on the result from his Everton club-mates.

The early pattern of the game saw England launch wave after wave of attacks. However, goalkeeper Tommy Godwin was in inspired form, Carey, Martin and Bud Aherne proved difficult men to get past and wing-halves Willie Walsh and Tommy Moroney gradually took the sting out of the English front line.

Sensationally, on 33 minutes, Peter Desmond, a Corkman who had been playing earlier in the year with Shelbourne before being transferred to Middlesbrough, burst into the England penalty area and was brought down. Martin converted the spot kick.

The ferocity of England's attacks increased but the Irish held out and Martin recalled: 'Early in the second half when I intercepted a pass from Jesse Pye, I remember thinking, "Hey, we're not playing badly, we have a chance here."'

With five minutes to go, Tommy O'Connor slipped the ball to Farrell and his shot beat Bert Williams for a clinching second goal.

'A cute lob, all the papers called it,' recalled Farrell, 'but I'm not going to pretend it was. I just closed my eyes and banged it.'

England thus sustained their first defeat on home soil by a team from outside Britain.

'This win gave the FAI a real place in football and the fact that the receipts were over £9,000 should bring added warmth to their success,' wrote Bill Murphy in the *Irish Independent*, indicating that the financial ramifications were as important to the FAI as the result.

For Farrell there was the added satisfaction of collecting on the bets of his club colleagues but there were no big after-match celebrations for the Irish players.

'I got a lift from West Brom's coach back to Birmingham after the game,' recalled Con Martin, 'and I was in for training the following morning. England were the big team of the time but I don't think the enormity of what we had achieved sunk in for a long, long time.'

While left-winger O'Connor went back to Shamrock Rovers and his job as a compositor with the *Irish Times*, his Rovers' team-mate, goalkeeper Godwin, was snapped up by Leicester City.

The World Cup campaign in 1949–50 proved memorable in more ways than one. Occurring as it did in the year the Irish Free State formally embraced the status of Republic, it was always likely to be a minefield for the legislators. So it proved, but not before the Republic's interest in the competition ended. The return game with Finland was played on Sunday, 9 October in Helsinki, the team and officials flying out on an Aer Lingus charter which cost the FAI £1,040. On a bitterly cold day – the temperature was barely above freezing – the Irish had their first experience of poor World Cup refereeing, something which was to haunt them in later years.

Inconsistency was the problem, with the referee erring in the home side's favour when he disallowed a Dave Walsh goal following a fumble by the Finnish goalkeeper and then, in the last minute, with Ireland winning 1–0, he allowed Finland an equaliser when a couple of Irish defenders were put into the net as well as the ball following a cross. The Irish protests fell on deaf ears.

Farrell had opened the scoring in the 65th minute from a pass by Drumcondra wing-half Tim Coffey, a replacement for Eddie Gannon who was not released by Sheffield Wednesday. It was not a particularly noteworthy display by Ireland but captain Carey was presented with a cup at the after match banquet, having been named the best Irish player by the Helsinki Sports Club.

Ireland had to beat Sweden in Dublin if they were to bring the Swedes to a play-off at a neutral venue. Because of this, and the team's historic win over England, there was very close to a record attendance at Dalymount Park on Sunday, 13 November.

The selectors had picked the Goodison XI again but an injury to Moroney forced him to cry off and Reg Ryan of West Brom was called up for his first cap in the left-half slot. Ryan had been in line for a call-up for the trip to Finland but, on that occasion, West Brom informed the FAI that they were only prepared to release one player and the selectors opted for Dave Walsh.

The odds were stacked against the Irish. Seven of them were engaged in tough English games the day before and, when they arrived in Liverpool for a specially arranged flight, they discovered that flying was out and spent Saturday night wondering if they would be able to get to Dublin in the morning. Meanwhile the Swedes were sound asleep in their Dublin hotel.

The Irish were still rubbing the sleep from their eyes when Sweden went ahead in the fourth minute through teenaged striker Palmer and despite strong pressure – the corner count at half-time was 9–0 to Ireland – the home side were two goals down at the break in unhappy circumstances.

Five minutes before half-time, a spectator on the terraces blew a whistle and the Irish defence stood still, expecting a free-kick, while Palmer went through to score his second. It was an up-hill battle after that but the Irish plugged away and got one back 16 minutes into the second half when Nordahl held Walsh to concede a penalty, which Martin converted. However, nine minutes later, an uncharacteristic error by Carey was punished by Palmer for an emphatic 3–1 win for the Swedes, who distinguished themselves in Brazil where they finished third.

The following Wednesday, 16 November at Maine Road, England put an end to any Irish interest in the World Cup when they annihilated what Charlie Buchan described as 'one of the weakest ever Irish teams' 9–2 in the IFA's second British Championship match.

No doubt in the belief that they would be arguing from a position of power, the FAI decided to re-open negotiations on an All-Ireland team. Plans were laid in January 1950 for a letter to be sent to the IFA inviting them to a conference and informing them that notice of the invitation would not be divulged to the press until they had been assured the letter had been received.

However, the leaks which were to bedevil the FAI over the years, were soon apparent. Secretary Joe Wickham reported to the international affairs committee that he had been informed by a pressman that he already knew all about the matter. If that was discouraging, the response from the IFA was worse. Rejecting the idea of a conference, the Belfast body stated 'no new facts or suggestions have been presented that would justify recommending that a further conference be called to deal with matters which have already been discussed and on which the Council of the Association has consistently stated its views.'

That blunt statement was endorsed the following month by the IFA's selection committee who chose five players from the Republic – Carey, Aherne, Martin, Ryan and Dave Walsh – for their final British Championship – World Cup tie against Wales in Wrexham on Wednesday, 8 March.

Carey was withdrawn by Manchester United, who were chasing the league title and were due to play Aston Villa the same day. Villa, surprisingly, gave permission for both Con Martin and Trevor Ford, the Welsh centre-forward, to miss the league game and play in Wrexham, where their duel was considered the highlight of the 0–0 draw. Charlie Buchan, who named Martin and Ford the men of the match, noted that 'a much-changed Irish side produced the better football in a dull, lifeless game'.

The four Republic players made a little bit of history, becoming the first players to play for two different associations in the same World Cup tournament. The possibility of this anomaly being allowed to continue was a red rag to a bull as far as the FAI were concerned and a letter of protest was sent to the English FA and telegrams to the English, Scottish and Welsh FAs and to FIFA.

Not prepared to stand idly by while these bodies dithered, apparently afraid to offend the IFA, Shamrock Rovers' Chairman Joe Cunningham wrote to each of the Republic's English-based players asking them to declare their intention to play for the FAI only in future.

Cunningham was the instigator, but it fell to Aston Villa's Con Martin to be the catalyst of change, as he explained: 'I always had a great relationship with the IFA, we were treated very well and always liked playing for them but the night before the game in Wrexham I got a phone call from Dublin asking me to refuse to play. I said that it was difficult to give an answer because this was my work, my profession.

'However, when I returned to Aston Villa the morning after the game I was approached by the Chairman, Fred Normansell, who asked me to refuse to play for Northern Ireland. Surprised at this coming from him, I asked him why and he said that Villa would not be welcome in the Republic if I continued to play for Northern Ireland.

'At the time there was a big connection between Villa and Shamrock Rovers and it was Rovers who were making the running on this issue. I suppose it did not help either that Manchester United had beaten Villa the same night and they hadn't released Carey, while Villa had been short of two key players, myself and Trevor Ford. And about this time I had got a lot of threatening letters and was called a Judas for playing for 20 pieces of silver.

'The Chairman got me to make a statement and before I knew what had happened it was sent out over Reuters and that was me finished with the IFA. It all happened so quickly that I can't help feeling it was all set up between Normansell and Cunningham. Some of the other players were reluctant to follow me but eventually they all did.'

While the FAI were pleased to receive Martin's letter confirming his intention not to play for the IFA, they also received a letter from Major Keyes, the

Chairman of West Brom, complaining about Cunningham sending a letter to Reg Ryan and asking what action were they taking on the matter. They took no action, waiting instead to see how the players would react.

One by one, the players decided to fall in with Cunningham's suggestion but, when the selectors sat down to name their next team – away to Belgium on 10 May – they had several absences to contend with. Carey, who had been ever present since his debut in November 1937, was currently in Canada; Farrell and Eglington were unavailable; and Swansea pair Keane and O'Driscoll, were both in hospital.

So the team selected to face Belgium was an unfamiliar one, featuring four new caps – Mattie Clarke and Bobby Duffy (Shamrock Rovers), Terry Murray (Dundalk) and Martin Colfer (Shelbourne) – and a new captain, Con Martin, whose elevation to this office was well deserved but unfortunately linked by the media to his role in the 'Cunningham letter' affair.

It did not prove a happy occasion for Martin and his team-mates as they were soundly beaten 5–1 by the speedy Belgians, with centre-forward Mermans taking a hat-trick from his duel with the Irish skipper. The game was the first an Irish team played under floodlights, which were switched on for the last half hour.

There was a sensational development later that month when a telegram arrived from FIFA enquiring if the FAI would be prepared to compete in the World Cup finals in the event of a vacancy. The international affairs committee decided by three votes to two to accept but planned to investigate the matter further and meet again two days later. In the meantime no acceptance was to be sent.

When the IAC met again, the Honorary Treasurer M.J. Kenny had prepared a report on the cost of involvement which he estimated to be £2,700. He said that it would bankrupt the Association. When the matter was discussed by council, Kenny's view prevailed, but diplomatically it was announced that 'the Association was unable to accept the invitation owing to the short notice received'.

Oh, for the wisdom of hindsight. Far from bankrupting the FAI, participation in the 1950 World Cup finals would have proved a major financial boon. Such was the hunger of fans for the first finals since 1938, especially in football-mad Brazil, that world record attendances and receipts were set in the new Maracana Stadium.

Only 13 countries took part instead of the intended 16 and so successful was the tournament that all expenses had been paid before the final group games, assuring each of the finalists a handsome profit.

Instead of an interest in football in Rio, the FAI's sole interest was in the politics of football, especially its dispute with the IFA. Unable to afford to send a delegate to FIFA's Congress, they entrusted their case to English delegate, Arthur Drewry, President of the Football League.

The IFA, meanwhile, were not trusting to others to make their case. Their

President, Fred Cochrane, travelled to Rio and, before leaving, he put the IFA point of view forcefully at the Annual General Meeting of the Irish League.

'Our friends in the South have tabled a motion which, if carried, would prevent us from playing certain players in international matches,' he declared. 'I am going to oppose that motion and to endeavour to see that they will not, in future, be able to call themselves the FA of Ireland. If the FIFA carry out their rules they must support the parent Association of any country and the parent Association in Ireland is the IFA.'

FIFA, while upholding the FAI point of view, attempted to please both parties, deciding that the IFA could use the name 'Ireland' in British Championship games, but otherwise it must be 'Northern Ireland'.

The matter did not end there, for the IFA were not going to give in easily. The first opportunity they got the following season they tested the water by selecting Sligo-born Sean Fallon and Dubliner Nicholas 'Johnny' Matthews for an IFA XI to play the British Army on 14 September.

Matthews was the best centre-half in the Irish League, while Fallon was a full-back who had only recently been transferred from Glenavon to Celtic. Both played against the British Army in a 0–0 draw and, as a result, Fallon was chosen to play the following month in Belfast against England.

Fallon was an interesting character. As a boy, he had dreamed of playing for Celtic and yet when he was first offered terms by the legendary Jimmy McGrory he turned them down. He also took four years off his age, thinking that Celtic would not retain their interest in him if they knew he was 26.

'I had two passports – one for football and the real one,' he said.

He had never been selected by the FAI but when news of his selection by the IFA broke, Cunningham sent him one of his famous letters, which in effect told him to pull out.

'I was to get a cheque for £1,000 from Glenavon and a wrist watch in honour of the occasion,' recalled Fallon, 'but as my father was in politics in Sligo and this was a very hot potato at the time, I very reluctantly pulled out. I was the last player from the Republic selected by the IFA and I felt I had let them down as I had said I would play.'

It was the end of an era. There would be no more all-Ireland teams. The split had been confirmed and the island would in future field two distinct teams in international competition, differing in this respect from most other sports. Since 1949–50, both associations have gone their separate ways but one cannot help feeling that should the right administrator come along, the breach could be healed, and the game and the island would be the better for it.

Northern Ireland were beaten 4–1 by England on 7 October and three days later, the council of the IFA decided to break off relations with the FAI. One of the first casualties was the inter-league series between the League of Ireland and the Irish League and this was not repaired until April 1953.

Fallon's reward was to be chosen as reserve against Norway at Dalymount on 26 November and when he arrived in Dublin he was met by the legendary Mary Jane

Cunningham (wife of Joe), who informed him that Con Martin had been injured, so he was in.

It proved a difficult debut for Fallon, who recalled: 'I was breaking in new boots because my old boots were drying out after the game the day before and I lost my two big toenails as a result.' However, he acquitted himself well in a game in which Ireland went 2–0 down after only 12 minutes and came back to earn a 2–2 draw with goals from Carey (penalty) and David Walsh, the latter a magnificent headed effort from an Eddie Gannon cross.

Carey's penalty was the first he had ever taken. In the absence of usual penalty-expert Con Martin, Carey, as captain, had asked Eglington to take any penalties but he was not keen. Carey had then gone around the other players until one of them had said, 'Why don't you take the penalties yourself?' In such haphazard fashion were decisions made in those days.

For the first time, no League of Ireland player was selected. This set a precedent which the selectors were keen to follow, but they were often frustrated due to injuries or the unwillingness of English clubs to release players.

The background to the Norway game is also interesting as in August the FAI decided to play Yugoslavia on that date. However, on 1 September, Secretary Joe Wickham reported that objections had been raised in view of the recent persecution of Catholics in Yugoslavia by the communist government of Marshal Tito.

Following a discussion, it was agreed unanimously that 'this match not be played' and it was decided to accept Norway's offer to play on that date instead. Five years later, amid more public controversy, the FAI finally kept their date with the Yugoslavs.

6

One Step Forward,

Two Steps Back

The early 1950s were trying times for the international team. For every step forward it seemed to take two or even three backwards. Football elsewhere seemed to have progressed to a plateau beyond the Irish grasp.

One of the main reasons for a series of heavy defeats was the increasingly high age profile of the team, the nucleus of which had remained constant since the war. Full-backs Carey and Aherne were well into their 30s, while Farrell, Eglington, Martin, David Walsh, Moroney and Gannon were all hovering around the 30 mark.

Fortunately, there was evidence of young talent coming through, while an Irishman was discovered who had emigrated at a young age and played all his football in England – flying winger Alf Ringstead.

Another drawback to progress was the failure of the FAI to arrange regular games. After the glut of eight games in 1949, it was back to a diet of crumbs with an average of three games a year, down to two in 1954. New players had to adapt straightaway or they might not get another chance, which militated particularly against the part-time League of Ireland players.

In August 1951, the FAI appointed former Celtic full-back and Scottish athletics coach, Dugald Livingstone, as national coach to both the FAI and the League of Ireland. The Scotsman set himself the target of putting Ireland back on the soccer map.

'In recent years, other countries have assumed the attitude that they are merely fulfilling obligations by playing against Ireland,' he said, 'but I want to see the time when they will consider it an honour to play against us.'

The appointment of Livingstone was the first in a series of cosmetic exercises by the FAI. All were doomed to failure as they did not include the FAI's relinquishing of the ultimate power – the power of team selection.

The problem of putting Ireland on the map proved beyond Livingstone and he moved on within two years to guide Newcastle United to FA Cup success in 1955. Later he became manager of Fulham.

The visit of Argentina in May 1951 was secured by offering a guarantee of £1,500 or half the gate, if greater, less match expenses. The interest in the first visit of a South American team was so great that Dalymount hosted its first all-ticket international, which attracted a crowd of 40,000 and, at increased prices, record receipts of £7,000.

The fare provided did not meet expectations apart from the lively contribution of newcomer Ringstead, 23, who was the son of an English jockey and had left Ireland when he was two. He had signed for Sheffield United in November 1950 and his international debut capped a meteoric rise to fame as a free scoring outside-right.

Against Argentina, according to the *Independent*'s Bill Murphy, 'Ringstead was positively brilliant, fast and direct with some lovely curling crosses that brought moments of real worry to the visiting defence. Here at last we have found the right man for the right wing but the trouble now is to find somebody to play with him.' Unfortunately, of the other forwards, only Kit Lawlor played well, and he was winning his third and last cap. The game was decided by a 54th minute goal scored by Labruna when the Irish offside trap failed because of Bud Aherne's delay in stepping out.

There was, however, a fairytale first cap for goalkeeper Freddie Kiernan, two months short of his 32nd birthday. A civil servant, he had spent 10 seasons in League of Ireland football when he was given a free transfer by Sligo Rovers at the end of the 1949-50 season. He signed for Leinster Senior League side Grangegorman and was spotted by Paddy Coad who brought him to Shamrock Rovers where he produced the best form of his career. He earned an inter-league cap and proved to be the star of an honourable 1–0 defeat by the English League a month before the Argentina game.

Kiernan won a further four caps and in October 1951, at the age of 32, was transferred to Southampton for a record League of Ireland fee for a goalkeeper of £4,500. He played almost 150 games for the Saints before retiring in 1955.

On a less happy note, there was evidence that Irish captain Carey was becoming vulnerable as well as venerable, as he received his second 'roasting' from a Latin left-winger inside 18 months, this time from the nippy Loustau.

The selectors switched Carey to centre-half for the game against Norway in Oslo on Wednesday, 30 May, dropping the dependable Con Martin. There were first caps for Limerick inside-right Tim Cunneen and Everton right-back Tommy Clinton, but Cunneen's debut lasted only 42 minutes. He was a victim of the rule which decreed that substitutes could only be used in the first half. A half-time massage could well have had him right again, but trainer Billy Lord quickly decided that Coad should come on when Cunneen got his knock. It proved to be a matchwinning move.

Norway took the lead twice, through Sorensen and Huidsten, and were hauled back to level terms by Farrell and Ringstead. The deciding goal came eight minutes from time when Coad went on a run. Looking up for someone to pass to and finding nobody in position, he advanced to the edge of the box before unleashing a terrific left-foot drive which tore into the roof of the net.

As a result of this game, the FAI insituted their scheme of honouring a player's 25th cap. They learned that Norway's FA presented their players with gold watches for 25 caps. At the time, Carey was the only player who qualified and, with games hard to come by, it would take the next recipients, Farrell and Martin, another few years to achieve the honour.

Farrell took over as captain for the home game against West Germany on Wednesday, 17 October 1951. Ireland were the fourth country to play the Germans following their reinstatement by FIFA in 1950.

It was a game of high drama. For Bud Aherne the drama began the previous day when he spent six hours grounded by London fog before catching a flight to Dublin. Undeterred, he turned in one of his best displays, eliminating the danger of right-winger Gerritzen.

A Wednesday game always levelled the playing field, with none of the usual two games in 24 hours that applied to Sunday fixtures, and it was the Irish players' fervour, enthusiasm and tenacity which overcame the Germans' better technique. Florrie Burke, who had been magnificent against the English League, once again rose to the occasion and had a magnificent game in what, surprisingly, proved to be his only international. Eglington and the recalled Arthur Fitzsimons were the matchwinners in attack, with Eggo's dribbling skills turning the Germans inside out and Fitzsimons showing his colleagues how to shoot.

The Irish got off to the best possible start, when Posipal, under pressure from Fitzsimons, turned the ball into his own net. Five minutes before the break, Fitzsimons notched number two with a cracking left-footed drive from the edge of the penalty area.

The Germans, who included five of the players who were to win the World Cup in 1954, got back on terms in the second half.

Fritz Walter, the German captain, finished off a pass from Morlock in the 63rd minute – his 21st goal in 28 internationals – while Morlock shot the equaliser after a period of heavy pressure in the 75th minute.

However, the fighting Irish were not to be outdone. With five minutes to go, Farrell brought the ball out of defence to Eglington, who put it through for new cap Dessie Glynn to chest down, round goalkeeper Turek and place in the net, a score that was greeted with an invasion of delighted fans.

Kiernan had to be at his best in the last minute to turn a Morlock shot around the post. The corner was on its way across when referee Ling of England blew the final whistle, denying Walter who turned the ball into the net only to find that it did not count.

This win was considered among the best displays ever by an Irish team. However, there was no hope of building on it as the next game was not until the continental tour in May 1952 and that brought the team quickly back to square one. The Germans got their revenge with a 3–0 win in Cologne. Posipal, the scorer of the own goal which set Ireland on the way in October, opened the scoring after 32 minutes. Second half goals by Ottmar Walter and Termath completed the rout.

An everyday expression, used in innocence by an FAI official, caused a bit of a stir media wise. When asked about relations between the two countries, he replied that they were getting along 'like a house on fire'. The literal interpretation brought back harrowing memories for the Germans of the Allied firebombing of Dresden just seven years previously, considered by many a war crime of the same magnitude as Hiroshima or Nagasaki. Fortunately all was smoothed over.

The players had only three days to recover from their exertions in Cologne before facing Austria. The game was played in the Prater Stadium, Vienna, located in what was then the Russian zone. Russian soldiers were everywhere and the signs and symbols were all in the language of the Soviets.

Although there was an improved display from the Irish, it was not reflected on the scoreboard as Austrian centre-forward Huber helped himself to a hat-trick between the 22nd and the 25th minute of the first half; Haummer added another before half-time and Dienst scored twice after the break, all without reply. It equalled the worst defeat previously suffered.

The selectors had less than a month to come up with a winning formula for the visit to Madrid on 1 June but the only new cap was Everton's 20-year-old goalkeeper Jimmy O'Neill, who won his place thanks to a good display in the Jimmy Dunne Memorial game. O'Neill, who had joined Everton from schoolboy club Bulfin United, was a son of former Irish professional golf champion, Moses O'Neill.

Coach Livingstone brought the team together for a week's training before departure to Spain, but the benefit was not obvious as the Spaniards proved to be streets ahead of the Irish in the things that mattered – skill, speed and shooting power. Once again it was Gainza who did the damage, scoring one and laying on two other goals in the first 13 minutes, and generally giving the unfortunate Sean Fallon a rough ride. Con Martin had one of those days he prefers to forget.

'It got to such a state with the heat that I couldn't have cared whether we won or lost,' he recalled. To make matters worse, he missed a penalty just after half-time when Fitzsimons was taken down. His kick hit the crossbar and Fitzsimons, from the rebound, hit the upright.

The selectors had arranged that, 'if any change was necessary during the match', Jack Traynor, the Chairman of the selection Committee, and FAI Secretary Joe Wickham would decide 'after consultation with the captain'. Rarely was this procedure invoked; there was still a marked reluctance to use substitutes. With Fallon in such difficulty, and with another right-back, Tommy Clinton, on the bench, a fresh pair of legs might have helped to curb Gainza's influence but no move was made to rectify the situation.

However, the selectors made a move in the right direction for the next game which was against France at Dalymount on Sunday, 16 November, when they requested – and received – the release of their players from English league duty the day before. There were first caps for Seamus Dunne, the Luton Town right-back, and Sean Cusack, the Limerick left-half, and a recall for Johnny Gavin of Norwich City, while Fallon was tried at centre-forward.

The game with France attracted a crowd of over 40,000 not all of whom paid as the gates were broken down. Receipts were £7,000 but, to put that into perspective, the England-Wales game at Wembley the same week had a crowd of 94,094 and receipts of £43,600.

One of the most hectic first halves ever seen in Dublin produced plenty of fireworks, not all of the football variety. The highlight was the sight of Bud Aherne chasing French winger Raymond Kopa down the tunnel after play had been stopped for a foul. Kopa ran for his life after upsetting Bud once too often. The crowd loved it! However, the selectors failed to see the funny side and Bud was told that a repeat would end his international career.

Fallon opened the scoring after 24 minutes when his header from Gavin's cross was deflected into the net by Jonquet. Piantoni equalised in the 69th minute, and the French were only denied a win by the brilliance of O'Neill on his home debut.

The game was still fresh in the memory when the World Cup draw was made and Ireland were paired with France and minnows Luxembourg in Group Four, with one to qualify for the finals in Switzerland.

Only one game was arranged before the World Cup qualifiers, but it was a good one – the return with Austria. The Austrians were among the favourites for World Cup honours but nothing went right for them on their visit to Dublin.

They played a 0–0 draw with West Germany in Cologne on Sunday, 22 March, and were due to fly to Dublin immediately after for the game on Wednesday, 25 March, but fog prevented them taking off. Instead, they travelled overland to Amsterdam, flew to Manchester and caught the boat to Dublin, only arriving on the day of the game.

The Irish selectors, meanwhile, had chosen a record five players from Everton – O'Neill, Clinton, Farrell, Eglington and new cap George Cummins, a 22-year-old inside-forward who had been signed from St Patrick's Athletic. However, a suspension incurred following a sending-off over a month previously cost Cummins his first cap. Clinton had to cry off and was replaced by Seamus Dunne, while Aherne also cried off, letting in Fulham's Robin Lawler, a former Drumcondra and Belfast Celtic player, who was receiving his first cap at the age of 27. Ringstead was recalled to take Cummins's place.

Before a crowd of 40,000, the Irish fought hard to keep the visitors at bay in the first half but the home side stormed into the lead on the resumption and went on to record a famous 4–0 win.

Ringstead showed why he was such a regular scorer in England with two opportunist goals, while Eglington, in his 17th international, at last got the goal he had long threatened. Frank O'Farrell's late, long-range effort was the icing on the cake. The jubilation in the Irish camp was justified although the retirement of Carey – going out on a high – meant that the selectors would have some thinking to do before the World Cup began in October.

Once again, the financial aspect was allowed to take precedence over everything when it came to arranging dates for the World Cup games. Ireland's best results were achieved in midweek when the release of players was not a problem, yet they fixed the most important game, the surefire sellout against France, for a Sunday and the loss-making Luxembourg tie for a Wednesday.

With the French game less than a month away, the FAI announced the appointment of Alec Stevenson as national coach in succession to Livingstone, but the French made a more important move when they opened their World Cup campaign with a 6–1 win away to Luxembourg.

The selectors said they would consider only players released from their clubs' Saturday fixtures for the game against France on 4 October, and straightaway ran into trouble when two of the stars of the Austrian game, Ringstead and Lawler, were not released. Tommy Moroney, then with Evergreen United, took Ringstead's place, while Bud Aherne, 34 and nearing the end of his career, was recalled in place of Lawler.

Farrell took over as captain from Carey, who had been appointed manager of Blackburn Rovers, while Con Martin resumed at centre-back. A record attendance of 45,000 produced record receipts of £8,235 and gave the home players, who were receiving £30 for their efforts, every encouragement.

However, it was France who made most of the running. Their outside-right Ujlacki was their star, and he gave Aherne a torrid time, scoring two second half goals. Glovacki gave France the lead after 22 minutes, Penverne added a second in the 40th minute and Ujlacki made it 3–0 five minutes into the second half.

Moroney was switched to the wing in the second half, with Fitzsimons moving inside. This led to some improvement and Ryan opened Ireland's account when he struck home the rebound after his 58th minute penalty had been saved. Any hopes of an Irish revival were quickly shattered when Ujlacki notched his second goal and Flamion made it 5–1 with a quarter of an hour to go.

The Irish threw everything at the French in the last 15 minutes and were rewarded with goals from Walsh – following a Moroney cross – after 83 minutes, and O'Farrell – a long-range effort in the 89th minute. It was a case of too little, too late and back to the drawing-board for the selectors.

Three new caps were introduced for the visit of Luxembourg on 28 October – West Ham's 21-year-old defender Noel Cantwell, who was chosen at centre-half; inside-forward George Cummins, who had moved from Everton to Luton Town; and Shamrock Rovers' 19-year-old striker Liam 'Mousy' Munroe, who took the outside-right spot. An attendance of 20,000, the smallest for some years, were treated to a stonewalling display by the visitors, with the home side not very skilled at breaking them down. Eglington, who ran his marker ragged, and Fitzsimons were the exceptions.

Fitzsimons' 18th minute goal, which opened the scoring, was a magnificent individual effort. In a dribble along the back line he beat three men, then switched the ball to his right foot to make a better angle before shooting into the net.

A Ryan penalty three minutes after half-time and further goals by Fitzsimons and skipper Eglington ensured a comfortable home win but there was little indication that the talent was there to turn the tables on the French in Paris the following month.

With centre-half proving to be the selectors' biggest headache, Everton played Clinton in that position in a reserve game to enable Capt. Tom Scully and selector Liam Rapple to run the rule over him. They obviously approved as Clinton was chosen at No 5 as the selectors opted for experience for the visit to Paris, with Farrell, Ringstead and Walsh all recalled. However, an injury to Rory Keane forced a re-shuffle, with Clinton moving to his usual right-back spot and the veteran Con Martin coming in at centre-half.

The Irish party had an unhappy experience *en route* to Paris. Weather conditions were so bad that it was touch and go whether their flight from London would go ahead and there was very nearly a tragedy on arrival when the plane appeared to be coming down on a block of flats and had to go back up again. Some of the players and officials were so shaken that they refused to return by plane.

Before a record midweek attendance, the Irish contributed handsomely to a lively, open game in which the defence played magnificently. O'Neill made some marvellous saves, Con Martin was back to his majestic best and Robin Lawler put the clamps on first-leg matchwinner Ujlacki.

The goal which secured France's place in the World Cup finals was an unsatisfactory affair as Ujlacki fouled Lawler before crossing and Clinton headed straight to Piantoni, who accepted the gift and shot in to the net.

France duly beat Luxembourg 8–0 in their final qualifying game in December, which meant that Ireland's visit to Luxembourg on Sunday, 7 March 1954 was an opportunity for the selectors to blood some new talent.

Six new caps were chosen, four of whom were never capped again, but it was not the intention to introduce so many new faces. They had asked for and been refused the release of Gannon, Ringstead and Lawler. Because of the position of their clubs, the selectors did not request the release of Ryan (West Brom) or Fitzsimons (Middlesbrough). Neither did they request any of the four Everton players although they had been assured they would be made available.

The new caps were: Southend United goalkeeper Tommy Scannell, a native of Youghal; Southampton left-back Tommy Traynor, who had won an FAI Cup medal with his native Dundalk in 1952; Hibernian half-back Matt Gallagher, who remains the only native of Arranmore Island, Donegal, to be capped; Millwall half-back Pat Saward, a native of Cork; Dubliner Noel Kelly, an inside-forward with Nottingham Forest, who had previously played for Bohemians, Shamrock Rovers, Glentoran and Arsenal; and Cork-born Fred Kearns, who was transferred from Shamrock Rovers reserves to West Ham United, where he moved to centre-forward with some success. Kelly was receiving his first cap at the age of 32. Only Saward and Traynor were honoured again.

Luxembourg put up a brave rearguard action and it was not until the 62nd minute that the deadlock was broken, with George Cummins driving the ball low into the right corner of the net.

It was an unsatisfactory end to a campaign which had shown again the FAI's inability to make the most of the talent at its disposal. Between March 1953, when they had the thrilling win over Austria, and October, when they met France, the team had no game. Preparation was condensed in to a couple of days' training under a new coach, who had not even had time to get to know the players individually.

The decision to play France on a Sunday was justified by officials on financial grounds but this game would have attracted the same crowd in midweek when a full squad of players would have been more readily available. Playing Luxembourg on a Sunday would have made more sense. As it was, the FAI reported a profit of only £200 on the season, with losses incurred in both games against Luxembourg.

On a hopeful note, £440 was spent sending a youth team to a tournament in Germany. Two members of that team – Mick McGrath and Joe Haverty – later became regular members of the international team, while another, Ronnie Whelan, won two caps.

North–South relations improved a little, but not much. In March 1953, the IFA removed its October 1950 ban on games with teams from within the jurisdiction of the FAI and straightaway the Irish League agreed to resume its home and away series with the League of Ireland.

In November 1953 FIFA's ruling that the FAI should play as Ireland and the IFA as Northern Ireland was finally passed at a congress in Paris but IFA President Fred Cochrane's response was: 'It makes no difference. We will continue to play as Ireland. They have been playing under that name for years anyway, only we have been doing it for almost 50 years longer.'

This business of titles was finally resolved in 1954 when FIFA's Executive Committee decided that in future the teams should be Republic of Ireland and Northern Ireland. This was acceptable to the FAI but the IFA continued using the title Ireland in their British Championship games to the annoyance of the FAI who protested to FIFA. However, FIFA ruled in favour of the IFA in this matter.

7

Up the Republic

On Sunday, 7 November 1954, a new era began for the FAI and with it a new determination to end the folly of asking players to turn out for their country 24 hours after playing a tough league game across the channel. The game, against Norway, was the first played under the title Republic of Ireland.

The selectors insisted that players would have to be released by their clubs from their Saturday games and report to the Secretary on Thursday. Sean Fallon (Celtic) and Arthur Fitzsimons (Middlesbrough) were the only players whose clubs would not release them, Everton going so far as to release four players although they were due to play at Portsmouth.

Team captain Peter Farrell was one of the Everton four, as was new cap Don Donovan, a full-back from Cork. There were two other new caps: Fionan Fagan, the Manchester City right-winger whose father, John 'Kruger' Fagan, had played in the FAI's first international in 1926, and Shamrock Rovers' centre-forward Paddy Ambrose.

Norway took the lead after 13 minutes through Olsen and it was not until the 59th minute that the Republic got back on terms, Con Martin heading in a Fagan corner. The match was decided seven minutes later when the unfortunate Svennsen, who had conceded a penalty in the 2–2 draw at Dalymount in 1950, pushed Ambrose to concede another one which was despatched by Reg Ryan.

Not surprisingly, a letter of complaint was sent by the English League over the FAI's action 'in securing the release from a Saturday league fixture of four players of the Everton club'.

Waterford centre-forward Jack Fitzgerald was the only new cap for the next game, at home to Holland on Sunday, 1 May 1955, as the selectors tried again to find a successor to David Walsh. Fitzgerald had built up a tremendous understanding with Scotsman Jimmy Gauld in a free-scoring Waterford team.

Holland, not the attraction of later years, drew the smallest international crowd since 1929 – a mere 16,680 – but the faithful few saw a 79th minute bullet-like header by Fitzgerald from a Con Martin free-kick decide the issue. It was a memorable occasion for Big Con as he became the second player to reach the 25 cap mark and qualify for the FAI statuette.

71

For the tour to Norway and Germany at the end of May, the selectors chose a squad of 14 but it did not include Fitzgerald. He had broken his ankle playing for the League of Ireland in Germany so his place at centre-forward went to teak-tough Sean Fallon.

Fallon, who did well on this tour in the troublesome centre-forward position, decided to keep his jersey after the Norway game, which the Republic won 3–1 with goals from Cummins (2) and Ringstead. Fallon, supported by O'Farrell, laid it on the line to the FAI officials that if they met their commitments and paid the £2 a day pocket money which other international teams received they could have their jerseys back.

A hastily convened meeting resulted in a 'you can keep the jerseys' decision. Fallon, despite playing his best football in the next two seasons, was never capped again; O'Farrell was dropped for the game in Germany, and won a meagre four caps after that.

Peter Farrell's brilliance in Germany, where the Republic lost a thriller 2–1, prompted the selectors to nominate him as their first choice when asked by UEFA for candidates for the Rest of Europe team to play Great Britain in Belfast on Saturday, 13 August, for the IFA's 75th anniversary celebrations. The other players nominated were Fitzsimons and Eglington.

The FAI trio were ignored and the FAI itself received no invitation to the celebrations. Yugoslav striker Vukas scored a hat-trick as the UEFA team slammed Britain 4–1, a feat which did not do the advance publicity for the Republic's home game with Yugoslavia on 19 October any harm at all.

However, the publicity which the FAI received in the run-up to this game had little to do with football. The renowned Archbishop of Dublin, John Charles McQuaid, made a request to the FAI not to proceed with the game on account of the persecution of Catholics in Yugoslavia.

In his approach, Dr McQuaid was ahead of his time. The use of a sports boycott as a weapon against persecution would not be used effectively until the 1970s when South Africa's apartheid laws were the target and even FIFA, so slow to act in these matters, suspended the errant nation.

When the FAI decided to go ahead with the game, Dr McQuaid brought the matter to the attention of Taoiseach Eamon de Valera. De Valera's response was to withdraw permission for President Sean T. O'Kelly to attend the game, an action which prompted Northern Ireland politicians to denounce the Archbishop.

Feelings ran high in some quarters, including at Radio Eireann where regular commentator, Philip Greene, felt so strongly on the issue that he refused to broadcast the game.

The Catholic lay organisation, the Legion of Mary, picketed the laneway leading to the ground but there was no trouble, although the crowd was a disappointing 22,000. However small in numbers, they made their voices heard by giving a thunderous welcome to FAI President Oscar Traynor when he walked on to the pitch to be introduced to both teams, the role traditionally undertaken by President O'Kelly.

With all but two of the players based in England, the team was not greatly affected by the controversy and new cap Liam Tuohy typified the attitude of the home brigade when he said: 'The only way the controversy affected me was that I was afraid they might call the match off.'

The game itself was all over after 14 minutes, by which time Milos Milutinovic, an older brother of USA World Cup manager Bora Milutinovic, had scored twice. When Fitzsimons replied, Milutinovic completed his hat-trick just before half-time. Veselinovic, with another clinical finish, emphasised the difference between the teams when he completed the scoring in the 76th minute.

'The reason we got hammered was that we were a collection of individuals playing against a team,' recalled Tuohy, adding about his own introduction to international football: 'I got a couple of kicks and a header and a wallop from the full-back. He ran into me and shipped me about 20 yards; he sorted me out early on. After that I was essentially an observer.'

The comprehensive nature of the defeat led some commentators to call for an end to the selection committee and a change to the continental style of a team manager/coach picking the team.

Significantly, the IFA had recorded a 2–1 win over Scotland – their first win since they started fielding a Northern Ireland team in 1949 – and a lot of the credit was given to team manager Peter Doherty even though he was not a selector. The FAI decided to follow the IFA's lead and offered the position of team manager to Jackie Carey, whose acceptance was noted 'with pleasure' at a selection committee meeting on 8 November. Carey's reign, which began with the game at home to Spain on 27 November, 1955, lasted over 10 years – longer than any subsequent manager – but he had little or no power and his contribution to the team is, to this day, the subject of debate among the players he managed.

With England due to play Spain three days after the game in Dublin, Associated Rediffusion, with FAI permission, filmed the match, for a later TV showing, for the princely sum of 30 guineas.

This first TV deal was handled by the international affairs committee who, at the same meeting, had an application from Radio Eireann to broadcast a commentary on the Spanish game. In a decision which illustrates the depth of feeling engendered by the Yugoslav controversy, permission was granted 'provided Mr P. Greene is not the commentator as he is not acceptable to our Association.'

To their discredit, the international affairs committee were keen to make Greene eat humble pie on a matter of conscience and when he asked for a personal hearing he was kept waiting. After he explained that he had never intended to cause any trouble to the FAI, he was given the go-ahead to broadcast on 27 November.

Charlie Hurley, the 19-year-old Millwall centre-half, was the only new cap named to play Spain. Unfortunately, his youthful enthusiasm delayed his debut.

'I was on National Service with the Army Catering Corps,' he recalled, 'and our Battalion had a match on the Wednesday. Major Evans said, "you mustn't play with your big game on Sunday" but I said I needed the work-out. So I played and did my knee ligaments so badly I thought I was finished.

'I was out for 15 months. Finally I went to a rehabilitation centre in Watford and exercised my knee for a fortnight and, thank God, never looked back from that. I got through with a dodgy left knee until I was 34. It was never 100 per cent right from the time I came back but my spring was not affected as I jumped off my right.'

Con Martin was recalled to take Hurley's place against Spain who were, as ever, popular visitors. The crowd numbered over 40,000, many of whom were admitted free as the gates were broken down.

It was the custom for the players to report to the Gresham Hotel after Mass on Sunday and Carey requested they meet there at 12.30. He was there, the players were there – all except centre-forward Shay Gibbons. Finally, at 1.15, Shay arrived. Carey straightaway asked Gibbons if he knew the meeting was fixed for 12.30.

'Yes, Boss,' he replied, 'but I did not know it was High Mass.'

Fitzsimons opened the scoring after eight minutes, but goals by Pahino after 24 and 44 minutes had Spain in front at half-time. A lull in the excitement ended when Ringstead equalised in the 76th minute and, in a thrilling finish, Ireland might have won.

With an eye to the future, the youthful defence gave most satisfaction, with goalkeeper Jimmy O'Neill and full-backs Seamus Dunne and Noel Cantwell promising many years of good service.

Carey's position was clarified by the selection committee at his request. They decided that his current appointment would apply to the game in Holland on 10 May, that he would be paid the same fee as the players, and that his position would be ratified by council at the start of each season. There was no mention of him having any say in the selection process.

Adding interest to the game against Holland, the World Cup draw on 27 April paired the Republic with England and Denmark. Three new caps were chosen: St Patrick's Athletic wing-half Tommy Dunne, a son of the legendary Jimmy Dunne, Arsenal left-winger Joe Haverty, a former youth international, and Manchester United inside-forward Liam Whelan.

For Con Martin, captain in the absence of Farrell, it proved a traumatic occasion.

'My sister died and I was going to cry off but Joe Wickham persuaded me not to,' he recalled. 'I attended the funeral on Tuesday and then left by plane for London, on to Amsterdam and from there by car to Rotterdam, arriving at four in the morning.' He had just a day to recover and get into the right frame of mind, as the game was on the Thursday.

Carey's tactics were simple: 'You are smaller and lighter than the opposition so don't try to batter yourselves to defeat. Use the ball and the open spaces.'

To facilitate this, centre-forward Jack Fitzgerald was detailed to act as a link, coming off the centre-half and leaving the space for inside-forwards Fitzsimons and Whelan to come through.

The result was one of the Republic's most impressive away performances. Fitzsimons and Whelan created havoc, with the Middlesbrough player thriving on the slide rule passes of his teammate, who had a magical debut. Seven minutes after half-time Fitzsimons opened the scoring, Haverty made it 2–0 after 60 minutes and Fitzsimons and Ringstead had the Republic 4–0 ahead before Appel got a consolation goal for the Dutch.

It was considered a triumph for Carey who, for the first time, sat on the touchline with the trainer and the reserves, puffing his pipe. It was also a special day for 33-year-old Con Martin, who bowed out of international football on a high note just as his manager had done three years earlier. In his 30 appearances, Martin had served Ireland well in a variety of positions from goalkeeper to centre-forward, a genial giant who earned the respect of opponents in hard battles splendidly fought.

'While waiting at London airport for the flight to Paris for the World Cup tie in 1953, a Millwall supporter came over to me and said, "Charlie Hurley will be taking your place one of these days," and it suddenly dawned on me that I couldn't go on forever,' recalled Con.

However, with Hurley unable to step straight into Con's shoes, the selectors had to look elsewhere for a centre-half. Two magnificent performances by the League of Ireland in September 1956 against the English and Scottish Leagues prompted the selectors to utilise the league's entire half-back line of Tommy Dunne, Gerry Mackey and Ronnie Nolan, for the opening World Cup tie at home to Denmark.

'When we were having our shower after the game against the Scottish League, Joe Cunningham came in and said "Well done, lads, it will be the same half-back line against Denmark",' remembered Dunne. 'Once Joe said it we knew we did not even have to look in the papers for the team.' Cunningham, the Shamrock Rovers' Chairman, was not even a selector, but he remained one of the main power brokers in Irish soccer until the late 1960s.

The League's centre-forward, Dermot Curtis, was also chosen but, with five changes from the team which had done so well in Holland, it was not surprising that they never functioned as fluently. Whelan and Fitzsimons did not come up to their Rotterdam form, and Cantwell was the only one to enhance his reputation.

Nonetheless, a 2–1 win was achieved, thanks to goals from Curtis after 28 minutes – when a Fitzsimons shot was deflected to him – and a Johnny Gavin penalty just before half-time when Haverty was taken down running on to a Fitzsimons pass. Denmark's consolation goal came with four minutes to go.

Money, rather than the points won, was the issue at the following council meeting. Noting the small profit on the game (£1,023) led on to a discussion about the expenses claimed by the selectors. For the Denmark trip this amounted to £223 which was considered 'too high and unnecessary' by one delegate. The Chairman pointed out that selectors had to travel to watch certain players but added that the council could if it wished, decide that they should not do so. The matter went no further. The discussion was a reminder that, with an overdraft of £320, the FAI was not in a position to be generous.

Carey must have been aware of that for he refused to accept his fee for the following game against West Germany because he felt he had not been able to give it sufficient time. This was noted at the international affairs committee meeting on 3 December, and a letter of appreciation forwarded to him.

For the visit of the world champions on Sunday, 25 November the selectors increased the number of League of Ireland players to six, with first-time caps for goalkeeper Alan Kelly and outside-right Jimmy 'Maxie' McCann. A further honour for the home brigade was the nomination of centre-half Mackey as captain. When Manchester United refused to release Whelan, his place was taken by Shamrock Rovers' Noel Peyton, another new cap.

Training in Milltown led to an unusual situation, which Haverty recalled: 'We were training there one day when a young fellow came into the dressing-room and got stripped. The cross-channel players thought he was a League of Ireland player and the League of Ireland players thought he was a cross-channel player but after we had done the first lap and he said "Take it easy there" we realised he was just a passer-by. That was how casual it was.'

That Sunday proved to be a great day for the Irish. In the first half, they could not make the breakthrough but 12 minutes into the second half there was a great roar from the 35,000 crowd when Curtis, who was proving a handful for the Germans, was sandwiched in the penalty area and the referee pointed to the spot.

Cantwell duly obliged to put Ireland ahead and two cracking goals in the last four minutes settled the match beyond doubt. In the 86th minute Haverty scored after a great Fitzsimons pass and two minutes later McCann, following a short corner which was returned to him by Tommy Dunne, hit the net with a blistering left-foot shot.

The first signs of a Green Army travelling in support of the Irish team came at the council meeting on 14 March 1957, when it was noted that '3,000 tickets had been applied for and paid for' in respect of the World Cup tie at Wembley. A request was sent to the English FA for some extras for late applications.

With the prospect of two of their biggest ever pay-days in sight, the FAI decided to increase the players' fee to £50 for the World Cup matches with England. A further £600 was allocated to sending a youth team to a West German tournament.

When the World Cup panel of 22 was announced it included seven League of Ireland players. A surprise omission was Luton Town's George Cummins, who was listed for stand-by duty even though there was a severe shortage of first division players. Although Hurley was fit again, the selectors kept faith with Mackey, presumably on the basis that he had done a good marking job on the England dangerman Tommy Taylor in the inter-league game the previous September.

However, it proved to be Taylor's day. A loser in the Cup final with Manchester United, he quickly put that disappointment behind him with two goals in the opening 18 minutes.

In the 38th minute Kelly could only palm a Finney cross as far as John Atyeo who made no mistake for number three and, two minutes later, Taylor headed a Finney corner practically out of Kelly's hands for number four.

It was a disconsolate Kelly who sat in the dressing-room at half-time, head in his hands as he muttered to Noel Cantwell: 'If this is English football I don't want to know.'

After the break, Ireland fought back, with Curtis giving Billy Wright a hard time. Fitzsimons brought the best out of Alan Hodgkinson before Haverty, in the 55th minute, beat Jeff Hall beautifully and crossed for Curtis to head powerfully into the net. There were chances at both ends after that but no further score until the 90th minute when Atyeo linked up with Finney and blasted the return past Kelly.

'The result was flattering to England, 4–2 would have been fairer,' said Carey. 'We had the outstanding player on the pitch in Haverty. The second half showed England can be beaten and there is no need to be despondent about meeting them in Dublin.'

With Cantwell keeping Stanley Matthews quiet, in front of him Haverty was able to produce his most elusive form against a bewildered Jeff Hall but elsewhere the Irish defence did not fare so well, with Finney a constant problem for Don Donovan, while Taylor and Atyeo ran Mackey and Saward ragged. In attack, apart from Haverty, Whelan and Curtis showed up well.

For the FAI the attendance was a 'disappointing 54,000', which gave them almost £7,000 as their share of the £18,000 receipts. No doubt they were thinking of the 100,000 who had attended the Cup final the previous Saturday with receipts of almost £50,000.

Among the 5,000-plus Irish fans was Charlie Hurley.

'I went along because I was told there was a chance I might get in for the game in Dublin and I wanted to see what I was letting myself in for.'

When he picked up the paper the following Monday he read of his selection for his first cap.

'That made my father the happiest man in the world. He always said I'd wear the green jersey. For four weeks from the time I was picked he never did a day's work. He worked in Fords and the factory was full of Irish. He sat in a corner talking to all of them about his son – and the fact that I had a good game gave him the two weeks after. He was king for a month.'

Four changes were made for the return game: Hurley for Mackey, Tommy Godwin for Kelly, Seamus Dunne for Donovan and Ronnie Nolan for Farrell, with Cantwell taking over the captaincy from the veteran Farrell, whose distinguished career ended at Wembley.

Sunday football was still taboo at Lansdowne Road so every effort was made to increase the capacity of Dalymount Park. An all-ticket record crowd of 47,500 eventually crammed in, providing an atmosphere which proved hugely uplifting to the home team.

After only three minutes, Whelan passed to Fitzsimons and his cross from the end line flashed across goal to where Ringstead coolly drove it past his Sheffield United team-mate Hodgkinson.

In an enthralling game, with Ireland giving as good as they got, it was end-to-end stuff after that, with Godwin and Hurley performing heroics in the Irish defence, Whelan running the midfield, and Haverty and Curtis taking up where they had left off at Wembley. While Seamus Dunne had to stop a Ronnie Clayton effort on the line, Wright made an even more dramatic save from Haverty, diving almost full length to head away the little winger's goal-bound shot.

The 90 minutes were up when Finney turned to Cantwell and said: 'Well done, you deserved to win this.' In the press box the journalists were debating where the play-off would be held, with Windsor Park and Hampden mentioned. The Dalymount Roar, which reached new dimensions on this historic day, was building up to an unprecedented crescendo, and then in injury time, came the moment which remains one of the darkest memories of all Irish fans, those present and the countless thousands more listening to Philip Greene's commentary on the radio.

An Irish attack broke down and Hall played the ball up to Finney. What happened next is engraved on the memory of Irish captain, Cantwell.

'He beat me and eventually got past Pat Saward. I had got back to him again and, as he crossed, the ball hit the lace of my boot and lifted over the heads of Charlie Hurley and Tommy Taylor who were running to meet it at the near post and it went on to Atyeo, the big man with the brown boots and probably the worst player on the park and he was on his own to head the equaliser.'

Ireland, he believed, were denied victory by the width of his laces for had the ball not been deflected he is convinced Hurley would have headed it away, having beaten Taylor to every other cross in the 90 minutes. The resulting silence, it was noted, could be heard a mile away at Nelson's Pillar in O'Connell Street.

'It was an emotional game,' recalled Cantwell. 'We did well, but it was an effort, we were poles apart in ability. We only had two or three first division players in the team. Liam Whelan was a quality player and gave Duncan Edwards a roasting.'

Hurley, thrown in at the deep end on his debut, recalled it as one of the great games of his career.

'I actually surprised myself. I was a third division south player and these were first division giants.

'I was marking Tommy Taylor, one of the greats of the day, but his strength was my strength – in the air – and that was the compensation. To come away from the game and Taylor not having had a chance in the 90 minutes was very pleasing.'

It was some consolation to the Republic that, in Hurley, they had discovered a world-class centre-half, 'a colossus who could grace any international team', as Liam Tuohy put it.

While they missed out on the World Cup finals, the FAI at least had plenty of money in their coffers. The annual report for 1956–57, which did not include the games against England, showed a profit of over £3,000 from the international scene; the profit the following year was almost three times that amount. Referring to the Dalymount game, the 1957 report stated it was 'possibly the greatest display ever by an Irish team. This was a game to be remembered and it aroused more enthusiasm than any other previously played on this ground.'

The World Cup campaign concluded on a controversial note in Copenhagen on 2 October. A fine Irish victory, secured by second-half goals from the recalled George Cummins (53 minutes) and Curtis (62 minutes), was spoiled by time-wasting tactics which incensed the Danes and led to a near-riot situation.

'We were under pressure and a few of the old pros went down with injury to upset their rhythm. Suddenly the crowd started throwing apples at us,' recalled Hurley. 'The goalmouth was covered with apples and Tommy Godwin, who had no teeth and would remind you of a corpse when you looked back at him, picked one up and pretended to eat it.'

This infuriated the crowd even more and resulted in a caution for Godwin, who later explained: 'I would have eaten an apple, but it would have taken me 20 minutes. With no teeth I would have had to crush it to death.'

After the game the Irish party – team, officials and press – had to be smuggled out across an adjoining football ground by Danish officials to avoid an angry mob waiting outside the main arena.

On the same night, Shamrock Rovers played Manchester United in a European Cup tie at Old Trafford. The selectors decided not to call on players from either team and so Ronnie Nolan and Liam Whelan, two of the heroes of Dalymount, were replaced by O'Farrell and Cummins.

The following week the League of Ireland visited Elland Road where they were beaten less than convincingly 3–1 by an English League team of 'young hopefuls'. Taking part in the match were Jack Charlton and Liam Tuohy, whose paths were destined to cross again at Elland Road in controversial circumstances.

Another new source of competitive internationals was found when the council decided to enter the new Nations Cup. Together with the World Cup, this competition would in time completely overshadow the friendlies which for so long had been the FAI's staple diet and main source of income.

The Munich air disaster of 6 February 1958, which claimed the lives of eight Manchester United players, was a tragedy for soccer worldwide as United's young team had been blossoming into one of the all-time great combinations. Among the victims was 22-year-old Dubliner Liam Whelan and, although he had played a mere four games for the Republic, he was a huge loss. Many thought he was destined to become one of the mainstays of the side for the next decade.

Sir Matt Busby paid Whelan the highest compliment when he said: 'The tragedy is that he had the ability to be one of the all-time greats. He had amazing natural ability. I always said that Billy (Liam) would be our di Stefano and Bobby Charlton would be our Ferenc Puskas, the two key men in Real Madrid's great team.'

In fact, Whelan had not been long at Old Trafford – sent by ace scout Billy Behan – when Busby turned down an offer for him from a Brazilian club.

'He was their type of player – he had all the Brazilian skills. They offered me a blank cheque but I told them that all the money in the Bank of England wouldn't buy him,' recalled Sir Matt.

Whelan's individual ability and his scoring record – 43 goals in 79 league games – give some idea of his talents. His dribbling was said to be on a par with that of Finney and Matthews; his shooting from 30 yards out was compared with that of Jack Rowley and, in a great United team, he was the playmaker who made it tick.

While United could dip into the transfer market to replace such talent, however inadequately, that option was not open to the Irish selectors. They had to wait for someone displaying similar talent to emerge from the ranks of schoolboy footballers. When other great players came along, such as Johnny Giles, it only underlined the tragedy, prompting thoughts of what might have been had Giles and Whelan lined up together in the green jersey.

Sadly, the FAI were not always conscious of the need to encourage young talent. Despite their new-found wealth after the World Cup bonanza, they decided against sending a youth team to an international tournament in 1958. Charlie Liddy's spirited appeal on behalf of youth football was turned down and it would be some years before the Republic resumed participation at that level.

Carey's influence was evident when the selectors discussed the 1958 tour to Poland and Austria. It was agreed that 14 players should make the trip and be paid £30 for each match whether they played or not. 'Changes to be made in the second match, if considered necessary, by the manager, in consultation with Mr W. McCormack and the Secretary', the minutes of the selection committee meeting of 10 April noted.

The Republic made history on 12 May when they became the first team from the west to play in Poland since the war. The Slaski Stadium in Katowice was packed to its 100,000 capacity but the facilities were more wild western than western.

'We had to change in our hotel,' recalled captain Cantwell, 'and after playing in something like 100 degrees, at half-time we retired to tents set up in the stadium, with only a bucket of water and a sponge between all 11 players.'

In the hot and sultry conditions, the fans were treated to a masterly display by Hurley, whose coolness and confidence were an inspiration to his team-mates. Curtis was once again the star of the forward line, heading in the first goal after 12 minutes from a Ringstead cross, and leaving his marker trailing after 49 minutes to set up the second goal for George Cummins.

Poland earned a 2–2 draw with a 74th minute goal by Zientara but it was the Irish the fans saluted with cries of 'Bravo, Bravo' at the end of the game.

'The heat made all the difference,' said Cantwell. 'We tired in the closing stages.'

To play another hard match just three days later was asking a bit much of the players but this was the case, with Austria providing the opposition in Vienna. It was an example of the kind of false economy and poor planning which would remain a problem right into the 1980s.

Only two changes were made from the team that did so well in Katowice. Jimmy O'Neill replaced Godwin in goal and Mick McGrath came in for his first cap at right-half, in place of Ronnie Nolan, decisions to which the manager had an input.

McGrath played a storming game, laying on some beautiful passes for the forwards, but Hurley, up against a speedy opponent who matched him in height and physique, was never the commanding figure of the Poland game. He was not helped by a bad crack he received in a clash of heads in the first half.

This was Austria's first floodlit international but the lighting left a lot to be desired. Korner (20 minutes) and Buzek (59 minutes) had them in control before Curtis replied with a header from a Ringstead cross in the 70th minute – his fifth goal in seven internationals. A late Korner goal confirmed Austria's superiority.

A rare show of player power occurred on this tour when spending money was applied for and a payment of £1 per day was granted by the travelling officials, who were already in receipt of this allowance.

The FAI had its own peculiar way of dealing with players' expenses, as Haverty recalled: 'When I was with Arsenal the FAI never questioned my expenses but when I was with Millwall they docked £5, probably on the basis that I should have been glad to play for Ireland while I was at the Den. Then, when I was playing part-time for Shelbourne I had to take a week off work to play for Ireland and they wouldn't allow the expense. That was a sore point for League of Ireland players as they needed the money more.'

In its budgeting the FAI had a willing ally in the manager as Fitzsimons recalled: 'Each player filled in an expenses sheet and gave it to the manager. Players coming from London would have most expenses getting to Dublin. We claimed for meals and taxis and they might come to £10 or £12 and Carey would say they were a bit much and would you knock off that taxi.'

On 4 September 1959 the council addressed the question of the official party for continental matches. They decided it would be the chairman of council, one other honorary officer, the chairman of the selection committee, two members of council (by rota) and the secretary. Add in the trainer and the manager and it meant there would be more than one official for every two players. While council was good at looking after its own interests, the players' interests were neglected. The question of a medical officer travelling, for instance, was not even considered. It was some time before this omission was rectified.

For the return game with Poland on 5 October at Dalymount, the selectors were able to name the same forward line – Ringstead, Fitzsimons, Curtis, Cummins and Haverty – for a fourth successive game. Shay Keogh (Shamrock Rovers) was introduced for the unavailable Hurley.

Considering this line-up represented the nearest thing to a settled team in years, it proved a big disappointment on the day. The game was one of the worst for a long time and the forwards took most of the brickbats. In fact, it cost centre-forward Dermot Curtis his place at both club and international level.

He had moved to Ipswich Town from Bristol City and they were scheduled to play at Swansea on 4 October. When Curtis discovered he would not be able to make it to Dublin in time, he asked manager Alf Ramsey for his release.

'He told me he was leaving it up to me, but that if I decided to go to Dublin he couldn't guarantee me my place back.'

Curtis, who had made a promising start at Ipswich, lost his place as a result of his commitment to Ireland and, subsequently, lost his place on the international team because he was not playing first-team football.

It proved a bad day also for goalkeeper Jimmy O'Neill, who was at fault for the goals which gave Poland a 2–0 lead after just 19 minutes. Then, in the 65th minute, he was injured making a save and had to retire, with Waterford's Tommy Taylor coming on.

Taylor's appearance raised a chuckle or two among the fans, and caused questions to be asked at the following council meeting. It was all to do with his playing gear which did not exactly meet the accepted standards.

'There was no reserve gear,' recalled Taylor, 'so I used Bohemians' gear. I came on the field with the red and black socks down around my ankles and wearing a tracksuit top, which I removed when I put on Jimmy O'Neill's jersey. I borrowed a cap from one of the photographers behind the goal because the sun was straight into my eyes.' By coming on for the last 20 minutes, Taylor's fee increased from £10 to £30, earning him over £1 a minute.

Cantwell salvaged a draw with goals in the 26th and 31st minutes, the first a penalty, awarded when Fitzsimons was sandwiched going through, and the second a volley when a Seamus Dunne free-kick was cleared to him.

The overall display caused the selectors to discuss policy for future games at their next meeting on 28 November. The need to watch up-and-coming players was mentioned. It was thought that a League of Ireland v cross-channel players match would be helpful, but the main problem – that of asking the players to play twice within 24 hours – was not discussed.

The dates for the preliminary round European Nations Cup tie with Czechoslovakia were arranged on 28 October. The home game on 5 April 1959, should have been the first in the new competition, but the Soviet Union had played its first-round first-leg tie against Hungary in Moscow on 28 September, winning 3–1. The Soviets' second-leg game was not played until the following September, which meant that Ireland's matches, with the away game on 10 May, were the first to be completed.

Good displays by League of Ireland players in inter-league and B internationals were reflected in the team chosen and one of the victims was Curtis, whose record at international level was second to none. He was replaced by Shelbourne's Christy Doyle, who had scored in B games against Iceland and South Africa. He was following in the footsteps of his uncle, the great Jimmy Dunne. Shamrock Rovers' forwards Tommy Hamilton and Liam Tuohy also got the call.

Former Shelbourne player Brendan McNally won his first cap, taking over at right-back from Seamus Dunne, the man he had replaced in the Luton Town team in its run to the FA Cup final.

The attraction of a competitive game boosted the attendance to 37,000 and they were well pleased with what they saw. In defence, the big men, Cantwell, Hurley and Saward, were superb and Cummins was the star of the front line, always constructive and displaying ball control of the highest quality.

The problems for players making their debuts for the Republic at that time were put into perspective by Christy Doyle.

'It was both an ordeal and a great day,' he said. 'It was like being transferred to another team. I was playing as a twin striker with Shelbourne, but in that international side the two inside-forwards, Tommy Hamilton and George Cummins, were really midfield players, so I was a lone forager up front, a role which wasn't best suited to my game'.

To Tuohy fell the honour of opening Ireland's account in the new competition and he did it, in the 21st minute, with one of his trade-mark goals – a far-post header from a Hamilton cross. Cantwell converted a penalty awarded for handball in the 41st minute to complete the scoring.

For the return game in Bratislava on Sunday, 10 May, the selectors surprisingly dropped Saward to the reserves, bringing in O'Farrell. Doyle was also replaced, by Fitzsimons, winning his last cap and playing for the first time in the number 9 jersey, 'the position I had started out in with Johnville as a schoolboy,' he said.

A further change was required with the defection of McNally who, along with Cummins, was on the losing Luton Town side in the FA Cup final on 2 May. This let in former B cap, Dick Whitaker (Chelsea), for his one and only cap.

The FAI had not done their homework regarding the venue. The team was billeted in a hotel in the centre of town; it was festival time and bands were playing outside all night. The players found it impossible to sleep.

Undermining Ireland's hopes of holding out for an aggregate win was the poor form of defensive kingpins Hurley and Cantwell. In the fourth minute

Hurley dummied to let the ball run over the end line, but Pavlovic somehow got to it and crossed to Bubernik whose header O'Farrell had to save with his hands. Goalkeeper Stacho scored from the spot kick.

It was 1–0 at half-time and all to play for but the sluggish Irish, for whom McGrath and Fitzsimons were the only players to show their true form, were eventually worn down and conceded three goals in the last 23 minutes.

It was a disappointing end to the Republic's first Nations Cup engagement. With such a small pool of players, if one or two were off form or were missing, it made the difference between victory and defeat. The absence of leading scorer Curtis from both games was a silly, self-inflicted wound, compounded by the omission of Saward for the more attack-minded O'Farrell, evidence of poor tactics. However, even if they had played it is quite likely that the bands of Bratislava would still have sounded the Last Post for Ireland.

Early hopes that Carey's managership would revitalise Ireland had not quite materialised. The loss of Liam Whelan was, of course, incalculable. Looking to the future, Carey, in his position as manager of Blackburn, had given a young Bray lad, Andy McEvoy, his first-team debut at the end of April and he had scored twice in a 3–1 win over Cup finalists Luton; at Old Trafford, another young Dublin-born inside-forward, Johnny Giles, was about to make his mark. The big question was: would these players blossom in the Irish set-up?

8

The Giles Era Begins

The first of November 1959 was an important day in the history of the Republic of Ireland international team, for it was on that day that the career of Johnny Giles was truly launched. Over the next 20 years, Giles was to have a vital influence over practically every event of note regarding the international team.

Born in Dublin the son of former Bohemian and Shelbourne footballer Dickie Giles, Johnny was a precocious talent, a prodigy whose effectiveness never waned throughout a long and illustrious career. A player of exceptional vision and passing ability, his two-footedness enabled him to change the direction of play with pinpoint passes to either wing. Small and stocky, he was an inside-forward of the old school, he loved to have a crack at goal and was possessed of a tremendous shot, but he later adapted to a more withdrawn, midfield-general role as the game changed in the mid '60s.

Signed by Manchester United through ace scout Billy Behan's friendship with his father – they had played together at Shelbourne in the early 1930s – Giles had played only twice for the first-team when he was suddenly catapulted on to the international scene. And what a match for an 18-year-old to make his debut – at home to World Cup runners-up Sweden, who had just confirmed their well-being by beating England 3–2 at Wembley, despite travelling with only three of the players who had contested the World Cup final the previous year.

On the Wednesday when Sweden beat England, Giles was helping a Manchester United youth side beat Home Farm in Dublin. He was due back at Old Trafford before returning for Sunday's international, but fog prevented a quick return and Jimmy Murphy told him to take a few days off at home.

It was the ideal preparation but Giles was one of only three Irish players who did not have to line up for their clubs 24 hours before they faced Sweden. Charlie Hurley's predicament was typical. After a hard game at Roker Park for Sunderland, he had to get a taxi outside the ground and rush, with a police escort, to the station to catch the Holyhead train. He arrived in Dublin at seven o'clock on Sunday morning, having had little or no sleep.

Ireland's good home record, plus the introduction of new caps Giles, Noel

Dwyer and Joe Carolan, allied to Sweden's defeat of England, meant that interest in the game was at fever pitch. An attendance of over 40,000 crammed into Dalymount.

For manager Carey there was time only for a quick talk with his players, most of whom had seen televised highlights of Sweden's Wembley victory. The dangerman in that game had been centre-forward Simonsson, who had scored twice, so a lot depended on how Hurley handled his man. When Sweden scored twice in the first 13 minutes, captain Noel Cantwell turned to Hurley and said, 'There's still 80 minutes to go.' The Irish were in trouble and if inspiration was not found from somewhere, a humbling home defeat was in store.

Four minutes later, Giles provided that inspiration when he made his first dramatic intervention in international affairs. A Fagan cross from the right was headed clear by Johansson under pressure from Curtis. It dropped to Giles 30 yards out. He allowed it to bounce and then struck a classic drive which was in the net before goalkeeper Nyholm could move.

It was a goal to set any game alight, and the Irish team suddenly caught fire. Just before half-time, a move involving Cantwell, Saward and Curtis brought the ball to Giles and he flashed it out to Haverty who immediately crossed for Curtis to run, jump and head a truly magnificent equaliser. If ever a goal could be said to lift the roof off Dalymount, this was it.

The Republic resumed the second half in the same mood and, after eight minutes, were rewarded when Cummins ran on to a long throw-in from Saward and brought the ball to the end line before flicking it across to Curtis who had only to tap it into the net. It proved to be the winning goal.

Simonsson, who had been a doubtful starter with an injury picked up at Wembley, was asked after the game if his injury was the cause of his problems. His reply was a fitting tribute to Hurley: 'It was not my foot; it was my shadow!'

Manager Carey commented: 'I consider this the best football an Irish team has played at Dalymount Park.' The most pleasing aspect was the much-improved play of the forwards. Haverty was back to his best; Curtis looked a more confident leader; Cummins had the ability to hold the ball; Fagan did well on the right wing, and Giles had a dream debut. All the hopes that had been invested in Giles were seen to have substance. Things could only get better, it seemed.

Unfortunately, this encouraging win – it does not merit the appellation 'great' despite the excitement it generated at the time – only served to paper over the cracks of what was not a good Irish set-up.

As Giles recalled: 'I was lucky to come into an experienced side for my first match, but unlucky in that Pat Saward went out of the side soon after. I hardly played with Georgie Cummins again, likewise Dermot Curtis and Fionan Fagan. There was no continuity in those days. The structure was not there for players to come in and enjoy the continuity that we had later on.'

The selectors did make an attempt at continuity by naming the same team for the next game on 30 March 1960, at home to Chile. However, when Blackburn were unable to release McGrath, their plans were thwarted and he was replaced by Ronnie Nolan.

The FAI, which had been making overtures through Sir Stanley Rous for games with any of the British Associations, were elated in January 1960 when they received word that Wales would visit Dublin on 28 September.

Both the Wales and Chile games were fixed for midweek, representing a growing trend which would prove of some help to the selectors. It also underlined the need for floodlights at Dalymount Park.

Against Chile, Giles was again the star, playing even better than on his debut, while Cantwell, Hurley and Saward also showed their class in a 2–0 win which extended the Republic's unbeaten home record to eight games. Cantwell opened the scoring from a needlessly conceded penalty, and Curtis added the finishing touch nine minutes from time with a powerful shot after being put through by Saward.

Giles and Carolan were unavailable for the Republic's tour to West Germany and Sweden in May. It was only a minor hiccup in Giles's career but Carolan never again featured on an Irish team. He was transferred at the end of the year to Brighton before dropping out of league football while still a young man.

Saward proved an inspiring captain against West Germany with a wonderful display combining cool defensive work with adventurous attacking sorties. Hurley was an able accomplice in thwarting German attacks, but the man who really won the hearts of the 51,000 fans in Dusseldorf was goalkeeper Noel Dwyer. On West Ham's transfer list, Dwyer gave one of the best displays of goalkeeping the Germans had ever seen. In keeping a clean sheet he so impressed the German coaches that they subsequently used film of his performance to illustrate the art of goalkeeping.

The only goal came on the half-hour when Fogarty played a corner short to Peyton, whose curling centre was punched clear by Sawitzki, under pressure from Curtis, only as far as Fagan who shot right-footed in to the net.

A delighted Carey told his players they could have the following day off, a concession which Dwyer took literally – he disappeared from the team hotel! When he returned to the hotel two days later his left elbow had swollen to the size of a handball, an injury for which he had been receiving treatment at West Ham. Cantwell was also having treatment for an ankle ligament injury but when Carey left the decision to the players, they both declared themselves fit.

This gave the selectors the chance to experiment against Sweden on 18 May, with Cantwell at centre-forward. Against West Germany, Curtis had been the tallest forward, and he was only 5ft 9ins; Cantwell, at over 6ft and 14 stone, gave the forward line more potency in the air . . . such was the theory of the selectors and it probably had the backing of Carey.

Cantwell was injured early on in a clash with goalkeeper Nyholm and Dwyer also suffered a recurrence of his injury shortly after the start but no change was

87

made until near half-time when Peyton came on for Cantwell. Maurice Swan replaced Dwyer at the break. The Swedish part-timers, who included farmers, engineers, office workers, salesmen and a labourer, were 3–0 up by then, but the changes brought an improvement and the Irish fought back, gaining some reward when Fagan scored from the penalty spot after Curtis had been brought down. Dunne's last-minute, misplaced back pass enabled Boerjesson to notch the Swedes' fourth goal.

Dunne had played his last game for Ireland – just a month after his 30th birthday. While 30 was always regarded as a dangerous age for professional footballers, it was particularly so for those hoping to win favour with the FAI's selectors. Dunne was only one of many to be discarded once they reached 30; team-mates Cummins and Curtis were soon to follow. This policy contrasts starkly with the success enjoyed by later Irish teams which had an age profile of almost 30, with half the players over that age.

The game against Wales on 28 September was marked by one of the most unusual dilemmas the selection committee was ever likely to face. Leeds United's Peter Fitzgerald was chosen to lead the line, the unfortunate Curtis losing out again despite his excellent record. Fitzgerald, 23, was a member of a famous Waterford footballing family – his brother Jack had been capped in the mid '50s and two other brothers had won amateur caps. He had just signed for Leeds from Sparta Rotterdam.

A tall, strong, speedy striker, Fitzgerald was a worthy choice. What made his selection unusual was that his father, M.J. Fitzgerald, was a member of the selection committee! Another selector, Sam Prole, had a similar experience the following February when he was one of the selectors who chose his son Robert to play for the Republic's amateurs against England.

It was the natural bias of players to say that selectors knew nothing about football. Right or wrong, it was a handy defence in case of bad results, and it also ensured that the players got the praise in the event of a win. Peter Fitzgerald had no hesitation in attributing the same lack of football knowledge to his father.

'He did not know a lot about the game even though all his sons played,' Peter said. 'He would have been happier playing golf, and only came into football in the latter years when Tom, Denny and Jack made their name with Waterford. He was introduced to the club through my brother-in-law, Ben Wadding, and became a director.'

MJ spent some years as a director, was elected to the FAI Council and, from there, to the selection committee. It was a simple progression, with a willingness to spend time at council and selection committee meetings of more importance than any perceived football knowledge.

With Cantwell and Cummins unavailable, the Republic lost its proud five-year unbeaten record at Dalymount. New full-backs Phil Kelly (Wolves) and John O'Neill (Preston) had an unhappy baptism as Wales owed their 3–2 win to wingers Cliff Jones, who scored twice, and Terry Medwin. Phil Woosnam scored the third Welsh goal. Fagan was the marksman for the Republic, the first a blistering left-footed shot from 35 yards and the second from the penalty spot after Giles had been tripped by Stuart Williams.

Amends were made with the visit of Norway on Sunday, 6 November. Giles and Fagan showed the way with some magnificent shooting; the Republic overcame the loss of an early goal and some uncertain defensive play to win 3–1.

Fagan scored the first Irish goal with a classic left-footed shot from a pass by new cap Johnny Fullam (Preston). It was Fagan's fourth successive scoring game. Fitzgerald was the hero, scoring twice, the first after goalkeeper Ashjorn Hansen had parried a Fagan shot and the second from a pass by Giles.

'I was delighted with my performance.' Fitzgerald said. 'But when I met my father after he was more interested in the result of Waterford's game that day. He said I should have scored four, probably because someone had made that observation in his presence. He was a hard man to please.'

While the win over Norway was a timely boost for the forthcoming World Cup games against Scotland and Czechoslovakia, the defence again exhibited a certain frailty. Filling the right-back spot was proving difficult.

Meanwhile, the Old Trafford Irish contingent grew stronger as Cantwell was transferred from West Ham for a record fee. Earlier in the year, Matt Busby had, on the advice of Billy Behan, also signed Shelbourne full-back Tony Dunne. The concentration of so many Irish players at one club was to have its disadvantages. These were not immediately apparent as United were struggling, but once they resumed their successful ways, their players were not as readily available for international duty. This trend was followed by most successful clubs and did not apply just to the Republic. It would ultimately lead to direct action being taken by FIFA to ensure the release of players for competitive games.

Boosting Irish hopes for the World Cup tie against Scotland at Hampden on 3 May 1961, was the timely return to action after a serious injury of Giles, and also of Georgie Cummins, who had missed most of the season following a cartilage operation. However, the selectors were in a quandary over ace goalgetter Fagan. Having scored five goals in the previous four games, he should have been a certainty, but he was in dispute with his team, Derby County and had not been playing any football. The selectors opted for Giles at outside-right, much to his disgust. 'I played outside-right at United because I couldn't get into the team otherwise.' he explained, 'but that shouldn't have applied to the Irish team. I had never played outside-right before for Ireland and it was not my best position.' Thus were sown the seeds of his disenchantment with the selection committee system.

Fitzgerald also had his problems. He had been told to report to the Irish hotel in Glasgow on Monday, 1 May, at 11 a.m. His Leeds team-mate Billy Bremner offered him a lift and promised to call for him at 6 a.m. Fitzgerald was up at 5.30 and waited until 8.00, but there was no sign of Bremner.

'By then I had missed the morning train and I did not arrive until the players were going out for training. I remember I was more afraid of my father than the FAI. I was fined £30 and named as one of the reserves for the game. I was so upset I told Noel Cantwell that I was going home but he persuaded me not to do that, not to embarrass my father.'

When Fitzgerald later wrote to the selectors regarding the withholding of his match fee, he apologised for his late arrival at the hotel and explained how it came about. However, it was decided unanimously 'that no fee be paid'. By this time, his father was chairman of the selection committee, but he ensured that, like Caesar's wife, he was above reproach on this contentious issue.

The Irish fans travelled in large numbers, but the Rangers duo of David Wilson and Ralph Brand spoiled their day. They tore the Irish defence apart; Wilson, in particular, had a field day against McNally. But for a magnificent display by goalkeeper Dwyer, ably supported by the classy Hurley, the final scoreline would have resembled a massacre.

Two goals from Brand put Scotland 2–0 up at half-time. Haverty converted a Giles cross to make it 2–1 after 52 minutes, but further goals from Wilson and David Herd gave the scoreline a more Scottish slant.

The selectors made four changes in their bid to repair the damage for the return game in Dublin the following Sunday, 7 May. There was a first cap for Everton half-back Mick Meagan; Phil Kelly replaced McNally, and Fagan and Fitzgerald were recalled in an attack which had Giles back at inside-forward.

Unfortunately, the big crowd (36,000) was treated to practically an action replay of the Hampden game. Scotland, two goals up after 16 minutes, rode their luck in each case, Young seeming to be offside for the first and Wilson appearing to let the ball roll over the end line before whipping in the cross which Young converted for the second.

The expected Irish fightback never materialised, and the crowd let their feelings be known with the slow handclap. Brand finished the scoring in the 86th minute. Only Dwyer and Hurley emerged with credit.

Czechoslovakia, the other team in the group, filmed both games, and their coach had no hesitation in stating that they would beat the Irish 'unless they found some new players'. It was transition time for the Republic, with the backbone players – Dwyer, Cantwell, Hurley, McGrath, Giles and Haverty – urgently in need of reinforcements.

The selectors turned to Shamrock Rovers in their crisis. Ronnie Nolan was named at wing-half for the home game with the Czechs on Sunday, 8 October. His team-mate Frank O'Neill was chosen at centre-forward, although outside-right was his best position.

On the Saturday, in the British championship, Scotland trounced Northern Ireland 6–1 in Belfast, and the Scottish journalists travelled *en masse* to Dalymount in the hope that the Republic would secure a World Cup ticket for their Celtic neighbours by taking a point from the Czechs.

The Irish had to overcome a third-minute setback when Scherer's shot deflected off Hurley past Dwyer. Giles, who was back to his best with quick bursts and powerful shooting, equalised just before half-time with a tremendous drive, but the second half was a stroll for the Czechs as the usual problem of two games in 24 hours took the zip out of most of the home team.

Kvasnak, with two goals in nine minutes, proved the matchwinner for the visitors and ensured that they needed only to beat the Irish in Prague to earn a play-off with Scotland for a trip to the World Cup finals in Chile.

To the surprise and dismay of many fans and scribes, the selectors named the same team for the return game on 29 October. A lot of the criticism from the first game had focused on the lack of fighting spirit in the team and, to the Irish fan, this is the unpardonable sin.

Not surprisingly, Giles disagreed with that view.

'The problem was that we did not have a great selection of players. There was a dip in standard from the time I made my debut in to the '60s, and other teams became more organised. We stayed as we were while others improved. We had some good players but never had enough organisation, and things weren't done professionally enough to make use of the players we had.

'The defeat by Czechoslovakia shouldn't have been any big surprise when you compare their preparation to ours. It was no contest.' It certainly was no contest. The Czechs took the Irish apart. A record 7–1 defeat could have been even more.

Hindsight can be a great healer and it helped in this case when Czechoslovakia went on to beat Scotland 4–2 in the play-off and became one of the great European teams, going all the way to the World Cup final in 1962, eventually losing 3–1 to Brazil. Eight of their final team had played in Dublin.

On 7 March 1962, the Dalymount floodlights were officially switched on. The FAI now had the alternative of a midweek arrangement for its important fixtures, but they were slow to take advantage of this option, persisting with Sunday games for a further three years.

The weakness of the Irish attack in the 1961 World Cup ties convinced the selectors of the need to move Cantwell to centre-forward for the game against Austria at Dalymount on Sunday, 8 April. This was the most notable result of their deliberations, which also produced two new caps, right-back Tony Dunne and inside-forward Alfie Hale.

Inspired by the magnificent Hurley, the Irish gave a heartwarming display. Cantwell had a good day in attack, scoring with a spectacular 40 yard shot from near the left touchline that went in off the post. He provided the second for Tuohy when his bullet-like drive came back off the bar. Tony Dunne was also a success, his decisive tackling and speedy recovery marking him out as a star of the future.

With the score at 2–2 and the Irish pushing forward for a winner, they were caught out by a long ball which left Hof in the clear. He stepped inside Hurley, who was rushing back, and gave substitute goalkeeper Dinny Lowry no chance.

THE BOYS IN GREEN

Meanwhile, at FIFA's congress in Santiago, England's proposal on qualification for international matches was passed. The new rule stated that 'qualification shall be birth within the area of the national association. In the case of subjects from abroad, their nationality shall be decided by the nationality of their fathers.' The new rule, which came into force for the 1966 World Cup, opened up a new avenue for the discovery of talent by the FAI.

After five consecutive defeats, the Nations Cup visit of unrated Iceland on Sunday, 12 August, offered a chance to get back on the winning trail. The selectors pinned their faith on the team that had done so well against Austria, the only change being the lively Amby Fogarty for the unlucky Curtis. While victory was duly achieved, the final score of 4–2 was not as convincing as it should have been and the usually reliable Cantwell missed a penalty. Tuohy opened the scoring after 11 minutes when he headed in a Giles cross; Fogarty scored the second by finishing off a Cantwell header and Cantwell made up for his penalty lapse with the other two goals, one a well-placed ground shot and the other a header from an Alfie Hale cross.

A depleted Irish side travelled to Reykjavik for the return on Sunday, 2 September, with McNally, Nolan, Curtis and Peyton in for Dunne, Meagan, Hale and Giles. After 38 minutes Curtis cut in along the end line and crossed for Tuohy to head in to the net and continue his impressive scoring record. Iceland equalised in the 57th minute, but the Republic's progress to the second round was never in doubt. Honour, it appeared, had been satisfied all round for the home fans gave their team an ovation as they left the field.

In May, Cantwell followed in the footsteps of Carey when he captained Manchester United to FA Cup victory, with Dunne and Giles also in the team which beat Leicester City in the final. Cantwell owed his elevation to the captaincy to a match United played in Dublin in February. Maurice Setters, who was to enjoy many happy days in Ireland as assistant to Jack Charlton, was United captain at the time of that game but his lack of co-operation with young Dublin autograph hunters was spotted by United's Irish scout Billy Behan and reported to Matt Busby. As a result, Setters lost the captaincy, with Cantwell taking over.

Scotland's visit to Dublin on Sunday, 9 June, led to a split within the selection committee. With the game being played out of season, there were no problems of availability, and the selectors restored Haverty to the left-wing position, even though Tuohy had scored in each of the last three games.

Tuohy's demotion was too much for Capt. Tom Scully (Shamrock Rovers), the chairman of the selection committee. He resigned in protest, and did not resume as a selector until the 1964–65 season. For Tuohy, the loss of his place on the team was hard to take because selector Billy McCormack had told him: 'You are being brought in to score goals. If you score you'll stay in. It is up to yourself.'

The selection committee, with its members' club allegiances, left the way open for trade-offs to be made to get 'your man' on the team. Tuohy, as a former Shamrock Rovers player, would have had the support of Capt. Tom Scully, but Haverty, a former St Patrick's Athletic player, could depend on Billy McCormack. In this case, McCormack had his way.

There was only one new cap on the team: speedy inside-forward Paddy Turner who, on the day the team was named, was transferred from Morton to Celtic. The ninth of June turned out to be a glorious summer's day and 26,000 shirt-sleeved fans witnessed another of those special days that the Republic served up from time to time.

After only seven minutes a low Haverty corner was mis-hit by Turner, but Cantwell collected the ball and swept it into the net. That ended the scoring but not the excitement on what proved to be a wonderful day for Cantwell, who became the first member of that team to win the coveted 25-cap statuette.

Alan Kelly was another star. He made a brilliant save from Millar just a minute after Cantwell's goal and, all through, his handling of crosses and shots was perfection.

Sustained Scottish pressure meant that the second half was a holding operation for the Irish and, as the closing minutes brought to mind the agony of the game against England in 1957, Hurley intervened.

'We were having a spell where we needed the crowd on our side,' he recalled, 'and I wanted to gee up our players. So I went to the terraces and shouted "Come on," with arms upraised, and the noise started with a rumble and built up into a roar and you could feel it lifting the players.'

It was one of those magical Dalymount moments, with the communion between fans and players helping to reduce the talented Scots to fumbling wrecks. Magical? Yes, because three days later, Scotland, with only two changes, slammed Spain 6–2 in Madrid.

Injuries and club calls reduced the selectors' options for the Nations Cup tie in Vienna on Wednesday, 25 September. Three League of Ireland players were called up – Ronnie Whelan (St Patrick's Athletic), Tuohy (Shamrock Rovers) and amateur defender Willie Browne (Bohemian FC). The only new cap was 26-year-old QPR defender Ray Brady.

Relentless rain turned the pitch into a quagmire and reduced the crowd from a possible sell-out 60,000 to 25,000. But the Republic's players had to get back to their clubs, so the game went ahead. Conditions were ideal for Brady and Hurley at the back to get stuck in and it was on these two that the Austrian attacks foundered. The home team's frustration flowed over, with their fans' hoots and boos echoing around Prater Park as the game became more and more bad-tempered.

Brady, who was man of the match from an Irish point of view, was the villain of the piece according to the Austrians, who labelled him the 'Assassin of Vienna'. He tackled ferociously, but when an Austrian player kicked him from behind he lost his temper.

'You had him chasing the guy who kicked him and the referee chasing Brady,' recalled Hurley. 'It was comical. Ray was lucky he did not catch the guy or he would have been sent off – and the Austrian was lucky Ray was not the fastest.'

Tuohy recalled another incident: 'Ray tackled this guy very hard and a little mêlée developed. He was being pulled out of it and turned and kicked the player who was pulling him only to discover it was Hurley. So Hurley was the only one to get injured in the mêlée.'

Another key figure was Giles. He slowed the pace of the game in the manner of a great inside-forward and, in the last 10 minutes, showed his true brilliance when, on two occasions, he lifted the siege with huge kicks to the corner flag, with no Austrian within 30 yards.

For all the pressure they had to endure, in the end the Irish could have won. Curtis twice hit shots straight at Fraydl and then Fogarty brought a fantastic save from the Austrian goalkeeper after he had parried Curtis's shot.

For Curtis, then with lowly Exeter City, it proved to be the last of what seems, in hindsight, a meagre 17 caps. He scored eight goals, a terrific ratio at a time when the Republic was not particularly strong, and was a constant thorn in the side of any defence he opposed. Although only 5ft 9ins tall, he was, according to Haverty, 'one of the best headers in the game, every bit as good as Tommy Lawton. You could just fling the ball over and he'd get it. He also gave the centre-half as much trouble as the centre-half gave him; he could take the stick and give it back too.'

While the 0–0 draw was hailed by some commentators as akin to the 1949 victory over England, Giles did not see it that way: 'Unfortunately for us, the way things were going, it was the worst thing that could happen to us. It only encouraged the FAI to go on the way they were going.'

There was no place for Browne, Whelan or Tuohy in the team named to play Austria in Dalymount on Sunday, 13 October. The selectors instead turned to the team that had beaten Scotland, with one change: Brady in at half-back and McEvoy moving to inside-forward to the exclusion of Turner.

Although McGrath was injured after only 16 minutes – he received nine stitches in a head wound after a kick by Jank – the Republic survived on the wave of euphoria which gripped the 40,000 fans who paid to get in and the thousands more who got in free when the gates broke down yet again.

Fogarty, at the 'dangerous' age of 30, was winning only his 10th cap. In the opinion of Haverty, he should have won many more.

'He was one of our most underrated players. He gave 120 per cent home and away. While he was not a graceful player, if I was in the trenches, he'd be the one I'd like with me. He tackled like a full-back, covered every inch of the ground and he made sure you did not shirk. He made other players play.'

With the game balanced on a knife edge, Cantwell having equalised Koleznik's 40th minute goal just before the break, Fogarty came into his own with a storming second-half display. After 65 minutes, when Giles back-heeled a Haverty corner, Fogarty forced the ball home for the lead. Flogel shot the equaliser in the 82nd minute and, with only a minute left, a Haverty shot hit

Frank on the arm and referee Poulsen (Denmark) pointed to the spot. In the ensuing pandemonium the crowd invaded the pitch.

It took four minutes to clear the pitch and, even then, the area behind the goal was full of enthusiastic fans waiting to congratulate the successful penalty taker. If ever there was a need for a cool head, this was it. Cantwell was the man, placing the ball on the spot, turning his back on the goal and then crashing the ball in to the roof of the net.

In what was clearly an intimidating situation for him, Austrian goalkeeper Fraydl was humorously described by Irish fans as having made sure he dived the wrong way! It may have been funny for the Irish, but the Austrians had another name for it. Herbert Meisel, sports editor of the *Daily Kurier*, wrote: 'The match ended in a unique scandal before 40,000 fanatics. The referee, who should have abandoned the match, apparently lost his nerve in the turbulent final phase.'

The draw for the quarter-finals threw up the alluring prospect of an FAI–IFA encounter, for the Republic were to meet the winners of the Northern Ireland–Spain tie. Northern Ireland earned a magnificent 1–1 draw in Spain, but their hopes ended in Windsor Park when Gento scored the only goal.

The Republic were to see a lot of Spain for when the draw for the 1966 World Cup was made in February 1964, they came out in the same group as Spain and Syria. Syria later withdrew, leaving it a straight fight between the Republic and Spain for a place in the finals in England.

Complications set in for the selectors when Manchester United and Sunderland had to go to a second replay to resolve their sixth-round FA Cup tie. This was fixed for Monday, 9 March, two days before the Nations Cup quarter-final against Spain in Seville. Dunne and Cantwell were withdrawn from the Irish squad by United, leading to a first call-up for Northampton Town full-back Theo Foley.

Hurley, despite his exertions two days earlier for Sunderland, lined up against the speedy Spaniards for his third game in five days; but it proved too much, and he was less effective than usual. In fact, it was his square pass intercepted by Amancio, which led to the first goal after 13 minutes.

Two minutes later Fuste added another, but a neat chip by Giles, which was taken and controlled on the run by Andy McEvoy brought Ireland back into the game after 22 minutes.

In the wet, greasy conditions, Amancio sparkled on the right wing and, in a three-minute spell on the half-hour, he scored one and laid on another for Marcellino. To cap a miserable night, Traynor deflected a Marcellino shot past Kelly in the 88th minute.

The 5–1 defeat made the second leg a formality, and the only hope for the future was in McEvoy's goal, his first for the Republic. A prolific scorer for Blackburn Rovers in the first division, his previous four caps had been at wing-half. His goal showed that, even with limited opportunities, he could get his name on the scoresheet.

Wholesale changes were made for the return at Dalymount on Wednesday, 8 April, a game which was played partly under floodlights. Another capacity 40,000 crowd attested to the drawing power of the visitors, but they saw little to cheer about, apart from some fine goalkeeping by Kelly. Once again it was a right-winger who did the damage. Zaballa, deputising for Amancio, capitalised on crosses from left-winger Lapetra after 24 and 87 minutes to earn Spain a 2–0 win and a place in the semi-finals on a 7–1 aggregate.

Fortunately, Spain were not due in Dublin for the World Cup tie for another 14 months, giving the selectors time to look at the talent available and, with four friendlies lined up, hopefully achieve a winning blend. The first chance was a tour to Poland and Norway in May.

With Carey on club duty with Nottingham Forest, the two most experienced players, Cantwell and Hurley, were appointed 'to look after the pre-match training and the players' general conduct'.

The selectors called up two League of Ireland players. Shelbourne's Freddie Strahan was earning his first cap, while Shamrock Rovers' Paddy Ambrose got a surprise recall at the age of 34, nine years after his previous honour. Ambrose was called in due to Cantwell suffering a recurrence of back trouble.

The game against Poland in Cracow was decided by defensive blunders, Brady and Hurley gifting goals, but, on the bright side, Tony Dunne came of age as an international with a polished display.

Brilliant work by McEvoy set up the Irish goal for Ambrose. He killed a long pass from Strahan with the outside of his foot, beat two defenders with a quick feint and pushed the ball through for Ambrose, who committed the goalkeeper and then hit the ball over him into the net. Later Ambrose had another goal – again set up by McEvoy – controversially disallowed. That would have tied the scores. Instead, the Poles managed another to win 3–1.

For the game in Norway, Hurley moved to centre-forward, with inside-forward Fullam dropping back, but it was an enforced change.

'The food was terrible in Poland,' recalled Hurley, 'and I got food poisoning. I was on the toilet all night. I was so weak I said to the selectors I wouldn't be able to play centre-half but stick me up front and I'll play as long as I can.'

With Haverty turning it on for a watching pen-pal, the Republic won 4–1 with goals from Hurley (2), Giles and McEvoy, raising expectations for the visit of England to Dublin on Sunday, 24 May. Billed erroneously as the FAI's 100th international – it was the 98th – the game was an all-ticket affair.

The visitors, under Alf Ramsey, were building a formidable team and their task was made easier by the absence of Hurley through injury. Willie Browne took over at centre-half and Eddie Bailham was awarded his first cap at centre-forward after finishing top scorer for a Shamrock Rovers side that had swept all before it.

On a pleasant, sunny day, the game was not without controversy. Haverty started as he had in Oslo and twice got past George Cohen in the first couple of minutes. The next time he got the ball, Cohen caught him and his ankle was broken.

Top left: Bob Fullam: scored Ireland's first goal; *Top right*: Frank Brady: great-uncle of Liam and captain of Ireland; *Bottom left*: Billy Lacey: Liverpool legend and Ireland's oldest cap; *Bottom right*: John 'Kruger' Fagan: War of Independence veteran whose son Fionan also played for Ireland

Top: Tom Farquharson, the Dublin-born goalkeeper who refused to play for the IFA
Bottom: Dr Douglas Hyde, President of Ireland, was banned by the Gaelic Athletic Association
for attending the game against Poland in 1938. He is seen being introduced to Willie Fallon by
captain Jimmy Dunne. A youthful Jackie Carey is on the extreme left (*Sunday Independent*)

Top: The FAI's first World Cup team, which drew 4-4 with Belgium on 25 February 1934 in Dalymount Park. From left: (*front row*) Billy Kennedy, David 'Babby' Byrne, Paddy Moore, Tim O'Keeffe, Jimmy Kelly (*back row*) Miah Lynch, Joe Kendrick, Jim 'Fox' Foley, Tom Burke, Joe O'Reilly, Peader Gaskins (capt), coach Billy Lacey
Bottom: The team that beat England at Goodison Park in September 1949. From left: (*front row*) Peter Corr, Tommy O'Connor, Jackie Carey (capt), Peter Desmond, Peter Farrell, David Walsh (*back row*) Con Martin, Thomas 'Bud' Aherne, Tommy Godwin, Tommy Moroney, Willie Walsh (*Sunday Independent*)

The last All-Ireland team: the IFA team that played Wales on 8 March 1950 in Wrexham (0-0). The FAI players included are Reg Ryan (*extreme right back row*), Con Martin (captain), 'Bud' Aherne and David Walsh (*last three on front row*)

The team that scored a pulsating 1-0 win over the Soviet Union in the World Cup in September 1984. From left (*back row*) Mark Lawrenson, Seamus McDonagh, Liam Brady, Chris Hughton, Ronnie Whelan, David O'Leary (*front row*) Michael Robinson, Tony Grealish, John Devine, Mickey Walsh, Tony Galvin (*Sunday Independent*)

Top: Don Givens completes his hat-trick against the Soviet Union in the European Championship in October 1974
Bottom: The goal that silenced Dalymount: England's John Atyeo, third from left, about to head the last minute equaliser in the World Cup tie in May 1957 (*Sunday Independent*)

'I had only to finish the game to get a contract with Celtic,' recalled Haverty, 'and I could turn it on in those circumstances. But after I had twice gone past Cohen he decided he did not want to get a chasing so he got me.'

It did not help that Haverty's replacement, Ronnie Whelan, had never played on the left wing or that he was not 100 per cent fit, having been injured in an end of season friendly. He had considered pulling out but was persuaded to stay in the squad by his club's selector, Billy McCormack.

'I did not feel right and I couldn't believe it when Joe was injured after five minutes and I was told to go on,' Whelan recalled, while Haverty jokingly remarked: 'I was fitter going off than Ronnie was when he came on.' It was another indictment of the selection committee system and the FAI's failure to appoint a medical officer.

England's attack led the Irish a merry dance early on, capitalising on Browne's uncertainty. John 'Budgie' Byrne, back in his parents' home town, showed no mercy, laying on the first goal after nine minutes for George Eastham and scoring the second after 22 minutes from a Jimmy Greaves pass.

A switch between Browne and Cantwell improved matters and, with a minute to go to the break, Strahan struck for an incredible goal. Receiving the ball on the half-way line, he dribbled to the penalty area, brushed past Ray Wilson and Bobby Moore and shot past Tony Waiters. It was real Roy of the Rovers stuff and raised hopes of an Irish revival in the second half, but a Greaves goal after 56 minutes completed the scoring. The difference in class between the teams was obvious, but more apparent was the fact that England were a team, while the Irish were a collection of individuals brought together on the day in the hope that they would click.

The start of the 1964–65 season offered some hope, with the League of Ireland in sparkling form in a 2–2 draw with the Scottish League at Dalymount, and Shelbourne advancing in the Fairs Cup at the expense of Belenenses. These games brought Jackie Mooney (Shamrock Rovers) and Jackie Hennessy (Shelbourne) to the fore while, in England, McEvoy continued where he had left off the previous season and was topping the goal charts with Blackburn Rovers.

Mooney and Hennessy were duly rewarded with their first caps when the team to play Poland at Dalymount on Sunday, 25 October was announced. Injuries to Hurley and Giles, brought in Theo Foley and Frank O'Neill, the latter only learning of his elevation on the morning of the match.

The Poles came with an unbeaten record in '64, but only 25,000 attended a thrilling contest. Lubanski started as though he was going to tear the Irish apart. Poland were 2–0 up after 22 minutes with goals from Lubanski and Pol, but Cantwell managed to put Lubanski off his game. When McEvoy revealed his goal-poaching genius in the 26th minute, the game was back in the melting pot. A through ball from Mick McGrath was deflected by Hennessy into McEvoy's path and he took it wide of goalkeeper Kornek before shooting from an acute angle.

The roar which greeted this goal – his first at Dalymount – was testimony to the fans' excitement at seeing for themselves the Blackburn goal-machine in action as much as to the fact that the goal brought the Republic back into the game.

The second half was Ireland's, but it was not until the 81st minute that the equaliser arrived, a Tony Dunne cross being flicked in to the net by Mooney. A minute later, the great comeback was completed when Foley whipped over a cross which Mooney headed in. Substitute goalkeeper Foltyny blocked the ball, but McEvoy was in like a flash to finish it off.

The threat of McEvoy, who had hit it off with Mooney up front, was emphasised by the fact that, apart from his goals, he also hit the post with a header and crashed another shot against the bar. With four goals in six appearances as a forward, he raised hopes that he was the answer to the Republic's attacking weakness. But, in that Irish set-up, it was not possible for a striker to prosper.

'With club sides, chances are being made all the time,' McEvoy said, 'but, with Ireland, so few were made and then, when one was, there would be a man marking you and another one behind you.'

Hero against Poland, McEvoy was villain in the next game, on Wednesday, 24 March 1965, against Belgium, when his unexpected back pass fooled Alan Kelly and gave the visitors the lead after 15 minutes. In this first fully floodlit international at Dalymount, there was to be no comeback by a weakened Irish team. A brilliant individual goal on the hour by Jurion, who cut inside and let fly from 25 yards, completed the scoring.

However, the early part of 1965 offered hope for the future in other games. The Republic's amateurs, so often a source of future internationals, were narrowly beaten 3–2 by England, with Jimmy Conway and Turlough O'Connor starring, while at youth level, the Republic finished seventh in the UEFA Championship, with Terry Conroy, Eamonn Rogers and Mick Leech prominent in a team which beat a Holland side containing the great Johan Cruyff.

Meanwhile, the FAI were anxious to take advantage of FIFA's parentage ruling and an ideal candidate had come to the fore in Manchester United's Shay Brennan, whose parents came from Carlow.

'I received overtures from Joe Wickham asking me if I would like to play for Ireland,' recalled Brennan. 'I did not have much chance of playing for England even though I had been in the 40 from whom the 1962 World Cup squad was chosen. I had attended a week's session in Lilleshall that year and played one or two representative games for the League v the Army, but Jimmy Armfield was a permanent fixture then and George Cohen took over from him.'

United won the League in 1964-65 with Brennan and Tony Dunne the full-backs and former Shamrock Rover Pat Dunne in goal. The FAI selectors chose them *en bloc* for the World Cup tie against Spain at Dalymount on 5 May, with United reserve Cantwell at centre-forward.

The number of Irish players with a first division pedigree had risen to nine, with League of Ireland players Frank O'Neill and Jackie Hennessy making up the numbers. Spain travelled without Italian exiles, Del Sol and Suarez and the injured Gento and Amancio but, as usual, they attracted a full house of over 40,000 to Dalymount.

The game was never a classic in strictly football terms, but as a contest it was riveting. The Spaniards were in control for most of the 90 minutes and it required excellent defensive displays from new caps Brennan and Pat Dunne and the veteran Hurley to keep them at bay.

However, the real hero for Ireland was Giles, back in his best role as midfield playmaker. His ball control and speedy penetration were the only threat to the visitors as McEvoy and Cantwell were marked out of the game.

The result hinged on a bizarre incident in the 63rd minute, which emanated from a foul on Giles as he made a run down the right touchline. O'Neill took the free-kick and floated the ball into the six-yard box. To the observers on the terraces, it was a poorly placed kick, being too close to goalkeeper Iribar. Cantwell realised this, too, but decided to challenge anyway. 'I remember running at Iribar and then, when I was not going to get the ball, I shouted at him. I can't remember what I shouted, I just wanted to put a bit of fear in him. He put the ball in the net — and afterwards called me an animal although I never got near him.'

The unhappy Spaniards refused to swap jerseys at the final whistle.

'We did not want any ill-feeling to be carried into the second leg,' recalled Giles, 'so we tried to get them to change their minds a little later. However, we found they had locked their dressing-room door, and because of the row going on inside we did not pursue the matter any further.'

With goal difference not applying, the Republic were sure of a play-off if they lost in Seville on 27 October. But the Irish cause was not helped when the majestic Hurley succumbed to injury and could not be considered. Shay Brennan was also injured and in the subsequent re-shuffle, Foley and new cap Eric Barber (Shelbourne) were called up.

Barber, rated by many as the best centre-forward in the League of Ireland in the 1960s, had an unfortunate introduction to the international scene.

'We were to meet at Dublin airport on Monday at one o'clock, and on Sunday night I developed toothache,' he recalled. 'On Monday morning I went to Mercer's Hospital, they gave me a shot and I passed out. I woke up in a bed, looked at my watch and saw that it was ten past one. Despite the pleas of the nursing staff that I was not fit to get up, I jumped out of bed, ran out of the hospital, and hailed a taxi.

'When I arrived at the airport I discovered the plane had been delayed. I remember running across the tarmac with photographers running alongside me. I had dark sunglasses on and was holding my swollen jaw. I probably looked as though I had been to a nightclub and been beaten up!

'Noel Cantwell came down the aisle to let me have it for delaying the flight but he was very understanding when I explained. They gave me two penicillin injections each day, but it was a mistake for me to play. They left the decision to me and I was too anxious to get my first cap. It was the only game I ever wished to be over. I must have been the worst passenger ever, I only touched the ball about five times.'

The Spaniards dominated the first half – corner count 14 to one – but they had Portuguese referee Freitas to thank for their 2–1 half-time lead. In the 19th minute he disallowed McGrath's goal after the Blackburn player had hit a quickly taken O'Neill free-kick in to the net. Freitas claimed he had not given a signal, yet in the 44th minute he allowed Spain's second goal to stand when he again gave no signal and a quick free-kick went to Zoco whose shot was parried by Pat Dunne, but only as far as Pereda who scored.

It wasn't as though the Spaniards needed the help of the referee, despite the Republic taking a surprise 26th minute lead when McEvoy finished off a Giles cross. It took Spain until the 40th minute to equalise despite all their pressure, and the controversial 44th minute goal gave them the lead, with second half scores from Pereda (completing a hat-trick) and Lapetra giving an accurate reflection of the trend of play.

On the same night, a League of Ireland team played the English League in Hull. The Irish, captained by Liam Tuohy, went down 5–0, with Leeds' centre-half Jack Charlton claiming one of the goals.

Agreeing on a venue for the 10 November play-off, to decide which team went forward to the World Cup finals in England the following year, took some long, hard negotiations. It was not until 3 a.m. on Thursday that a decision was finally made – Paris.

The Republic again had to do without Hurley and he was joined on the injury list by McGrath and Alan Kelly. Fortunately, Shay Brennan was available again, and the only new cap was a frail but skilful inside-forward from fourth division York City, called Eamon Dunphy, a 20-year-old Dubliner who had been at Old Trafford the previous season.

Neutral Paris may have been, but it did not appear that way as 30,000 Spaniards took over the Parc des Princes. The Irish team were taken aback when they emerged from the 50 yard long tunnel on to the pitch to be greeted by a veritable sea of red and gold flags and banners.

Tactically, the selectors had chosen an extra defender, Northampton Town full-back Theo Foley, who played in midfield and did a marking job on Spain's playmaker, Luis Suarez. Haverty impishly recalled: 'Theo couldn't do anything but he could volley a good winger and he kicked Suarez out of the game.'

Allowing for poetic licence, Foley certainly put the clamps on Suarez who was in no way as effective as Giles. The little Dubliner produced his greatest display to date with a world-class exhibition of how to find space and how to use the ball. He was a constant thorn in the Spanish side.

Meagan was another to rise to the occasion. He displayed all his wiles to keep Pereda quiet and had excellent support from Cantwell, playing centre-half in place of Hurley, Shay Brennan and Pat Dunne.

However, this was no 90 minutes of defensive football, but a polished, all-round display by the Republic who gave as good as they got. Giles was narrowly wide with a header early on and then laid on two chances for McEvoy, the first of which was headed just over; the second was deflected inches wide by Zoco with Betancourt well beaten.

In the second half, Giles hit a long-range dipping shot which Betancourt touched over at the last minute, and then the Spanish goalkeeper just beat McEvoy to a Giles through ball.

An injury to Foley disrupted the Irish pattern and let Spain in for the decisive score. In the 80th minute, as Foley was coming back after treatment, Pereda crossed the ball, Cantwell got a touch, but only as far as Ufarte who slammed home the only goal of the game. It was a case of history repeating itself, for in the 1957 World Cup tie with England it was Cantwell's touch to Finney's cross which had carried the ball to Atyeo for the silencing equaliser that eliminated the Republic at Dalymount.

The mood in defeat was strangely euphoric, for this was a display to rank with the best ever by the Republic. The general feeling was that the players had done themselves and their country proud and, with a bit of luck, might have been in the World Cup finals.

One player who admitted his limitations was new cap Eamon Dunphy. Writing in the *Con Martin Annual*, he said: 'If ever a player was out of his class that night it was me. The pace of the game was far greater than I had ever experienced, the skill of the opposition was unbelievable and even my own colleagues, mostly from first and second division clubs, were geared to a far faster game than I had anticipated.'

Dunphy, later to make his name as a controversial commentator on football, added: 'It was an experience I'll never forget, a real baptism of fire and a game I am delighted to have figured in. I learned a lot from it.'

While commentators in general reflected an upbeat mood, one writer was looking down the road and painting a bleak picture of the future. Bill Kelly, the *Sunday Press* correspondent, pointed out that the team beaten by Spain was composed of veterans or near veterans.

'Noel Cantwell is nearing the end of his career. Shay Brennan, Theo Foley, Andy McEvoy, Mick Meagan, Charlie Hurley, Mick McGrath and Joe Haverty will be over the hill for the next World Cup.'

Arguing that it was time to start planning, he called for an end to the selection committee system. 'If I had my way, I'd appoint a one-man manager-selector who would have complete control of the team. Unless we are prepared to revolutionise our approach, we must be prepared to remain as "gallant losers", and "moral victors", while other countries are the factual and financial winners.'

Sadly, there was no indication that his voice was being listened to by the FAI who continued blithely on their way. The only changes made were in the personnel of the selection committee. In their opposition to real change, they were about to reap the whirlwind.

9

Decline and Revolt

After the near miss of the 1966 World Cup, the decline of the team proceeded gradually, delayed only by the presence of Giles. With defensive mainstays Hurley and Cantwell at the veteran stage and Hurley increasingly injury-prone, it was left to the diminutive Dubliner to provide the class and inspiration needed in an international arena which was becoming more and more competitive. Giles was the one truly world-class player in the team at this time; his value cannot be overstated. It was unfortunate for him that his best years happened to coincide with the break up of what had been a fairly useful team. Shay Brennan summed up Giles's unique contribution:

'Everything revolved around him. You could always find him, that was one of his gifts and he always seemed to have space – that's something you can't coach into anybody. He was the best ever to come out of Ireland in my time, him and Liam Brady.'

Spain visited Dublin for the first European Championship game on Sunday, 23 October 1966, and promptly indicated that they were taking no prisoners when, in the first minute, Santamaria laid centre-forward Ray Treacy low – out of the action, but not out of the game as he proceeded to prove his considerable fighting spirit by coming back for more.

It was as rough and tough an international as the 40,000 crowd (paying record receipts of £11,000) were ever likely to see, with the football suffering as a consequence and few chances being created. In the highly charged atmosphere, Cantwell proved an inspirational leader at centre-half in place of the injured Hurley, as the Republic battled to a 0–0 draw.

By playing Spain on a Sunday, the FAI had put profit ahead of preparation. The record receipts were to prove a short-term return, as the point dropped left the team without much hope of reaching the later stages of the competition, and the fans' expectations – raised by the World Cup near miss – quickly evaporated. For the next game, at home to Turkey (played on a Wednesday and won 2–1), the crowd was down to 25,000 and, following two away defeats, by the time Czechoslovakia arrived in May, support had dwindled to a mere 6,500, the lowest ever.

The team chosen to play Spain in Valencia on 7 December had Cantwell at centre-forward. When he reported injured, McEvoy was selected but, when he in turn was injured, the selectors had to find a replacement. They met on Sunday, 4 December and the minutes of their meeting state that Waterford's Alfie Hale was given the number 9 jersey, because 'this player had a passport and was ready to travel the following day'!

A 2–0 defeat was no disgrace, but it meant that a win was a must in Turkey on 22 February and, when this failed to materialise (Turkey winning 2–1), Jackie Carey announced his resignation.

Joe Kinnear, who made a fine debut that day and has since made his name as manager of Wimbledon, was born in Dublin but brought up in Watford from the age of 10. His father, Joe Reddy, was a goalkeeper with St James's Gate. When he died Joe's mother re-married and Joe took the name of his stepfather, Gerry Kinnear, a Tyrone man.

'That first game I played under Jackie Carey, a very laid-back manager, and in the side were five future Irish managers, Kelly, Meagan, Hurley, Cantwell and Giles. I wouldn't mind making that six. I remember Carey saying to me, "You've nothing to prove, go out and enjoy the occasion and make the position your own."

Limerick's Al Finucane, also making his debut, was disappointed with Carey.

'He was one of the heroes of the game for me. I had only read about him and I was in awe of him, but his management of the team was ordinary and his tactics mundane. That was one of the disappointments of my first international – he did not live up to my expectations.'

That criticism of Carey should come from a League of Ireland player is not surprising, as he seems to have been more comfortable with players from English clubs. He knew them and was able to keep in touch with their form, while, for the form of the League of Ireland players, he was at the mercy of the selectors.

Liam Tuohy was also disappointed with Carey.

'There never seemed to be a pattern of play indicated and the goalkeeper tended to be told to get it down the pitch. He said to the goalie before one match "This team are better than us so when you get the ball kick it as far away as you can because then it will take longer to come back." There was very little attempt by him to outline a plan of campaign and that was a disappointment to me because he was a great player and had a great reputation as a manager in England.'

Shay Brennan, who as a youngster on the Old Trafford terraces idolised Carey, remarked: 'It was not what he said, it was what he did not say that disappointed me. I thought that he was big enough in the game to have told the FAI that he was going to pick his own team.'

Giles, acknowledging the limitations imposed on Carey as a manager without power of selection, agreed with Brennan.

'The only criticism I have of Carey is that he did not seem to make any effort to change the situation. He seemed to accept that this is what is entailed in being manager of the Irish team and that's what he did.'

Andy McEvoy, who had experience of Carey as manager at Blackburn, adopted a less critical line.

'As a club manager he got out with us in a tracksuit. He had very good skills and got the lads to play as he wanted them to play. But with the international team we usually met on Sunday morning and he kept it very basic. He wouldn't say that much and wouldn't give you a bollocking at half-time as he would at the club.'

Mick Meagan also had Carey as his boss at Everton.

'I admired him as a manager. He was so proud of being Irish and always wanted you to make something of yourself. He used to tell us about the Blackburn player Dave Whelan who broke his leg and then opened a little stall in the afternoon – he's now a millionaire.

'With the international team I felt he did not want to confuse the players by trying to put a fortnight's work into a half-hour so he left you alone.'

Hurley, captain and defensive kingpin for many of Carey's games in charge, remembers him with affection, calling him 'the most laidback manager in football.'

'Carey's situation was different from that of a club manager. Quite often he'd turn up and find players missing, pulled out by their clubs on the pretext of injury even though they could play the following Wednesday. Carey knew this, and losing three top players must have been deflating for him, as it often meant taking the backbone out of the team. He was very calm about it but, deep down, he may have been seething.

'For Tony Dunne's first cap against Austria, we had a weakened side and Carey said, "We've not got much chance here today. Those who can play, play, and those who can run, run, and if we do those two things well, we've got a chance." We only lost 3–2.'

Cantwell was, perhaps, the player who got closest to Carey during his 10 year reign. He was captain for most of those years and was encouraged by Carey to speak his piece in the dressing-room. However, the Corkman's memories are not entirely uncritical.

'He was my idol as a young lad and, while I was at West Ham, I went to Highbury to see him play for Manchester United. He was a great passer and had a great influence on that team.

'When he was appointed Irish manager I thought it would be great to play under him and, as captain, I had more reason to consult him.

'One of the things about Manchester United under Busby was that there was very little coaching – you were left to yourself to do it out there. I always wanted to improve my knowledge of football so, whenever I got a chance, I sat and listened to Carey. I thought he would have a lot of ideas, but I soon got the impression he felt there was very little he could do with a team who assembled on the day.

'Before a game he would talk for a few minutes and then ask me to say a few words and I would often go on longer. I would emphasise what it meant to play for Ireland; the confidence you needed to show when playing and the aggressive nature we needed, especially against teams like Spain and Austria. We needed to hunt in packs and put them under pressure.

'I remember Carey having a team meeting and asking our forward line to stand up. They were all small and he asked; "Now, how do we play with you?"

'He often left the responsibility to the players themselves. I can appreciate players being disappointed with his input. He never raised his voice – he was not the enthusiast who transmitted his enthusiasm to the players. He was not a motivator, which was important. He never got excited. I've been in dressing-rooms after we've beaten teams and everybody is clapping themselves on the back and he remained the same calm Carey as before.

'He was a great father figure for the national team, but we probably needed a more aggressive coach and a stronger personality at the time. I wanted to change things and went to him with ideas, but he did not always back the players. Maybe he thought it was too much trouble. We couldn't even get a decent bus from the Gresham to Dalymount. That wouldn't bother him, but it bothered me.'

So Carey, the quiet, thoughtful, pipe-smoking lover of a passing game, was often bypassed by the pragmatic Cantwell whose team talk was based on 'the need to get the crowd on our side. I wouldn't bother talking about tactics. There was not enough time to worry about who was doing what. It was pointless to talk about free-kicks and throw-ins, so my talk was basically a rallying call and then, hopefully, I led by example.'

It is difficult to come to a verdict on Carey's contribution because he was a manager without any real power. Why he chose to remain so without any semblance of an attempt at rocking the boat is harder to come to terms with. His lack of ambition, or his gentlemanly nature, allied to his friendship with the selectors – whatever was responsible could be said to have held Irish football back at a time when even England, the great traditionalists, had seen the need for change.

The teams Carey had charge of can be briefly summarised as consisting generally of one or, at most, two world-class players, a further three or four of genuine international class, with the remainder selected in the hope that they might rise to the occasion.

The fact that most games were played in circumstances which reduced the hopes of success – home games 24 hours after the players had performed for their clubs, for example – must be taken into account when examining Carey's record. However, there is little evidence that he tried to effect change by insisting on midweek dates, or that he had any part in drawing up the team's fixture list, both areas which can make all the difference between victory and defeat.

The conclusion has to be that Carey was a passive servant of the FAI, and was quite prepared to let things go along as they were without attempting any real change. His acceptance of this role made the FAI's job easier, but was of little benefit to the players.

For the next game, at home to Czechoslovakia on Sunday, 21 May, the selectors turned to Hurley as Carey's immediate successor. They appointed him captain and coach for an extra fee of £20.

With Manchester United, Leeds United and Tottenham players all unavailable, it meant a complete re-vamp from the team that played in Turkey. Not surprisingly, the new-look side – even though it included only one new cap in Mayo-born Ollie Conmy (Peterborough United) – proved a failure, a lacklustre display earning the slow handclap from the 6,500 present (the smallest ever attendance at Dalymount for a competitive international).

The defence, with Hurley, Foley and Dempsey in form, kept the Czechs at bay, so it was rough justice that the two goals which decided the game should stem from defensive errors. In each case Al Finucane was the central figure. In the 16th minute he turned a harmless-looking shot into his own goal and, two minutes after the break, his pass was intercepted by Szikora who slipped the ball through for Masny to score.

There was no continental tour in the summer, but Shamrock Rovers, led by player-coach Liam Tuohy, were in the USA for a special tournament. They represented Boston. On 6 June, they lost 1–0 to Stoke City, who were representing Cleveland. The winning goal, two minutes from time, was scored by Stoke's captain and centre-forward, Maurice Setters.

The appointment of a successor to Carey exercised the minds of the selection committee when they met on 29 September, and Secretary Joe Wickham reported that he had received a phone call some days previously from Cantwell expressing interest in the position. He had advised him to forward a letter confirming his application and outlining his views.

Although Wickham had received no letter, the meeting agreed unanimously, 'that we recommend that Mr Noel Cantwell be appointed Team Manager for this season and that consideration also be given to an increased increment to him.' Within days, Cantwell had landed a second managerial post, succeeding Jimmy Hill as manager of Coventry City.

Wickham reported to the selection committee on 10 November that he had spoken on the phone to Cantwell. He relayed the manager's views on possible players and his hope that he would be able to travel to Czechoslovakia with the team for the final European Championship game on 22 November.

The selectors discussed the players available and the methods to be employed in the match and picked a team which included a fifth defender (previously tried with some success in the 1965 play-off game with Spain) and Fulham centre-back Dempsey at centre-forward. When Manchester United withdrew Dunne and Brennan, the team was re-cast, with Treacy and Fulham reserve Turlough O'Connor coming in up-front and Dempsey reverting to defence.

Cantwell, meanwhile, was having his problems at Coventry.

'I remember thinking that to go to Czechoslovakia would mean me being away for four or five days and it wouldn't go down well with Chairman Derrick Robbins. He wasn't the kind of man who would think much of me managing

Ireland. The Coventry job simply overtook everything.' In Cantwell's absence, Hurley was again appointed player-coach.

Czechoslovakia, on seven points, required only a draw to overtake Spain and clinch a place in the quarter-finals but their supporters were confident of administering another hiding to the depleted visitors. When the Irish team coach approached the stadium in Prague, the locals held up signs predicting a 10–0 win.

Despite tremendous Czech pressure – the corner count over the 90 minutes was 16–1 – there was no score at half-time, but disaster struck 12 minutes after the break when Dempsey volleyed a Meagan flick past Kelly for a spectacular own goal.

Hurley moved Dunphy to a more attacking role as he switched from a 4-4-2 to a 4-3-3 formation and, eight minutes later, it paid off with a goal which, even on paper, is thrilling in its brilliance.

Conmy brought the ball clear from his own penalty area and sent three opponents the wrong way before passing to Rogers near the half-way line. Conmy, still on the move, shouted for the return, but Rogers caught the Czech defence on the wrong foot by switching in the other direction to Conway and, from his pass, Dunphy crossed for Treacy to head home.

The Czechs' ace striker Szikora was carried off with torn ligaments after a clash with Hurley and the 10 men's world fell apart all together in the 85th minute when Popluhar tried to dribble past Treacy on the edge of his own area and was dispossessed. Treacy flicked the ball into the centre and O'Connor headed home. The two late call-ups had proved to be the matchwinners.

While the result had more significance for Spain, Hurley has always regarded it as the greatest Irish victory of his career. Meagan also regards it as one of the highlights.

'It had to be a great display to come from a goal down. The ground was frosty, so the light players like Conway, Dunphy, Conmy and O'Connor played great touch football. One of the best performances ever by an Irish player was that of Conmy, who was skipping by the Czechs. If this had happened at home a lot would have been made of it. I think the ground conditions were perfect for the likes of us.'

The final Group table showed Spain on top with eight points; Czechoslovakia next with seven; then the Republic of Ireland with five and Turkey with three. The three points lost at home to Spain and Czechoslovakia had proved costly. However, hopes of a new dawn were premature. The next Irish victory was 21 games and almost five years away! Spain lost out in the quarter-finals to England.

The friendly with Poland at Dalymount on Wednesday, 1 May 1968, proved to be Cantwell's only game in charge. With Manchester United and Leeds United in European action, there was a call-up for full-back Tommy Carroll, who had just helped Ipswich Town to the second division championship, and a recall for Johnny Fullam.

Mistakes by Hurley had Poland 2–0 up by the 24th minute but Dempsey justified the experiment of his selection at centre-forward by heading in a Fullam lob seven minutes after half-time, and impressive midfielder Dunphy brought about the equaliser. Receiving the ball near the right touchline with only a minute to go, he coolly beat four defenders before crossing to substitute Alfie Hale, whose bullet-like near-post header shot past Kostka.

The exciting finale, in which Hale justified Cantwell's decision to send him on for Eamonn Rogers, strengthened the manager's hand. The selection committee were anxious to renew his appointment for the 1968–69 season, which would feature the beginning of another World Cup campaign.

Again there was no close-season tour, but the disquieting news, when the selection committee met in August and September, was that Joe Wickham had received no response to letters and phone calls to Cantwell. Years later, Cantwell said: 'I find it staggering that they sent those letters to me and I never bothered to reply, because that's not like me.' With Coventry again in the relegation zone, Cantwell had to give his club priority, and the selectors finally gave up on him on 18 October and appointed Hurley player-coach for an extra fee of £30.

Ireland's visit to Katowice on Wednesday, 30 October, goes down in the record books as a 1–0 victory for Poland, but the date has more significance for the FAI as it was at this game that Joe Wickham collapsed and died. He was the longest serving secretary in world football, and over the years had been an excellent ambassador for the game and for Ireland. Wherever the Irish team went, Wickham was known and admired. He would be a hard act to follow.

Giles, who had missed the previous four games due to injury and club calls, was back for the home friendly against Austria on Sunday, 10 November, the last game before the start of the World Cup campaign.

For the third home game in succession, the visitors were given a two-goal start, Redl and Hof the marksmen. After the second goal in the 51st minute, Jimmy Conway replaced Jackie Hennessy and took over at centre-half, releasing Dempsey for another spell up-front. In a thrilling finish, Dunphy crossed for Rogers to crash a tremendous 20 yard shot in to the net in the 81st minute. Five minutes later, Rogers teed the ball up for Giles who dribbled through and shot against the post, with Hale finishing off the rebound for his second dramatic late equaliser.

The 2–2 draw and the inclusion of 10 first division players in the 22-man panel raised expectations for the opening World Cup game at home to Denmark on Wednesday, 4 December. However, while there was ample cover for all the defensive positions, the midfield and attack, apart from Giles, was mainly young and inexperienced.

In view of what was to follow, the World Cup campaign got off to an appropriately farcical start. With fog swirling around Dalymount, Scottish referee W.M. Symes delayed the kick-off for 28 minutes before giving the go-ahead. The Irish team gave their visitors their by now traditional welcome, conceding a goal to Wiberg after only 18 minutes. A Giles penalty for a handball offence equalised matters by half-time, and that's how it stayed as the game had to be abandoned six minutes after the break.

So the first World Cup tie became the home game against Czechoslovakia on Sunday, 4 May. It was only five months after the Denmark game, yet the selectors made five changes, two of them due to unfortunate injuries to in-form League of Ireland players Fullam and Hale.

The only new caps were Shamrock Rovers' 20-year-old goalscoring sensation Mick Leech, who had only recently returned after a seven-week lay-off with damaged knee ligaments, and his club-mate Paddy Mulligan, called in at left-back for the injured Mick Meagan.

The Czechs had a score to settle and they went about exacting vengeance in a crude way under the benign refereeing of Saldanha Ribeiro from Portugal, who lost control from an early stage.

It did not help the Czechs' equanimity that Rogers opened the scoring after 15 minutes, heading in an O'Neill cross. Shortly after, Leech beat a player on the wing and was going down the line when Plass came across, went right over the top and took him out of the game. It was a sending-off offence but the referee took no action. Leech, with a five-inch gash in his shin as a souvenir of his debut, had to go off and was replaced by Eoin Hand, another new cap.

The Czechs, aided by the referee, won the war; two second half goals won them the points also. The after-match verdict was that Hurley was past it and that Giles and O'Neill were the best of the attack. The following day, the selectors were given an encouraging hint of new striking talent when 19-year-old Don Givens scored twice in Manchester United's 4–0 defeat of Shamrock Rovers.

By his own admission, Giles had a quiet game against the Czechs, 'but this was understandable as it was my third game in six days. The others were Leeds' vital championship fixtures against Liverpool and Nottingham Forest, both of which took a lot out of me, mentally and physically.'

However, neither he nor the Irish public were prepared for the bombshell selectors Jack Traynor, Mick Toomey, Billy McCormack, Donie O'Halloran and Capt. Tom Scully dropped on 17 May when they announced the team to play Denmark in Copenhagen on Tuesday, 27 May.

Giles, O'Neill and Hurley were dropped, with Dunphy selected in Giles's role and Shelbourne's Billy Newman named as reserve midfielder, giving rise to the comment that 'the only people in this country who think that Newman is better than Giles would seem to be the selectors.' When Tony Dunne cried off, Newman was brought into the team in a re-shuffle and Jimmy Conway got the reserve spot. Suddenly, the selectors had discovered three No 10s who were better than Giles!

'I had never been dropped,' recalled Giles, 'but it was a time of inconsistencies in the game. I would have suffered because I was playing with a Leeds team which won the League that year, and when I came home they'd say why can't you play for Ireland like you play for Leeds.

'The difference was the very professional set-up at Leeds, with great players, so that you could perform as you wanted to, whereas the Irish team was very hit-and-miss. You were always up against it and the attitude was that I was not trying.

'It was a crazy situation. When I told Don Revie I was dropped he said "they must have some selection of players."'

For Giles, who was at the height of his powers as the playmaker in Revie's successful Leeds United, to be spurned by his own countrymen was impossible to accept. He had always had a keen awareness of his own worth – he had even parted from Manchester United to prove that point – and now, at 28, he was ready to take on and change the status quo within the FAI. A revolution was in the making.

Giles's first move was to make himself unavailable for the next World Cup tie at home to Hungary on Sunday, 8 June. For a player who loved wearing the green jersey, this was the supreme sacrifice, but he saw no other way of bringing matters to a head.

'I had given up on the system. I wasn't match fit as I hadn't kept in training because I thought if I was not in the 16 against Denmark what chance had I of being in the team the following month?

'That was a protest. I could have played. I was out of training because I was not that interested. I was sick of the way the team was being run. I couldn't say "I'm not playing because I was dropped," because people would say "Who does he think he is?" There was a lot of PR involved.'

Ireland lost to Denmark. The attack, even with the inclusion of new cap Givens, was no threat to the Danes, who scored once in each half through Soerensen. The only moment of light relief occurred just before the first goal when a female fan ran on to the pitch and set about man of the match Dempsey with an umbrella, apparently mistaking him for Newman who had just brought down Madsen!

The selectors shuffled their cards again for the game against Hungary. Apart from the recall of Giles, player–manager Hurley was moved to centre-forward. When Giles opted out, Rogers was called up from the reserves. The Manchester United full-back pairing of Brennan and Dunne were together for the first time in three years.

With Dempsey injured, Finucane took the number 5 jersey and had his best international against the Olympic champions. He subdued Dunai, while Mulligan put the shackles on Albert, and Brennan was so effective that Kozma was replaced by Farkas.

Despite going a goal down in the first half, the Irish were unlucky to lose. A lot of the credit for this was due to Dunphy, who filled in admirably for Giles. He did more work than any other player on the park, rarely wasted a pass and was the instigator of the move which led to Ireland's equaliser in the 59th minute.

Bringing the ball from his own penalty area, Dunphy spun an inch-perfect pass to O'Neill on the right wing. He in turn beat Szucs before floating a centre over the head of Meszoly to Givens who chested it down and volleyed into the net.

An unfortunate clash between Conway, running back, and Brennan after 80 minutes gifted the winner to Hungary. Farkas was left with time and space to measure his cross and Kelly, under pressure, could only knock it as far as Bene who accepted the opportunity clinically.

The game marked the end of Hurley's brief reign as manager but, more importantly, the end of his magnificent contribution as a player. At half-time he had taken himself off and brought on O'Neill.

Hurley at his peak was one of the few world-class players on the Irish side. He never missed a game except through injury and it was unfortunate that injury caused him to miss the most important game played during his career – the World Cup play-off in Paris against Spain in November 1965.

The influence of Drogheda director Charlie Walsh was evident in the selection of Hurley's successor. Walsh had persuaded Mick Meagan to return to Ireland as player–manager at Drogheda and then, in his role as an FAI selector, he was in a position to influence Meagan's appointment as international team manager for the 1969–70 season.

However, Giles remained the real kingmaker, and he saw in Meagan's appointment a chance to effect change. Ten years after his international debut, Giles had had enough of the amateurish FAI set-up, and was ready to act as the catalyst of change.

10

Meagan and Tuohy –
the Pioneers

The process of change speeded up considerably with the appointment of Mick Meagan, even though the FAI still kept their foot on the brake, unwilling to relinquish control totally.

Meagan's reign began on Sunday, 21 September, with a friendly against Scotland. He was quickly made aware of the problems to be faced when Tony Dunne, John Dempsey and Terry Conroy cried off. Meagan, with a welcome display of independence, chose himself in Dunne's position, even though the FAI had stipulated that the manager should not be a player.

After Scotland had opened the scoring in the eighth minute through Colin Stein, the Republic equalised in the 27th minute when Treacy and Hale combined in the penalty area to give Don Givens a chance which he converted at the second attempt. That ended the scoring, as the Irish were unable to maintain the hectic pace they had set. Meagan showed he could still do a job, but it was his last international, his 17 caps being a poor reward for a player of his talent.

Giles took the opportunity to initiate a players' meeting in the Four Courts Hotel.

'I thought it was about time something was done about the situation. We couldn't keep going on the way we were going. We formed a committee – Mick Meagan had to keep away because he couldn't be seen to be part of it – drafted a statement and went to the FAI. That was the start of the breakdown of the selection committee'.

On Thursday, 2 October, Giles and Frank O'Neill, two of the six-man committee, which also included Alan Kelly, Shay Brennan, Tony Dunne and Alfie Hale, had a formal meeting with the selection committee at which they presented their request for a sole selector of the international team, and offered the opinion that he should be, the then manager, Mick Meagan.

The selectors – Frank Davis, Michael Twomey, Billy McCormack, Charlie Walsh and Jim Younger – agreed to refer the players' views to council, and Giles and O'Neill expressed satisfaction at the hearing they had been given. However, O'Neill was probably not too pleased the following morning when he learned that he had been omitted from the 15 man squad to travel to

112

Czechoslovakia for the World Cup tie four days later, even though nine other players were unavailable.

With so many crying off, the last thing Meagan needed was a player who did not want to play, yet that was what happened in Prague during a 3–0 defeat in which Kinnear and Conway were the only bright spots in an otherwise dull show. Givens, after taking a couple of heavy tackles, was limping for the last minutes of the first half and had to be replaced. Andy McEvoy, then with Limerick, was the obvious replacement, but when Meagan told him to get ready, he refused.

'It was lashing rain,' McEvoy explained, 'and Meagan asked me to get out and run up and down but I said, "I'm not going out in that rain." So Johnny Fullam went out instead and he got on'.

McEvoy was one of the most talented strikers Ireland ever produced but he never realised his full potential. Al Finucane, his Limerick team-mate, explained: 'He was the most unassuming, introverted person you ever met. A lovely fellow, he was too shy to be an outstanding player. He was actually embarrassed by his own ability. When he was picked for that trip to Czechoslovakia he had already lost interest in the international scene and I'm surprised he even turned up.'

Giles kept up the pressure for change with a meeting in Manchester the day after the Prague debacle. O'Neill, Brennan and stand-in committee member Eamon Dunphy also attended. Strike action had been mooted, but Giles said after the meeting: 'There was never any question of strike action. We are prepared to accept the selection for Wednesday's game against Denmark.'

With Meagan consulted on the selection, a 4-3-3 formation was announced, with one new cap, Southampton's Tony Byrne. The FAI also filled a long-felt need with the appointment of Bob O'Driscoll, a Waterford surgeon, as team doctor. He had experience in a similar role with Burnley.

The game against Denmark was distinguished only by Givens' third goal in five internationals and Ireland's first World Cup point in a 1–1 draw. Mulligan was one of the better players, and he was transferred from Shamrock Rovers to Chelsea shortly after. As a result, there were no League of Ireland players in the squad which travelled to Hungary for the final World Cup tie on 5 November. That had not happened since the win in Prague two years earlier.

The Hungarians, intent on claiming a play-off with Czechoslovakia, made light of the Irish challenge and won comfortably 4–0. The game was marred by the sending off of Dempsey who disputed a free-kick in the 80th minute and seemed to threaten to throw the ball at Yugoslav referee Jackse. It was the first time a Republic of Ireland player had been sent off and, to rub it in, Kocsis put the resultant free-kick in to the net for Hungary's fourth goal. Hungary lost the play-off to Czechoslovakia.

Four games in less than three months, all against quality opposition, had meant a hectic start for Meagan. When he looked back, that was one of his principal regrets.

'There were no easy matches at that time; no breathing space to give you confidence. The Cantwell–Hurley era was over and we were effectively starting again. The likes of Dunphy, Treacy and Conway coming in could never get the tempo of international football because we were always chasing the game. It would have been nice to play Malta or someone like that. A few of those matches would have given the players confidence, but the FAI were only thinking of money and so they always went for the big teams for friendlies.'

The draw for the European Championship pitted the Republic against three more big names – Italy, Austria and Sweden – but there was a lot of quality in the 15 man squad chosen for the Continental tour in May 1970, only three of them lacking first division experience.

Despite the riches of a full-strength squad, the performance against Poland in Poznan on 6 May was so disappointing that the only redeeming features were the tremendous goalkeeping of Kelly, the midfield mastery of Giles and another goal from Givens.

The trip from Poznan to Berlin was a nightmare.

'It was the most horrific I ever experienced,' recalled Joe Kinnear. 'We travelled by train and it was overbooked, so we [the players] ended up in the luggage compartment for about three hours while the officials were in the regular compartment. Then when we came to the border we had to get out on the platform while the Soviets sent their tracker dogs in, and our passports were taken from us and checked and double-checked. Giles was complaining like hell.' It was not ideal preparation for the game against West Germany on 9 May.

An unfortunate deflection by Eoin Hand gave the Germans the lead, but it was the Irish, with Giles at his best ably assisted by Mulligan, who dictated the game to such an extent that the 73,000 fans jeered their World Cup bound favourites.

Franz Beckenbauer was lucky not to be sent off.

'He nearly broke my leg,' recalled Shay Brennan. 'Beckenbauer was coming through and the ball ran away from him but he continued right through on me. I was lucky.' Later in the game the German superstar escaped punishment again when he took Conroy out from behind with a crude tackle.

Loehr touched a Held cross on in to the net in the 82nd minute but the Irish were finally rewarded three minutes later when Mulligan headed in a cross from Dunphy.

Two months later the new selection committee of Charlie Walsh, John Farrell, Patsy McGowan, John McKenna and Seamus O'Brien announced that Meagan would sit in with them in future to name a panel from which he would then select his team. The first trial of this new system was a return friendly with Poland at Dalymount on Wednesday, 23 September. There were debuts for promising Liverpool winger Steve Heighway and Shamrock Rovers' Mick Lawlor, son of 1950s international Kit Lawlor. Both looked the part but Lawlor had to retire hurt at half-time.

By then Poland were 2–0 up and the Irish luck was out with Lawlor and Treacy hitting the post and Conroy having his shot taken off the line as Poland registered their first win in Dublin.

Meagan exercised his power for the first time when the 15 man panel for the opening European Championship game against Sweden was announced, dropping Brennan, Hand and Treacy. Unfortunately, Giles was still injured and his loss was keenly felt by Meagan.

'One of my regrets is that Giles was not available for all the games,' he said. 'He would have given the young players a great lift. They would look around and see Giles and know they could give him the ball.'

Still, there were enough plus factors to attract over 30,000 to Dalymount on Wednesday, 14 October. It was one of the biggest crowds for some time, and all went well for the first 45 minutes. Irish pressure was finally rewarded two minutes before the break when Dempsey was fouled following a corner, and Carroll converted the penalty.

The only sour note was the extremely crude treatment Givens was receiving from Nordqvist and Grip. This confrontation reached ridiculous proportions when Givens was booked for a foul, before the referee finally condescended to take Nordqvist's name. Givens had to retire seven minutes from the end following another foul, this time by Bo Larssen. It was a bitter lesson for the young striker.

Sweden equalised through substitute Brzokoupil on the hour and hit each post in turn as they threatened danger with every attack. In the end, a relieved Irish team settled for a point.

For the return a fortnight later in Stockholm, Meagan had problems, with Dunne, Kinnear, Mulligan, Giles and Conway unavailable. He called in Shelbourne centre-back Paddy Dunning for his first cap and recalled Limerick's Al Finucane in a defensive formation.

It turned out to be one of the better performances under Meagan, with Dunphy once again assuming the mantle of Giles and slowing the game down by using the ball well in midfield and working up and back to control and dictate in the fashion of the maestro.

Up-front Heighway and Treacy gave the Swedes some anxious moments, while at the back Dunning's excellent reading of the game allowed him to have a satisfactory debut. Unfortunately, all the good work came to nought when, 15 minutes from time, an Eriksson pass put substitute Turesson through to beat Kelly and supply retiring Swedish coach Orvan Bergmark with a less-than-impressive farewell victory.

For Meagan it was a fierce disappointment.

'The players had done everything right for 75 minutes and were looking like they might score and then from that high, bang! Sweden score! From believing in ourselves, it was suddenly a case of starting all over again.'

With the value of hindsight, he regrets that he did not adopt a more attacking policy.

'I often think we should have forgotten about the opposition and see if we could score a couple of goals. Sometimes we pay these teams too much respect. One of my regrets is that the emphasis was not more on attacking them and seeing what they had to offer then.'

While that attitude might have had some justification against the Swedes, who were mainly part-timers, it would have been considered foolhardy against Ireland's next opponents, World Cup runners-up Italy, who were parading their final team with the exception of broken-leg victim Riva, replaced by Prati.

Before 55,000 fans in Florence on Tuesday, 8 December, Italy clinically dismissed the Irish challenge. They were helped by a 23rd minute penalty conceded when Brennan handled, and a Dempsey mistake upon which Boninsegn capitalised two minutes before half-time. Just before the second goal, Dunphy, who was having another splendid game, was injured, and had to be replaced by Mick Lawlor. Prati wrapped up the points with a third goal in the 85th minute.

Italian goalkeeper Albertosi did not have to make a single save in the 90 minutes, prompting *Il Messagero* to reflect that the game 'was a good training session for Italy'. *L'Unita* awarded Conroy and Dunphy seven out of 10, only Prati, with eight, doing better.

For the return on Monday, 10 May, 1971, the FAI, aware of Italy's popularity, moved the game to Lansdowne Road. Meagan, although denied Conroy because of a club commitment, had the strongest squad he had yet been able to assemble.

Don Revie, still peeved at the treatment Giles had received two years earlier, released his midfielder provided he came unscathed through three games in five days – a league game against Nottingham Forest and testimonials at Hull and Glentoran. Meagan must have been seething at this petty point-scoring but diplomatically contented himself with the comment: 'He has problems like myself.'

Fortunately, Giles was available for the most extensive preparation the squad had yet enjoyed, with sessions on Friday, Saturday and Sunday. Only Heighway was unable to attend – he was playing for Liverpool in the FA Cup final. That game went to extra-time with Heighway on the mark but Liverpool losing out to Arsenal.

Giles led out the Republic before a large and enthusiastic crowd and proceeded to orchestrate as good an Irish performance as had been seen for some time. In this he had a skilful assistant in Dunphy and, between them, they set Ireland on the attack continuously.

However, the old failing of giving the visitors a goal start re-surfaced, with Boninsegna heading in a Mazzola free-kick after 16 minutes. Eight minutes later, the scores were level when Conway darted in to head a Dunphy free-kick past Zoff.

An injury to Rogers forced a re-shuffle at half-time. Mulligan, who had been playing excellently at the back, moved to midfield and Finucane came in. On the hour, from another Mazzola free-kick, Boninsegna headed down for Prati to smash the ball past Kelly.

It was heartbreaking for Meagan, who became aware that his time might be up.

'I could sense after the match this feeling all around — and especially from the officials — are we ever going to win?' That sentiment was voiced at the FAI council meeting the following Friday when Chairman Sam Prole allowed a discussion to take place on the international team's lack of success. As a result of the opinions expressed, Meagan offered his resignation, to take effect after the game against Austria on 30 May.

The FAI, celebrating its Golden Jubilee, arranged a special game at Lansdowne Road on 24 May. This should have been a full international but the hoped-for opposition from England amounted to something less than a B selection, featuring players from the lower divisions. It was a slap in the face for the FAI from their English counterparts. In the event, the only notable feature of the 1–1 draw was the fact that crowd-pleaser Heighway scored.

When the panel for the game against Austria was announced, the selection committee expressed their regret at Meagan's decision to resign and also registered their disapproval of Prole 'allowing a discussion at the council meeting on 14 May which resulted in the manager's resignation.'

Any hope that Meagan would leave on a high note was soon shattered for the 16,000 loyal supporters at Dalymount, the Austrians racing into a 3–0 lead after half an hour, courtesy of a penalty, an own goal and a goal scored following a corner. They eventually won 4–1, the Irish goal coming from a Rogers penalty after Byrne had been taken down.

The game was something of a shambles with the guidance of Giles missed, this time because of his involvement in the Fairs Cup final. Dunphy, his usually reliable replacement, chose this occasion to have a nightmare game, and was replaced at half-time by new cap Noel Campbell (St Patrick's Athletic).

In view of the fact that the team had, for once, more than adequate preparation, this performance was a bitter blow, and made a mockery of the Republic's aspirations to be taken seriously at international level. It was, in many respects, a watershed.

Yet the team which failed so miserably against the speedy Austrians included eight players who would figure prominently in turning around the Republic's fortunes, among them substitute Jimmy Holmes who, at 17 years and 200 days, became the youngest player capped by the Republic.

With two draws and 10 defeats from his 12 games in charge, what was Meagan's legacy, apart from being the first manager to pick the team? Most players point to his enthusiasm — he was so eager he would repeat himself in his team-talk — but there seem to be doubts about his tactical awareness. Above all, he is remembered as a nice man, an attribute which Alfie Hale regards as part of his downfall. 'For all his professional expertise, he was too nice a guy.'

Kinnear's assessment is in similar vein: 'He was very nice, very honest. He always encouraged me and kept telling me to express myself, that I had more ability than other full-backs. He was very hyper but would have had the respect of the players. He gave the impression that he was always under pressure from the powers that be and the media and never looked relaxed.'

Al Finucane was impressed by Meagan.

'He was very sincere and knew what he was doing. He was very well organised and astute tactically. He impressed me as a very good manager. The problem was the depth of talent was not there.'

Meagan, appointed on a match-fee basis, earned very little from a job which brought its quota of abuse and frustration. 'I went out as I came in,' he said. 'No fuss. There was no Press conference when I was appointed and there was none when I resigned. but I enjoyed every minute of my time in charge.'

As the pioneer who blazed the trail, Meagan is deserving of more credit than Giles gives him. Giles's assessment is of the damn-him-with-faint-praise variety.

'Mick was OK. He was better than anything we had before because he had more responsibility and more power. We knew who we were responsible to and we assumed he was picking the team and the squad – I wouldn't have agreed with anything else.'

In taking over from the selection committee, Meagan put an end to a certain attitude among the players, which was described by Joe Haverty: 'When you played for the international team you played for yourself first and if you had a good game you were in the next time. If you played for the team and the team lost you could be out and no one might hear of you again. Even Giles played for himself early on, but as player-manager he was half the team'.

Being responsible to a manager whose instructions you followed brought an end to selectors picking on the basis of crowd reaction, a system about which Alfie Hale once received advice from Charlie Hurley.

'He said to me before one game in Dalymount, "If things go wrong I'll do a few dribbles and get the crowd on my side and my advice to you is to do the same if you want to keep your place."

It was the end of an era in which club affiliations cost players caps. There were players in the 1950s and 1960s who were awarded caps without deserving them, and others who should have got caps and never did. Provincial players were most affected. Players like Waterford's Dixie Hale and Cork's Donal Leahy and Austin Noonan would all have been capped had they been with Dublin clubs. In fact, Sam Prole, chairman of the selection committee, promised Leahy his cap if he would sign for Prole's club, Drumcondra!

The system also failed because the players saw it as unprofessional compared to the managerial system at their clubs. As Shay Brennan put it: 'The officials were on the trips for a good time. The matches weren't everything for them and this translated to the players. I remember we were playing Italy and it was an early kick-off. We ordered a steak at 12.00 but when two of the selectors came in they were given the steak. They accepted it even though the players had to wait another three-quarters of an hour before being served.'

When the FAI council met on 2 July, the managerial vacancy was discussed, with John Farrell suggesting that a retainer of £500 per year be offered in addition to the match fee, while Liam Rapple wanted the appointment to be for at least three years. It was left to Farrell, Charlie Walsh and Frank Davis to draw up terms of reference.

The FAI received a number of replies when they advertised the position but, with his good record as manager of the League of Ireland team, Liam Tuohy was always the front runner and was duly appointed. Given full control, he set out to improve the team's preparation and, to that end, demanded that all future fixtures be played on Wednesdays.

Conscious also of the difficulties regarding the release of key players, Tuohy paid a personal visit to the English clubs involved 'so the manager would know the face at the other end of the phone when I rang him. I also made sure the players knew when a match was coming up because if a player wants to play he'll get his way.'

His principal target was Giles and that meant chatting up Revie. 'I wanted to get the position established that if he was fit he'd be made available and also to assure him that we were trying to get matches in midweek and have the players over for proper preparation. Revie said he felt the FAI had insulted Giles by not selecting him for a particular game and if that was their attitude they wouldn't have him. He said he had prevented Giles coming over and that he was happy for Giles not to be playing international matches.'

Notwithstanding that blast, Tuohy felt his mission had been a success, but his debut gave him no chance of putting that to the test as the return with Austria had already been fixed for Sunday, 10 October, in Linz. Only three England-based players were able to obtain their release. He called up Chelsea pair Mulligan and Dempsey, but the latter had to cry off, leaving Tuohy with a team of League of Ireland players plus Mulligan. Six were newcomers to international football.

It was a hopeless situation — his weakened side was defeated 6–0 — but that has never been taken into account when Tuohy's tenure as manager comes under scrutiny. It was a defeat entirely of the FAI's own making, a product of their amateurish approach to fixture-making.

Goalkeeper Paddy Roche was the star, but Irish hopes were effectively undermined by the brilliance of Ettmayer who gave Mulligan his most uncomfortable 90 minutes in the green jersey. However, it was not Mulligan who got the axe after this display but the League of Ireland players, Tuohy obviously reckoning there was more for the future in Mulligan. One player disenchanted by this was Al Finucane.

'I was a good player for a long time after my last cap but I was dropped after that game in Austria and never told why. I have always felt I was the scapegoat for Mulligan's poor display against Ettmayer.'

The World Cup draw paired the Republic with the USSR and France, only one to go through to the finals. With no room for a slip-up, Tuohy set out to discover the extent of the talent at his disposal.

His first opportunity came with the visit of the West German Olympic team on 4 January, 1972. Giles captained the side and, leading by example, was instrumental in setting up two of the three goals by which the Republic registered its first win in five years. Mick Martin, son of 1940s and 1950s hero Con Martin, opened the scoring; John Herrick, in for the unavailable Tony Dunne, struck the second and Mick Fairclough headed in the third from a Giles corner.

It was an invigorating display. Tuohy's 4-3-3 formation looked the part and raised expectations that the Republic would at least let the USSR and France know they were in a game when they came to Dublin.

'Essentially, a manager has a philosophy of play and picks players best suited to that,' explained Tuohy. 'My philosophy was to play from the back through midfield and have two wide players. I could never see the sense of having four midfielders and bypassing them. In those days we were always fighting to get a share of the game and it was essential that when we got the ball we did not give it away. So, when Giles played, we tried to work through him.'

However, when the Republic were granted the trip of a lifetime to take part in Brazil's mini-World Cup tournament in June, three of the key elements in his plans were missing. Liverpool and Stoke turned down requests for wingers Heighway and Conroy, while Giles helped Leeds win the Centenary FA Cup final despite a groin problem and then suffered the consequences, not even being fit for the start of the following season.

Tuohy was furious when Tony Dunne reported unavailable because he had booked his holidays for the period concerned. Significantly, Dunne never played under Tuohy. Tuohy knew that some players would never cry off but others, while happy to play in the home games, did not fancy tough away games which meant leaving London on a Sunday and not getting home until Thursday. It was not unknown for players to develop a convenient injury. Dunne became the first victim of Tuohy's new strict code, just as David O'Leary was later to become Charlton's *cause célèbre*.

Tuohy eventually travelled with a squad made up of four first division players, five from the second division, Noel Campbell from Fortuna Cologne and the rest from the League of Ireland. Among the latter was Waterford's Coventry-born goalkeeper Peter Thomas who had taken out Irish citizenship after spending five years in the country. He was the first to qualify for the Republic in this way.

One of Tuohy's strong points was his personality. He quickly developed a rapport with his players, having the ability to be one of the boys and at the same time clearly the boss. His droll sense of humour made him fun to be with.

Kinnear thought the Brazil trip was the first time the squad got to know one another.

'It was a super trip. I found Liam very bright, sharp, confident, with a good sense of humour and philosophical about things – a sort of light-hearted "let's go and get it sorted out and at the same time enjoy it" attitude'.

Training and playing in nearly 100 degrees heat was draining, with players losing six to seven pounds of fluid in 90 minutes. They were advised to take plenty of liquid and Tuohy had no objection to beer. The Iran and Ecuador players were staying in the same hotel and, when they came in from their training sessions, they were astounded to find the Irish in the bar tossing back the beer.

'They couldn't understand us having a drink even three nights before a game and a Brazilian paper called us the Irish football and beer team,' recalled Peter Thomas. But it was Ecuador, not the Irish, who had disciplinary problems, as they had to send two players home for violations of their code of conduct.

Team spirit soared and, after a tentative 2–1 win over Iran on 11 June in Recife, the football gradually improved. A goal down after nine minutes, a cracking effort by Leech produced the equaliser after 63 minutes and, four minutes later, Givens pounced on a defensive error to snatch the winner.

The game against Ecuador in Natal on 18 June was full of incident, with Rogers and Martin giving the Republic a 2–1 lead on the hour. Two minutes later Givens became the second Republic player to be sent off when he retaliated to some niggling fouls. Ecuador equalised, but Turlough O'Connor, who had come on at half-time for Treacy, scored a brilliant winner, lobbing the goalkeeper from 40 yards, with just four minutes left.

It was heady stuff, an understrength Irish team winning twice on foreign soil, a tribute to Tuohy's ability to get the best out of whatever players he had at his disposal.

With only three days rest before their next game against Chile in Recife, and with Givens suspended and Leech injured, the odds were against further success. They also found it difficult to contain Caszelly whose magical dribbling eventually wore down the Irish defence. He opened the scoring after 66 minutes and laid on another goal nine minutes later.

When the Irish fought back, disaster struck again. O'Connor's vivid recollection summed it up: 'I caught hold of the referee after I had been taken down in the area without getting a penalty and I was sent off before I realised what was happening.' That was in the 75th minute, but four minutes later, Rogers scored with a header from Martin's cross. However, they couldn't force the equaliser.

To remain in the competition, the Republic needed to beat Portugal by five goals in Recife on 25 June but, even with the return of Leech and Givens, they never looked capable of such a score. Portugal scored twice in three minutes from the 35th minute, Leech pulled one back almost immediately but the tired Irish could not lift their game for the equaliser. Portugal went on to the final in which they lost 1–0 to Brazil, while the Brazilian media chose Mulligan and Leech in their best XI from the Group.

It was an exhausting three weeks in unaccustomed heat. Tuohy and trainer Peter Fox worked the players hard. Despite that, the only casualty – apart from one or two cases of sunburn, and much to the players' amusement – was the manager himself, when he fainted following a routine injection and hit his head on a table. The wound required several stitches.

The boost which the Brazilian trip gave to morale was incalculable. The next game could not come quickly enough. Unfortunately, for the USSR's World Cup visit to Lansdowne Road three key players were missing. Givens was not released by his new club Queens Park Rangers – there was as yet no obligation for them to do so – and Giles and Mulligan were injured.

Tuohy called up Waterford centre-back Tommy McConville and kept faith with the midfield of Mick Martin, Noel Campbell and Eamonn Rogers that had done so well in Brazil despite the fact that Rogers had since been out of favour with his club, Charlton.

Kelly and his defenders were outstanding, keeping the Soviets at bay until the 55th minute but Rogers was only a shadow of his former self and it was no surprise when Leech replaced him after 62 minutes.

Conroy was the home star, displaying great dribbling skills and, despite shipping some heavy tackles, always willing to take on his man. He received excellent support from Treacy, but Heighway was a disappointment.

The spirited Irish performance failed to reap its reward as Kolotov added a second Soviet goal after 65 minutes from a suspiciously offside position. Conroy's 82nd minute reply, from a Leech pass, made for an exciting finish, but the Soviets were always in control.

The World Cup tie at home to France on 15 November marked the return of Giles, Mulligan and Givens. A stomach injury sidelined Heighway and forced Tuohy to opt again for a 4-3-3 formation. 'Had Heighway been available I would have been tempted to play 4-2-4,' he said later.

When a team goes six years without winning a game at home, the patience of the fans is sorely tested. However, the fans showed their appreciation of the team's performance against the USSR and turned up at Dalymount in large numbers in the hope that Tuohy's team could banish the home-town blues.

Led by Giles, around whom everything revolved, they proceeded to produce one of their most thrilling performances ever at World Cup level. They took the lead after 28 minutes when a Giles free-kick was blocked back out to him. He headed it into the penalty area where it was knocked down to Conroy who controlled it in a twinkling before hitting it in off the bar. When Larque volleyed a Molitor cross past Kelly for a 66th minute equaliser, the old anxieties returned for the fans. But eight minutes later the Irish struck for a spectacular winner.

Eoin Hand, who was operating in midfield, advanced on Rostagni who inexplicably hesitated in clearing his lines. Hand pounced to win possession near the right touchline and sent in a low near-post cross which Treacy met with a diving header, the ball looping over goalkeeper Carnus into the far corner. Hand later revealed the secret behind his contribution.

'The full-back should have cleared the ball but, 10 minutes before I had tackled him and probably shook him up. As a result, he was probably more conscious of me coming in on him than he should have been.'

Beating a major nation like France in a World Cup tie was so rare – the 1965 defeat of Spain was the only precedent – that it led to a new era of raised expectations where the fans were concerned. So, Tuohy's announcement on 1 December that he was resigning came as a bombshell. He had revived the team but he was also manager of Shamrock Rovers and a sales manager with HB Ice Cream and was over-committed.

'I had too much on my plate. Everything was suffering. I was not able to give my family or Rovers enough time. I would love to have stayed on but it was not practical to keep a job that was giving me £6 a week, and give up Rovers.

'The FAI had no money in those days. If the money had been there, yes, I would have stayed on. In the two years I was there I had nothing but co-operation from the FAI – they honoured everything they said they would. The problem was finance.'

FAI President Donie O'Halloran refused to accept the inevitable and persuaded Tuohy to delay his resignation until after the return World Cup ties in May.

Giles had a busy 1973. He helped Leeds reach the FA Cup final again – in which they were surprisingly beaten by Sunderland – and the Cup-Winners' Cup final in which they were due to play AC Milan in Salonika three days after the World Cup tie against the USSR in Moscow on 13 May. In addition, he was helping Derek Dougan select an All-Ireland XI for the visit of World Cup holders Brazil in July.

It was a relieved Tuohy who learned that Giles had been released for the Moscow game. But when Heighway phoned to say that he would 'like to play for Eire but I'm taking a rest this summer,' Tuohy blew his top.

'I deplore Heighway's attitude to the most important games Ireland have played over the last few years. The World Cup is the paramount competition and we have our best chance of qualifying for a number of years. If Heighway is too tired, then Giles must be a hospital case.'

In fact, Tuohy was not far wrong, as Giles recalled: 'I tweaked a hamstring the week of the Russian game, felt it a little going into that game and then pulled it and had to come off and missed the Cup-Winners' Cup final as a result.'

It was the one thing Tuohy did not want to happen for, apart from Giles's importance to the team, there was the thought of facing Revie's wrath. However, he need not have worried, as Giles recalled: 'Funnily enough, there was talk of Revie going to Everton at the time and his mind was full of that when I went to Salonika. I was dreading seeing him, but he did not say much. "If you are injured, you are injured." He was OK like that.'

That game in Moscow almost did not happen. The Russians made things as awkward as possible for the FAI, and matters came to a head when the press corps and the FAI group arrived at the ground and the press were refused admission. Exchanges grew heated until FAI President O'Halloran declared: 'If our press representatives don't go in, we don't go in. And if we don't go in, there will be no match.' That proved the open sesame, but the bad feeling lingered for the duration of the stay.

Going into the game, the Republic, the USSR and France each had two points from two games and, with the score 0–0 at half-time, the Republic were still in with a chance of a great result to keep their World Cup hopes alive. However, during the break, Giles and Conroy had to be replaced, Tony Byrne and Miah Dennehy taking over.

With Kelly brilliant in goal and Mulligan playing his best game ever, the Russians had to work hard for a breakthrough which eventually came in the 58th minute. A Muntian cross went over Carroll's head and Onishenko, standing behind him, took it down before cracking a rasper in to the far corner.

With nine minutes to go, the inspired Mulligan made another great run from the back and passed to Dennehy. But, with the defence out of position, the Corkman's control let him down and the chance was lost.

It was defeat with honour, but the team appeared to be only going through the motions when they played Poland at Wroclaw three days later. That game was notable only for the two goals scored by Lubanski – the second a particularly brilliant effort – and the international debut of midfielder Gerry Daly, recently transferred from Bohemians to Manchester United.

In the absence of Giles, the team's number one practical joker, Treacy and Givens had formed a partnership which was as lethal off the field as it was on. By the time the party moved to Paris for the final World Cup tie on 19 May the intrepid pair had chosen their next victim – new cap, Daly. It began with a phone call by Treacy, pretending to be Manchester reporter David Meek. He asked Daly all the personal details for which David Meek's column was noted, and said a photographer would be calling at the hotel to take some pictures. Borrowing a camera from doctor Bob O'Driscoll, they coaxed one of the hotel staff to act the part of the photographer and proceeded to line Daly up all around the hotel and finally in the foyer, to the amazement of the other guests and the amusement of his team-mates. Here he was pictured in his gear posing with one foot on a ball and Treacy even insisted on one with the crucifix he wore around his neck outside his shirt. For the onlookers it was uproarious stuff, the players sitting around laughing behind their newspapers. Treacy reminded Gerry, as he headed back to his room, to be sure to get after Meek 'as he can be a bit slow with the payment'.

Daly may have been the victim on that occasion, but he soon became as adept as any at pranks. On one trip when a member of the party accosted him on suspicion of knowing the whereabouts of his missing suitcase, Gerry replied: 'Oh, no, you've got the wrong man. I only deal in passports,' and opened his jacket to reveal a collection of about six passports in his inside pocket!

The Republic's visit to Paris served as a reminder to the manager why he had decided to quit. On his previous visit – in October to vet the France-USSR game – his dash back to Ireland had seen him arrive in Athlone at half-time for Shamrock Rovers' game and, on this visit, he learned that his wife had given birth to a son.

The players saw to it that Tuohy left on a high note. The superb defence shackled the French for long periods, and Dennehy, Givens and Treacy conspired to worry the home defenders often enough. It took a substitute, Chiesa, to find a way past Kelly, but the Irish response was magnificent. A Dennehy humdinger beat Carnus and rebounded off the bar for Martin to beat two defenders and head in to the net for a thrilling equaliser.

The impact of this spirited display extended farther than usual because the game was shown live on RTE. As a result, a new generation of children from all parts of the country were made aware of the Republic's soccer renaissance.

Everything about Tuohy's short term in charge was positive. He revitalised the squad and guided them to important victories, restoring morale and a much-needed belief among the players in their own ability to compete at the highest level.

'I like to think I left the international team in a healthier state,' he said. 'Morale was higher and preparation better. We started an upward trend and the FAI have to take their share of the credit because they went along with change and speculated a few bob on pre-match preparation.'

In 10 full internationals, Tuohy had three wins, a draw and six defeats. When his first game – the 6–0 defeat in Austria – and the friendly in Poland, are put aside, a clearer picture emerges of vastly improved competitive form in the mini-World Cup in Brazil and in Group 9 of the 1974 World Cup qualifiers. He never had a full-strength side, Giles being present on only two occasions and Heighway once. He has always regarded Heighway's absence as one of the big disappointments; he had gone out of his way to visit Liverpool manager Bill Shankly whom he had known as a player at Newcastle United.

'Outside Jack Charlton, Tuohy, with Giles, was the best tactician I've ever spoken to and the greatest motivator,' was Alfie Hale's tribute. 'He was at his best on the defensive. He couldn't afford to play with gay abandon because of the teams he managed. They weren't great teams.'

Treacy regarded Tuohy as the first excellent manager.

'The day he really got home to the players was in Recife. We were at the training ground and two or three FAI officials came over to where we were talking about the game and Liam came out with the statement: "Look lads, I've got the perfect relationship with these guys – they love me and I hate them." I remember thinking "That's some statement" but that was him and he was capable of getting away with it.

'Liam could drop you, he could give you the biggest bollocking you ever got in your life, and the medium he used, which is what he's brilliant at, was humour. He was caustic, cynical, but in a humorous way – and he had the ability to get through to you.

'He was the first to set a pattern of play. And again he made his point through humour. "Ray, my missus can run quicker than you" – which was probably a fact – "and therefore just get the ball and keep it simple."

'He would also talk to you about your strengths. He said to me, "Ray, you are the best header of a ball that I have seen, not just in terms of height but in terms of glancing headers, power headers or cushion headers or whatever." I walked out feeling 10 feet tall and feeling I could beat anybody. That's where Liam was great.

'He was the first strong manager. His organisational ability was excellent. He told the FAI what he wanted done for the players and he was the start of what's going on today.'

For the Republic's friendly on 6 June in Oslo, Bohemian coach Sean Thomas was appointed caretaker manager. The 1–1 draw was a disappointing end to an exciting season but some element of anti-climax must be allowed for. Also the players could be forgiven if they thought it was a case of back to the bad old days, as they were billeted on a university campus, an arrangement which would not have met with Tuohy's approval. Miah Dennehy opened the scoring after 17 minutes and it took all of Alan Kelly's brilliance to deny Norway until the 68th minute when Paulsen headed a rebound in to the net.

Sadly, this rather innocuous game proved to be Alan 'Jibber' Kelly's last stand. Injury forced his retirement early the following season after a record 47 caps. Peter Thomas was Kelly's understudy in Brazil and was highly impressed.

'He was probably the most underrated goalkeeper I've ever known. If he was playing for Ireland now he'd be a cult figure. He was a Peter Shilton in training – he pushed himself to the limit, which isn't easy to do. And his performances reflected his hard work when Ireland could have lost 6–0 and they were beaten only 1–0.'

The season finally ended on 3 July on a high note when the Shamrock Rovers' All-Ireland XI chosen by Giles and Derek Dougan met the World Cup holders Brazil at Lansdowne Road and were not disgraced in a 4–3 defeat with Martin, Conroy and Dougan contributing the goals. This out-of-season display against world-class opposition was another feather in the cap for the Irish. As Don Givens put it: 'It was a great performance considering the circumstances. Quite possibly we'd have got a better result if we had been fit'.

The Irish show was definitely on the road again. Tuohy was handing over to his successor a squad whose morale had never been higher and whose expectations matched those of the growing legion of fans.

11

Giles: So Near and yet so Far

The FAI changed their tune following Tuohy's success. In future, the Republic of Ireland's fortunes would be dictated more by the quality of the manager than the quality of the players. Tuohy had shown that, even without top-class material, a good manager could ensure that a team would be competitive.

A phone call was made in the summer of 1973 to the home of Leeds United midfielder Johnny Giles, and the position was offered to him. At 32, he had no managerial experience and he was still a key player with Leeds and the Republic, so it required some persuasion before he agreed to take over as player–manager, on a temporary basis.

It was a remarkable turn-around on the part of the FAI, whose selection committee had, four years previously, dropped the little Dubliner. It also ensured an about-face on Giles's part: his dismal record of availability over the previous four years was about to improve dramatically. The poacher had turned gamekeeper, and was himself the first to be taken in hand.

Giles's reason for taking the position gives some indication of how carefully he weighed up the proposition.

'The only reason I agreed was because, if I did not do it, it might go to someone I did not rate that much. I would have preferred Liam to stay on in the job. I was not touting for the job; I was either being offered it or not; I was not even keen on it.'

His first move was to gather his players at Bisham Abbey for a three-day session. The players left 'with a new sense of purpose and pride', according to Eamon Dunphy.

'John told us he believed we could become a world force. When we left we also knew we could be. He not only commanded our attention, but also won our respect with clear talking and intelligent views.'

For his first game, Giles could not have had a tougher assignment. Poland were the visitors to Dalymount on 21 October, and they had just eliminated England from the World Cup with an historic 1–1 draw at Wembley. In addition, the game was on a Sunday, meaning two games in 24 hours for most of the Irish players.

Displaying a thoroughness which would have done his mentor Don Revie proud, Giles left nothing to chance. He brought Leeds and England trainer Les Cocker to Dublin to reap the benefit of the notes he had made on the opposition.

'As a result, that was possibly Don Givens's best international, in a negative sense,' recalled Treacy. 'Their right-back was one of the original raiding, run-all-day types, and John asked Don to latch on to him. He made so many 50 yard runs back just chasing their right-back that he was eventually knackered and taken off but, in a team context, it worked for us.'

Waterford goalkeeper Thomas, who was one of two new caps – QPR centre-back Terry Mancini was the other – was impressed. 'Pre-match, Giles had a dossier on every player, man for man. Roaring and shouting was not his style.'

A hard-fought 1–0 win – the goal coming just after the half-hour from Dennehy who had replaced cartilage victim Conroy 20 minutes earlier – was highlighted by a superb display from striker Treacy, whose game showed a marked maturity in every respect.

The result generated a cherished spin-off for one of the players. Kinnear, who laid on the winning goal, recalled: 'I went into training with Tottenham the following morning wearing the Poland shirt to wind up the England lads. It did not go down too well as Chivers and Peters were still upset over being knocked out of the World Cup by the Poles.'

A new era was being ushered in, but how far could Giles take his team of mainly second division players? And which style of play would he adopt? Whatever the answers, the FAI council were among his supporters – they confirmed his appointment as manager at their November meeting.

The following summer, on a South American tour organised by his brother-in-law Louis Kilcoyne, Giles got his message across. Maintain possession, that was the order of the day, and it proved an absolute essential in the heat and humidity of Brazil, Uruguay and Chile. The players, practically in awe of their manager who had just added another league medal to his collection with Leeds United, were greatly impressed by his leadership, his tactics and his understanding of the problems to be overcome on away trips.

'He was probably the most tactically aware manager I have ever seen,' enthused Treacy. 'His reading of the game as a player was brilliant but he had the ability to take it a step further and put it across to his players. He would know as much about every position, with the possible exception of goalkeeper: what they should do, what they shouldn't. He would let players play and he would limit them to what they could do, for their own good.

'There were two fallacies about his style of play. One, everybody had to give the ball to Giles. That was nonsense. More often than not he was the most available player which is why he got it. Of all the players, if you wanted someone to do something with it you'd obviously give it to your best player and he was by a long, long way our best player. He was the one who was going to make it happen.

'Fallacy number two concerned passing the ball backwards. I worked longer with John Giles than anyone and he never once said pass the ball backwards.

Inset: Andy McEvoy, who refused to go on as a sub (*Sunday Independent*)

No one wore the green jersey with more pride than Liam Brady, but his commitment aggravated the flaw in his game (*Jim O'Kelly*)

David O'Leary oozed class from the first minute of his International debut against England at Wembley in September 1976 and his banishment by Jack Charlton was a tragedy for the player and his country (*Jim O'Kelly*)

Giles in classic pose, perfectly balanced and in full control (*Jim O'Kelly*)

Inset: Three greats and the scout who discovered them for Manchester United: John Giles, Jackie Carey, scout Billy Behan and Don Givens

No Irish manager was ever as much in demand as Jack Charlton, seen here surrounded by the media in Cagliari (*Sunday Independent*)

Top: Green giant in a sea of orange: Paul McGrath clears another Dutch attack
(*Sunday Independent*)
Bottom: Goalmaker: Charlton wanted to replace Kevin Sheedy in 1990 but he produced his
best form in the following two years (*Sunday Independent*)

The team that reached the last eight in Italia '90. From left (*back row*) Niall Quinn, Andy Townsend, Packie Bonner, Paul McGrath, Mick McCarthy (captain), Steve Staunton (*front row*) Kevin Moran, John Aldridge, Kevin Sheedy, Chris Morris, Ray Houghton (*Sunday Independent*)

Left: Andy Townsend took over from Liam Brady and proved an inspiring captain (*Sunday Independent*)

Bottom: Down but not out: Roy Keane recovers from a nasty tackle in Macedonia (Dara MacDonaill, *Sunday Independent*)

His philosophy was keep the ball. Go forward. If you can't go forward and keep the ball, go sideways. Only if you can't go sideways and keep the ball then go backwards and keep the ball.'

In South America, well away from the impatient fans whose constant demand was for the ball to be hoofed forward into the 'danger zone', Giles had the opportunity to convert players to his way of thinking. More importantly, it offered the opportunity to rid them of their inferiority complex.

'Beating Poland in our first match was no big thing,' he admits. 'We had beaten them before, but the tour to South America in the summer of 1974 was a big breakthrough for us.

'Brazil beat us 2–1 when they were preparing for the World Cup finals and then we went to Uruguay and that was a match we could have won. Don [Givens] missed a few chances.

'It's a psychological thing to lose when you should have won. I'd been through years of that. The people back home probably said, "Oh, 0–2, that's not a bad result," but we should have won the match and that's what I wanted to get into the team.

'I did not want any more "Oh, we could have won", or "They weren't so good". I wanted us to compete and do as well as we possibly could and if the match was there for the winning, to win.

'We played Chile in the next match – they had also qualified for the World Cup finals – and we went 1–0 in front. The crowd was geeing them up and the referee was giving them everything. They equalised and straight from the kick-off we scored. Paddy Mulligan went on a dribble all the way from the back – they had relaxed because they had just scored – and he laid it out to Terry Conroy who pulled it back for Jimmy Conway to score, and we hung on for a 2–1 win. I was delighted with that because it was a big match away from home even if it was a friendly, and it proved we could win.'

Thomas, who started as first choice goalkeeper but lost his place when he found he could not lift his arm after the Brazil game, recalled the lesson Giles taught on the way to the Uruguay game. 'We could not get into the stadium and I was banging on the door. Giles just summoned one of the FAI officials and told us to wait calmly. He explained that the delay was a deliberate ploy to try to upset us. It was only an hour before kick-off and we were kept waiting five to 10 minutes before we got in.'

Another area where Giles brought his experience to bear was in the post-game analysis. He was blessed with total recall, claimed Shay Brennan.

'After a game, he would sit the players down and talk to them about the game and show them where the mistakes were made. Even when playing he could remember everything.'

In South America, where even the substitutes on the line were sweating buckets, Giles had installed former goalkeeper Alan Kelly as his trainer and coach. It was a partnership which earned the immediate seal of approval from the players.

'It was a very professional trip – the best footballing one I've been on,' summed up Jimmy Conway.

It had not started out like that, with Eamon Dunphy trying to organise a boycott of the Chile game because of the executions held in the National Stadium the previous year by the military regime. However, the rest of the party showed no interest in Eamon's politics. For a few dollars more, they were prepared to emulate their predecessors in 1939 who obediently gave the Nazi salute in Bremen. It certainly was not the first time that fear of losing a place on the team had a stifling effect on conscience.

The 1974 tour proved a watershed for the team. The players acquired a new belief in their ability to mix it with the best, and in a style associated with the best continental sides. The tour was the ideal preparation for the European Championship in which the Republic had been drawn with the Soviet Union, Turkey and Switzerland.

Another big plus was the arrival on the scene of Liam Brady, an 18-year-old Dubliner many regarded as Giles's natural successor. Brady was the first of a trio of talented Dubliners to come off the Arsenal assembly line.

The question of who would make way for Brady was answered by Giles in a particularly droll way during training at Blackrock College before the 30 October Dalymount meeting with the Soviets. Hand, who had scored the first goal against Chile from a precise Giles corner, asked the manager if he would want him to go forward for the corners as in Chile. There was a pause, then Giles replied: 'That would be hard from the substitutes' bench, Eoin.'

It was a cruel lesson for Hand, but it was not lost on his team-mates – no one could take his place for granted any longer. Hand, a natural centre-back, was unfortunate that, at the time of Brady's arrival, he had been lining up in midfield and was the obvious candidate to make way for the Arsenal prodigy.

Giles opted for a team with a solid base of first division experience, midfielder Mick Martin, centre-forward Treacy and goalkeeper Roche, a Manchester United reserve, being the only players deficient in that area. His selection of Heighway, whose commitment had been called into question earlier, showed that Giles would judge the player on his performance on the pitch rather than his past record. For the South American tour he had also reinstated Tony Dunne.

The public turned out in huge numbers despite the Wednesday mid-afternoon kick-off. Sadly, the FAI slipped up again. Tuohy, who had done so much to get the show on the road, was not even given the option of a ticket and was only helped out of his predicament by a friend. Eaten bread is soon forgotten, seemed to be the FAI's motto.

When great games at Dalymount are recalled, the game against the mighty Soviet Union is always high on the list. For many this was possibly the greatest display ever by an Irish team. From the kick-off, when Givens played the ball back to Giles and the manager immediately passed it to Brady, this was a performance of awesome power. Chances were created early and often, with the skill of Giles in particular and Brady giving the home side the edge in midfield.

A number of chances were missed before Givens headed home a Kinnear cross. He added another goal when Treacy flicked on a long Heighway throw-in, and then centre-back Terry Mancini was sent off with Soviet defender Kaplichny for brawling.

The home side could not maintain the hectic pace, and the Soviets came more into the game. However, Roche proved his worth with some excellent saves and, after 70 minutes, Givens put the issue beyond doubt when he headed home a cute Giles free-kick. It was a terrific way for Givens to end an 11 game scoring drought. He became only the third FAI player to score a hat-trick – the previous was notched up over 40 years earlier by the great Paddy Moore.

Givens naturally earned most of the plaudits but it was a clear case of 11 heroes playing their hearts out. While Mancini was suspended for the game against Turkey in Izmir three weeks later – he never played for the Republic again – no other changes were expected. Giles had other ideas. Setting his stall out to take at least a point from Turkey, he dropped Treacy and brought in flying winger Terry Conroy.

Treacy, who had been one of the big successes against the Soviets, took a philosophical approach to his demotion.

'I was dropped so many times, most of the time it did not worry me. And the time I was least worried was when I was playing my best, like after the Soviet match when I was dropped because Giles was playing a different system with only one up-front.'

However, Treacy did not make it easy for him.

'He had this way, as you were jogging around, of calling you to one side and saying, "Look, I'm leaving you out," and he'd be embarrassed. So he'd try to catch my eye and I'd look away and then we'd be playing a five-a-side and I'd see him coming. I'd be on the right-hand side passing the ball to somebody and I'd see him making a move towards me and I'd just move away to the left until eventually he just stood on the centre circle and said, "Come here, you little bastard." So then I had to go to him. "Right, you are f***ing dropped." That was the sort of fun we used to have.'

Giles's tactics almost paid off, as the best chances fell to the reinstated Conroy but he failed to finish. With 70,000 Turks creating a very hostile environment, the Irish contained the Turkish attack until an unfortunate own goal by Mick Martin after 56 minutes. In the past this might have been the signal for heads to drop, but this side kept their composure, aided greatly by the skilful play of Giles and Brady and, seven minutes later, 'the little General', as Giles had become known, broke down the left to cross for Givens to shoot the equaliser.

A point away from home was rightly considered an excellent result. However, Givens summed up the new mood in the camp when he said: 'It was a good result but we weren't over the moon about it – the win was what we were after.'

Three points from two games was heady stuff and the increased public interest prompted the FAI to play their next game, home to Switzerland, at Lansdowne Road. The move was worth twice the gate receipts of a packed Dalymount and, in straitened times for the FAI, that fact weighed heavily. The players, who were on a bonus of 10 per cent of the gross gate receipts against Switzerland and Turkey if they qualified for the finals, were not consulted on the switch.

Kinnear's view was probably representative: 'I think we lost a bit when we went to Lansdowne Road, yet it was the right thing to do financially. There was something impersonal about it; there was something very personal about Dalymount, where you could touch the supporters around the pitch and felt they contributed to the team.'

The game had to be switched to Saturday, 10 May, as Sunday football was still not permitted at Lansdowne Road. It did nothing to diminish the interest, a full house of 50,000 attending as the FAI started the most important 12 days in its history.

A 1–0 victory over West Germany B in March had been the only get-together since the game in Turkey and the players were at the end of a long English season. However, Heighway was the only casualty, his injury allowing Treacy to resume his partnership with Givens.

In a strange game, the Republic threatened to run riot with a first-half display that was every bit as good as, if not better than, their display against the Soviet Union. Mick Martin opened the scoring after just two minutes with a diving header from a Treacy cross. Treacy added a second just before the half-hour when he finished off a Givens shot which had rebounded from the goalkeeper.

The Swiss were lucky to be only two goals behind at the break but, apart from a couple of early efforts by Giles and Givens, there was no attempt by the Irish to rub in their advantage. Instead a containment policy was adopted and almost led to disaster, with Muller reducing arrears after 73 minutes. The huge attendance, which had been entertained so well in the first 45 minutes, turned on their players in what was to be a foretaste of things to come for Giles.

Unbeaten after three games, having dropped only one point, they faced difficult games in Kiev and Berne which would decide their fate. The Soviets, forced into a re-think following the trouncing in Dublin, turned to the Dynamo Kiev side which had just won the European Cup-Winners' Cup.

Giles had Heighway back, but the Kiev players, backed by a capacity 100,000 attendance, threatened to overwhelm the Irish early on, shooting into a 2–0 lead inside a half-hour. But for some magnificent saves by Roche and a goalline clearance by Kinnear, the Soviets would have been out of sight. Instead, a Giles free-kick in the 79th minute fell to Givens who headed over the advancing Rudakov for Hand to shoot home. It was nearly a carbon copy of the Republic's display against Switzerland, with the Irish this time on the receiving end and almost upsetting the dominant home side.

132

The decision to play the Swiss in Berne just three days after the torrid affair in Kiev was a mistake on the part of the FAI, whose decision seemed once again to be based on short-term economics.

Kinnear was a food-poisoning victim in Kiev, allowing Jimmy Holmes to return at left-back, with Tony Dunne switching to the right, while the disappointing Heighway made way for Treacy up-front, as Giles looked for a winning formula.

With qualification up for grabs for the Irish, the tension was apparent in their play. They showed nothing like the composure displayed against the same opposition 12 days earlier and were fortunate the home side found it difficult to get their shots on target. Eventually, the game was decided by an unfortunate mix-up between Hand and Conroy. Both went for a cross, got in each other's way and Elsener was left on his own to shoot the only goal of the game after 76 minutes.

Giles then had to retire with a leg injury and was replaced by Daly, who had a late chance from a Conroy cross but headed wide. Defeat had often been the Irish players' lot but this time it was different. They had never been so close to an historic achievement before, and to see it slip away in this fashion was hard to take. Tears were shed in the dressing-room.

A glimpse of Giles's drawn and shattered countenance bore testimony to his commitment to the cause of leading the Republic into the Promised Land of soccer respectability. A week later, he suffered another major disappointment when Leeds United were beaten 2–0 by Bayern Munich in the European Cup final.

Looking back, Giles felt an important point was made in Berne. 'We did not play well on the night. It was disappointing because it put us out of the European Championship, but at least we were disappointed. We had expected to do it. That might sound trivial now but at that time it was a big breakthrough to have that attitude from the public and from the players.

'We were close but we probably weren't good enough. The Soviet Union qualified from that Group and they were a better team than us. At least we were in there having a go in the later stages. Before that we were never in the running.'

Mulligan had no doubt where to point the finger.

'It was bad organisation that cost us, and I mean off the field not on it. All we needed was a week's break between matches and we'd have hammered the Swiss but we weren't given it.'

The FAI's organisation was called into question again when the Republic completed their European Championship series with a home game against Turkey. With no hope of qualifying, Dalymount was chosen as the venue.

Match day, 29 October 1975, proved to be a red letter day for Don Givens, who equalled Paddy Moore's 41-year-old record by scoring all four goals in the 4–0 defeat of the Turks, but it was a black day for the FAI as crowd violence threatened to force Spanish referee Martinez to abandon the game in the second half.

The crowd of 23,000 was being treated to another spectacular show from Giles and his team, and Givens had already notched his hat-trick when Turkey's goalkeeper Rasim was suddenly pelted with missiles. While the Gardai tried to control this lunacy, the game was stopped twice, with the referee finally threatening to abandon the game in the event of a recurrence. A further delay was caused when the floodlights initially failed to function and the stoppages disrupted the flow of the game, with Turkey benefitting more than the home side.

However, after the visitors had a goal disallowed, the Republic regained the initiative. Treacy was taken down while rounding Rasim but Holmes's penalty kick was saved and the fourth goal was delayed until two minutes before time when Givens volleyed a Mulligan cross in to the net.

The team's performance left them one point behind Group Six winners, USSR, while the crowd's performance put a major question mark over Dalymount Park as a venue for future internationals. It would be many years before the Irish supporters would wipe the slate clean and re-emerge with credit.

Giles indicated his intention to retire as a player after this game and, with the next competitive game a year away, he started to have a look at the talent available. One of the first to suffer was full-back Kinnear.

'He sent me a letter,' recalled Kinnear, 'saying, "Thanks for the magnificent service you've given the country. I'm now taking the view that I'll persevere with the younger players. Good luck in your future with Brighton." It was his way of telling me my International career was over. I had a laugh at it myself because I was only 28 and he went on playing until he was 38!'

Despite this, Kinnear remains one of Giles's admirers.

'Everybody had such high regard and respect for him; he was probably one of the best ever to play for Ireland. He had the ability to mix with the players on social occasions and drink with the players as well as being manager. It was not a case of them and us.

'Tactically, he had great knowledge from his Revie days. He had been a winner and he advocated total football. He loved the side to pass the ball around. It was not as direct under John – he played a patient game.'

Installing Brady in the playmaker role, Giles introduced Tony Grealish and Mick Walsh in successive wins over Norway (3–0 at Dalymount) and Poland (2–0 in Poznan). The omens were good. Brady and Walsh scored against Norway, and Givens followed up with two in Poland to set an Irish scoring record of 15, beating the previous best set by Cantwell.

In between, the FAI had acknowledged Giles's contribution by granting him a testimonial, which took place at Lansdowne Road on 28 April 1976. The game attracted a crowd of over 40,000 who saw a Republic XI draw 0–0 with an England XI supplied by Giles's former mentor, Don Revie. It was a disappointing spectacle and fuelled resentment towards Giles which would only become apparent later.

In preparation for the World Cup tie away to France in November, the FAI lined up two difficult away friendlies. The first was at Wembley against England and was marked by the emergence of the second great Arsenal prospect, David O'Leary. The 18-year-old Dubliner had an outstanding debut at centre-back, a position usually entrusted to more mature players. O'Leary brought a touch of the continental *libero* to the Irish game, promising rich dividends in years to come. Defensively, he was also a tower of strength, one tremendous tackle on Kevin Keegan epitomising his excellent timing and sure-footedness in his own penalty area.

The Republic controlled the game but there was a lack of penetration up-front. It took a Daly penalty, after Heighway had been brought down, to earn a share of the spoils, Stuart Pearson having shot England into the lead a minute before half-time.

Giles, who had been persuaded to return to the International scene by former team-mates Cantwell and Hurley, had a calming influence on young midfielders Brady and Daly. The same midfield trio were in action for the friendly in Turkey the following month when Giles gave debuts to Joe Waters and yet another Arsenal prospect, striker Frank Stapleton.

For countries like the Republic, which have only a limited number of players to choose from, strikers are 'the last piece in the jigsaw', according to Giles. With Givens in such outstanding form, the need was for a second goalscorer who would take some of the weight off him and pose an extra threat to defences. Treacy was ideal for home games but lacked the pace necessary for away games when strikers feed off quick breaks. Stapleton was not any quicker but he had the advantage of youth.

For an injection of pace up-front, Giles relied mainly on Heighway. Unfortunately, Heighway failed to reproduce his club form for his country and was regarded as a disappointment by many fans who were well aware of his ability to score goals in vital European, Cup or league games for Liverpool, and contrasted that with his failure to hit the target in 33 games for the Republic. Giles is not among Heighway's critics.

'It was unfair criticism of someone playing with top-class players in his club, whereas with the Irish team against the top nations he wouldn't have been as far ahead of the opposition. In every way he had a better stage to display his talents on at Anfield. I thought he played quite well for Ireland.'

Heighway was not released for the trip to Turkey. In that game the Republic shot into a 2–0 lead with goals from Stapleton and Daly inside the first 15 minutes but then, inexplicably, let the home side take over. Mick Kearns was in great form in goal and saved a penalty but even he could not stem the tide and Turkey strode into a 3–2 lead by the 71st minute. A late Irish revival enabled Waters to snatch a surprise equaliser.

Going into the World Cup tie in Paris, the Republic boasted the proud record of a five-game unbeaten run in the previous 12 months, scoring 13 goals in the process. The only question mark seemed to be over the manner in which Turkey was allowed to regain the initiative in Ankara. If that little lapse was overlooked, there seemed no reason to doubt the team's ability to qualify from Group Five. The opposition, apart from France, was provided by Bulgaria.

With O'Leary and Heighway back, Giles fielded his strongest side at the Parc des Princes on 17 November 1976. Apart from O'Leary and Stapleton, each receiving their second cap, there was plenty of experience in the team, and player–manager Giles was winning his 47th cap, equalling Alan Kelly's record.

The game is remembered for two incidents involving the young Arsenal players. The first concerned O'Leary and occurred in the first half at a time when France were finding it difficult to create chances against a well-organised Irish defence. The French centre-forward, Lacombe, made a dreadful tackle on O'Leary, ripping his shinguard in two.

'If I hadn't got a shinguard my leg would have been broken in two,' said O'Leary.

Lacombe, lucky to stay on the field, was booked, but referee Maksimovic from Yugoslavia evened the score shortly after when he booked O'Leary for holding his tattered shinguard in his hand. 'He accused me of carrying a dangerous weapon!'

After a self-inflicted wound – a Mick Martin pass to Giles going astray and letting Platini in for the opening score three minutes after the break – the second major talking point arrived as the Irish valiantly chased an equaliser. Brady made a typical dart down the left and delivered an inch-perfect cross which Stapleton headed in to the net. The referee pointed to the centre circle, the Irish players celebrated; then the referee saw the linesman's flag raised for offside and the goal was disallowed.

To their credit, the Irish fought back, but in committing themselves to attack, they left themselves open to the swift counter and, with two minutes to go, Platini laid on a chance for Bathenay which he struck home from 20 yards.

A prestige friendly at home to Spain on 9 February 1977, gave Giles the chance to view some more new talent, including Fulham goalkeeper Gerry Peyton, who turned down an England Under-21 cap in order to play for the land of his Mayo-born father. However, in a 1–0 defeat, the most important fact to emerge was that the team did not function as well without Giles.

The following month, France were the visitors to Lansdowne Road for a game that attracted a sell-out crowd, despite being shown live on TV.

The Irish made their usual hectic start and, after 10 minutes, Brady scored a fine individual goal. He beat a number of defenders when the ball was cleared out to him, before slipping it under advancing goalkeeper Rey. It looked like the prelude to an avalanche, but the French weathered the storm and, as the Irish effort tailed off in the second half, they took control.

It required a brilliant tackle by O'Leary to deny Platini as he bore down on Mick Kearns; the goalkeeper also made a superb save from Bathenay. The final 10 minutes were agony for the home fans as the Irish were reduced to kicking the ball anywhere to relieve the pressure on their goal. When the final whistle went, with the score still 1–0, the release of tension was palpable.

While it was a famous victory, the fading of the midfield in the second half was a worrying factor for Giles to contemplate as he prepared for the vital game in Sofia against Bulgaria on 1 June. At 35, he was finding it hard to stay with the pace and was dropping deeper and deeper during the 90 minutes, while Brady appeared to have a stamina problem or else was not able to pace himself properly.

With Mick Martin required at centre-back, Giles had installed Gerry Daly in midfield but the Derby County player, while good going forward, was not renowned for getting back. The quiet, unobtrusive, but highly effective Martin was being missed.

A friendly against Poland on Sunday, 24 April, at Dalymount was notable only for the inclusion, for the first time, of centre-back Mark Lawrenson. Assistant manager Alan Kelly had spotted him at Preston and wasted no time in notifying Giles when he learned that Lawrenson's mother was Irish. Giles did not select many players on parentage grounds; Lawrenson was the most successful.

However, Lawrenson's inexperience ruled him out of the Sofia game, with Giles able to name his first-choice side. A small but growing band of supporters had begun following the team abroad and, with prices of £166 for a two-week holiday on the Black Sea plus coach transfer to the match and match ticket, there was a fair sprinkling of support among the 50,000 in the Levski Stadium.

Yet another self-inflicted wound after 13 minutes soured the proceedings. Heighway's inept back pass was finished off, after a slick three-man move, by Panov. When Givens was blatantly fouled but no penalty awarded three minutes before half-time, it seemed it was not to be the Republic's day.

However, all that changed two minutes after the restart when Givens equalised with a tremendous header from a Giles corner. It was his first goal in six games. The home side were now on the run; the Republic went for the kill. Twelve minutes later, a brilliant Heighway dribble ended with a cross to the far post, Daly was waiting to knock the ball back to Giles whose shot tore into the back of the net.

Referee Zlatanos from Greece at first allowed the goal but, after consultation with his linesman, awarded a free-kick out. This decision brought Bulgaria back into the game and, with luck on their side, they took the lead. Panov's indirect free-kick glanced off Giles and Jeliazhov pounced on the deflection to score.

'Five minutes after that,' recalled Brady, 'there was the biggest brawl I have ever seen or been involved in on a football pitch. Frank Stapleton, shielding the ball, had managed to dodge one malicious tackle when he was felled with a disgusting challenge. That signalled a free-for-all; we just ploughed in. The punch-up began on the pitch and finished up on the running track that circled it.'

Players traded punches, kicks and head butts and Bulgarian soldiers had to move in to restore order. When order was restored, Zlatanos sent off two players from each side, Mick Martin and substitute Noel Campbell being the unlucky Irishmen. Campbell had only been on the pitch for a minute and had not even kicked the ball. The main trouble-makers remained on the field as Bulgaria held out for two precious points.

French manager Michel Hidalgo commented: 'I thought it was disgusting. Ireland were robbed, for I saw nothing at all wrong with Giles's goal.'

That night, some Irish high jinks got out of hand and the hotel lobby was left in disarray. The following morning, the police were called in, and Giles had to do some hard bargaining to get the manager to accept a sum of $500 as compensation. As the players chipped in to raise the money, they could not wait to get home. Unfortunately, the incident proved to be a portent of worse to come.

Giles dropped a bombshell the following month when, after two successful seasons as player–manager of West Bromwich Albion, he announced he was returning to Dublin to take over as player–manager of Shamrock Rovers. His goal was to turn them into a full-time set-up and a force in European football.

With no international before the return game against Bulgaria, Giles agreed to a League of Ireland v International XI game at Dalymount on 21 September. The part-timers were not disgraced, losing only 2–1, and Sligo Rovers' striker Paul McGee did his cause a lot of good with his goal. Within months he was on his way to Queens Park Rangers, while Bohemian left-winger Gerry Ryan was transferred to Derby County.

McGee, while still at Sligo, was a newcomer to the international squad. He did not play against Bulgaria on 12 October at Lansdowne Road, but Mick Martin's suspension opened the way for Mark Lawrenson, then at Brighton, to win his second cap.

The Republic needed a big win to put pressure on France and Bulgaria, who were due to meet in Paris on 16 November. Despite dominating the game and creating a number of good chances, the Republic could not get the goal their play deserved, and their hopes of a place in the World Cup finals in Argentina were extinguished.

The following month France beat Bulgaria 3–1 and booked their place in the finals; they did not get past the first round. Only two points separated the Republic from a place in the sun, but the goal difference of minus two indicated that the high-water mark of Givens's potency had been passed, while Stapleton was still coming to terms with the international game. The two disallowed goals, both seemingly well constructed and clinically finished efforts, were the difference between qualifying and not qualifying. Luck, it seemed, was no friend of Giles.

12

Giles: Familiarity Breeds Contempt

Although he left Dublin as a 15-year-old, Johnny Giles always wore his Irishness on his sleeve. He was proud of his nationality. Visit him at home and you would be entertained by the music of Irish singers like Luke Kelly and Sonny Knowles. In over 20 years in England he retained his Irish accent; others lost it on a month's trial. It was natural that he should jump at the chance of returning to Shamrock Rovers, where he was guaranteed full control and provided the opportunity to put his theories into practice. It was too good to miss.

Returning home while still manager of the international team was a calculated gamble. Even the slightest falling off in standards – real or imagined – by his Rovers team would be used as a stick with which to beat him. And when it came to public relations, Giles was his own worst enemy. As Treacy put it: 'John did not want to know people. In those days he would have had five friends.'

Giles admitted himself that PR was not his strong point. However, as Treacy tells it he more than compensated in other areas: 'I got involved in a business while I was at Preston. It did not work out and I was broke. I had a mortgage to pay, a wife and two kids but I was too proud to ask anyone for money and I was not sleeping.

'Somehow Giles got to hear about it. He put a blank cheque in the post with a little note on it, basically saying you can write this for up to ten grand. He did not ask for collateral, he did not even say pay me back. It was just "there's some money" and he knew I'd pay him back, which I did. I'd love people who give him stick to know that.

'He doesn't make friends easily, he's always sceptical of people. He's a very private person, not good with the media and not good PR-wise but, as a man, he would rank among the best of the whole lot.'

The move to Milltown also raised crucial questions about Giles the player. Could he maintain the same high level of performance while competing in the part-time League of Ireland as he had during his years in the English first division? After all, at 37, he was now into the veteran stage.

Al Finucane contributed to this debate.

'Giles was totally selfless on the pitch. You could depend on him in any situation. When he was past his best he still picked himself probably because of his organisational ability, and I don't think the fans appreciated that at the time. He was so good at organising people and using the ball that he became a victim of his own ability because he probably stayed on longer than he would have liked.'

When the draw was made for the European Championship, the Republic were joined in Group One by England, Northern Ireland, Bulgaria and Denmark. The first meeting of the two Irish Associations in a major competiton was the main talking-point, and specifically because of the security problems due to the unsettled civil situation in the north.

Two preparation games in April were notable for the number of League of Ireland players – five – Giles introduced; of these only Bohemian full-back Eamonn Gregg got anything like a run in the team. Against Turkey at Lansdowne Road, the Irish were 4–0 up after 23 minutes and Treacy, who was on a hat-trick, should have made it five just after half-time but he kicked a penalty over the bar. Paul McGee (QPR), making his debut, and Giles also scored in a 4–2 win.

The following week an understrength side played World Cup bound Poland in Lodz. While the result was a predictable 3–0 win for the home side, the Irish contained them for long periods and made them look pretty ordinary.

The following month it was on to Norway for a friendly only three days before the European Championship game in Denmark. Giles fielded his first-choice team, with Derby County full-back David Langan and Orient midfielder Tony Grealish the significant newcomers.

Grealish had a good game; Langan, who was a bad traveller, did not and was replaced at half-time by Lawrenson. In an overall poor display, probably induced as much by the nearness of the Denmark game as the awfulness of the Oslo pitch, the 0–0 result was poor consolation, especially as key men Brady and Givens had to retire with injuries. Brady's ankle injury kept him out of the Wednesday, 24 May game in Copenhagen, but Givens managed to start and contributed handsomely before retiring at half-time in favour of McGee.

'If every international was that good, people all over the world would be happy,' said Giles after an exciting game in which the Republic raced into a 2–0 lead by the 28th minute, were hauled back to 2–1 and then seemed to have it sewn up when Gerry Daly made it 3–1 after 66 minutes. The Danes equalised with two goals in two minutes, the second a 30-yard rocket from left-back Soren Lerby.

It was an encouraging start, even if regarded as a point lost rather than a valuable away point gained. Although midfielders Grealish and Daly had been on target, it was a case of what might have been had Brady been available.

When the Republic's next game – at home to Northern Ireland – came around, once again an Arsenal player was missing. This time it was David O'Leary who, despite protestations to manager Terry Neill that he was fit, was refused permission to travel to Dublin. Giles called up his Shamrock Rovers team-mate Noel Synnott to play alongside Lawrenson in what was an historic, but tension-ridden, game before 46,000 fans at Lansdowne Road. With the fans carefully segregated, trouble was kept to a minimum by the presence of a large force of Gardai.

The game was boring, due mainly to the effective marking job David McCreery did on Brady and the resultant lack of penetration from the Republic's midfield. On the credit side, Lawrenson came of age with a commanding performance, despite requiring several stitches in the side of his head at half-time; the debit side included the booing of Giles by the fans, ostensibly because of the substitution of Heighway by Givens. It was a foretaste of what was to come.

The 0–0 draw was seen as a tactical victory for Blanchflower over Giles, and the loss of a point at home as extremely damaging to the Republic's hopes of qualifying from the Group.

To compound matters, an injury forced Giles out of the Republic's next game, at home to England, on 25 October.

The full house notices went up again as 50,000 fans crammed into Lansdowne Road. David O'Leary showed just what the team had missed by his absence against Northern Ireland with a display which had rival managers Giles and Ron Greenwood reaching for superlatives. 'Outstanding' was Greenwood's comment, while Giles said he must be as good as any centre-half in the world.

While the Irish effort was of heroic proportions as they held England to a 1–1 draw, again there was disconcerting evidence that they lacked staying power. A terrific first-half performance was followed by a handing of the initiative to the opposition. Magnificent defensive work by O'Leary, Mulligan, Lawrenson and Holmes, and some bad misses by England's attack, meant that England were unable to turn their superiority into goals.

Bob Latchford opened the scoring after eight minutes when he headed in following a corner by Trevor Brooking. The equaliser came in the 26th minute following a surging run by O'Leary. He was obstructed by Keegan on the edge of the penalty area and Brady played the free-kick to Daly who swept it into the net.

Although unbeaten after three games, the Republic had dropped points in games they might reasonably have hoped to win. Financially, the players were also in the also-ran stakes, receiving £100 per match compared to the £300 on offer to the England players.

The expectations Giles had raised were adding to his burden. Peter Ball, in an incisive analysis of Giles's work in *Magill*, recorded an exchange of views at a training session before the Republic's next game at home to Denmark on

Wednesday, 2 May, 1979. A journalist commented: 'We're not winning the vital matches,' prompting the pertinent retort from Eamon Dunphy: 'We've never been playing in the vital matches before.'

In a sense, both were right. Winning the vital matches would remain a problem for the Republic for many years, but Giles's achievement in bringing the team to the stage where it was regularly playing vital matches should not be overlooked or its importance understated.

The build-up to the Denmark game was a nightmare, with players dropping out day after day. The loss of his first-choice centre-backs, O'Leary and Lawrenson, was Giles's biggest problem, for the Danes included pacy striker Alan Simonsen, European Footballer of the Year for 1978.

When they first came together – against Bulgaria in October 1977 – O'Leary and Lawrenson seemed destined for a long run at the heart of the defence. O'Leary was the more natural defender of the two, but he was as good on the ball as Lawrenson, who had been converted from the wing while at Preston. Amazingly, while they were regulars in the squad over the next 70 games, they only figured as centre-back partners on 12 occasions, with Lawrenson switched to full-back and midfield on occasion.

On the credit side was the return after a two-year suspension of the wholehearted Mick Martin. Unfortunately, he broke his nose in training. However, Giles with no other option, selected him anyway at centre-back alongside the dependable Mulligan.

A makeshift side struggled in the first half against a Danish team that was in the process of becoming a force to be reckoned with. Then, a minute before the break, the home side took an unexpected lead. A Giles long ball was controlled instantly by new cap Austin Hayes, who drove the ball in from the right wing for the onrushing Daly to deflect into the net. It was against the run of play, but the Irish rode their luck and, in the 65th minute, Givens clinched a notable victory with a superb headed goal from a cross by Man-of-the-Match Daly.

Peter Ball, in his *Magill* analysis, noted that the cheers when Giles's name was announced before the game were mingled with boos, but stated: 'With the heart of the team, O'Leary, Lawrenson, Brady, Stapleton and possibly Daly, going to be available for the next ten years, and getting better, and a new wave of young players of outstanding potential coming along, the Irish team in a few years' time could be something.' In some respects, he was not far out.

With only a point separating the top three in the Group, Giles was understandably upbeat after this performance, but the preparation of some of his players for the next game, away to Bulgaria, must have dented his confidence.

Arsenal trio, O'Leary, Brady and Stapleton, following their success in the FA Cup final on Saturday, 12 May, were faced with this hectic itinerary: 14 May, away to Chelsea in the League; to Copenhagen the following day for a game that night; back to London on Wednesday; flight to Dublin on Thursday; on to Sofia on Friday for the game on Saturday, 19 May. Derby midfielder Daly was also globe-trotting, playing in the USA.

With so much at stake, it was a big blow when Stapleton joined Lawrenson on the injured list. He was replaced by Mickey Walsh, and there was also a recall for Heighway. Unsurprisingly in the circumstances when the crunch came, the team just did not have it. O'Leary and Brady, exhausted by their hectic schedule, were pale shadows of their usual selves, and if it had not been for a brilliant display by Peyton it would have been 4–0 instead of 1–0.

The corner count of 16–0 in favour of the home side gives an indication of the one-way traffic. Bulgaria's only fear appeared to be Heighway, and he was brutally taken care of in a number of early tackles which referee Bucek of Austria only acknowledged with a finger wagging to Jeliazkov. Badly though the Irish played, they managed to delay that score until the 80th minute.

The result, which effectively ended the Republic's interest in the Group, was overshadowed by the tragic accident to Jimmy Holmes whose leg was smashed in a tackle with Iliev in the 57th minute.

'When Steve Heighway came over and then looked away in horror, I sensed the worst,' recalls Holmes.

Holmes's agony continued on the flight home. The hospital staff in Sofia had put the plaster cast on too tightly and he endured so much pain that he was taken off the plane in Geneva and rushed to hospital where the plaster was removed and replaced. On his return to England he had to undergo further operations, and was out of the game for 11 months. Although he played once more for the Republic – in a friendly against Wales in 1981 – his career effectively ended that day in Sofia at the age of 25.

Holmes was one of the quiet, unsung heroes of the Tuohy–Giles revolution. He stepped into the left-back position and made it his own. A sweet striker of the ball, he was an excellent defender who always did a professional job for the Republic. It was fitting that the FAI granted him a testimonial in 1985, a game notable for the introduction of Tony Cascarino.

Sofia also marked Giles's last competitive match. He played in a friendly against West Germany in Dublin four days later and rounded off his career with a game against World Champions Argentina in aid of UNICEF a week later when the star attraction was 18-year-old Diego Maradona.

For Giles the manager, games against West Germany, Argentina, Wales and Czechoslovakia – the latter two away in September – afforded ample opportunities for experimentation. The one player to emerge with great credit was Tony Grealish, now a forceful midfielder after making his debut at right-back. With his powerful running and shooting, he made an excellent foil for the skilful Brady.

Apart from a 0–0 draw with Argentina, there was no joy in the other friendlies which were lost 1–3 (West Germany), 1–2 (Wales) and 1–4 (to European Champions Czechoslovakia). For the latter game, Giles selected four newcomers – John Devine, Pierce O'Leary, Fran O'Brien and Terry Donovan – while another two, Jeff Chandler and John Anderson, were introduced as substitutes.

Devine was the latest from the Arsenal assembly line; O'Leary was a brother of David; O'Brien was a brother of former international Ray; and Donovan was the son of 1950s star Don. The pedigree was right in each case, but only Devine enjoyed anything like a run in the team.

When Bulgaria came to Dublin for the return European Championship game on 17 October, they found Brady in irrepressible form. He dictated the play, ably abetted in midfield by Grealish and the ever-reliable Martin. Giles put Pierce O'Leary in beside his brother David and experimented with Ashley Grimes at left-back. He also gave QPR striker McGee a start, following his good display in Czechoslovakia.

Giles's experiments turned up trumps, although there were only 18,000 to witness a tremendous 3–0 trouncing of the Bulgars. Martin opened the scoring in the 40th minute, following a marvellous Brady pass; Grealish claimed the second a minute after the break with an enterprising run through the defence; and Stapleton headed the third in the 83rd minute from a perfect Brady cross.

England's 5–1 victory in Belfast the same night assured them of qualification. The Republic still had to visit Belfast and London, with the visit to the North on 21 November in the must-win category. As preparation, an understrength Republic played the USA at Dalymount on Monday, 29 October. The robust Americans proved quite a handful and took a 2–0 lead before goals from Grealish, Givens and Anderson – the latter two having come on as subs – saw the home side through.

It was an exciting match and a personal triumph for assistant manager Alan Kelly. Kelly, in charge in Giles's absence, was responsible for the matchwinning changes. One of the changes involved the introduction of Mulligan for his last appearance in an Irish jersey.

Mulligan was one of those players who, according to Giles, 'would die with the green jersey on him'. Capped 50 times, it would have been a lot more but for the fact that he did not sign for Chelsea until he was 24. He remained a fixture on the international team, at centre-back or either of the full-back berths, with an occasional stint in midfield, for 10 years. One of those rare players who seemed to be born to play international football, some of his best performances occurred at times when he was out of favour with his English club bosses.

When Brady failed a fitness test, the odds swung in the North's favour, but the Republic, with a midfield of Daly, Martin and Grealish, still produced most of the creative football. They were unfortunate to find goalkeeper Pat Jennings in inspired form. Gerry Armstrong headed home the one chance he got in the 54th minute from a Sammy Nelson cross. It proved to be the winner.

A minute earlier Daly had been struck by a missile thrown from the crowd. The resulting head wound required three stitches. Present-day retribution might have led to the game being re-played or Windsor Park being closed to international football for a spell but, in 1979, no great outcry was made over this disturbing incident.

Group One was rounded off with the Republic's visit to Wembley on 6 February 1980. The game, which attracted a full house of over 90,000, including a large Irish contingent, was billed as a duel between Brady and England's European Footballer of the Year, Kevin Keegan. On the night, however, it was Keegan who shone. A moderate England team made hard work of disposing of a young Irish team. Without Keegan, they might not have succeeded. He was creator and scorer, notching both goals in a 2–0 win that meant England finished top of the Group. His second goal, a delicate chip over substitute goalkeeper Ron Healy, was the highlight of the night.

With a World Cup series to be undertaken, involving European giants Holland, Belgium and France, it was time for Giles to indulge in some self-assessment; he was not all that pleased with his position. Criticism of himself and the style of play he had introduced was mounting, and he did not intend to hang around for the lynching party.

He remained in charge for the opening World Cup tie away to Cyprus on Wednesday, 26 March, which was won 3–2, but on the flight home he informed FAI officials that he was resigning. They were shocked; they would have been happy to see him remain in office and ride out what they considered a minor storm. But Giles's mind was made up, and that was that.

Although he went out on a winning note, he would have been happier with a bigger winning margin, as the Cypriots were the minnows in Group Two. Goals from McGee (2) and Lawrenson secured the points.

Looking back on his resignation, Giles said that it was a long process.

'I had been doing the job for seven years, I found there was a lot of criticism and I asked myself why was I doing it. It certainly was not for the money. I had the name for grabbing money and making this and that from the Irish team, which was completely false. The most I ever got from the FAI was £6,000 in any one year. I never did it for the money.

'What did me a lot of harm was that I came back to Shamrock Rovers, and familiarity breeds contempt. My observation was that whatever I did was not right, which happens to a manager who hasn't qualified. And I thought, well we've come from there to here and there's no real credit in that so I felt it wasn't worth it. I felt I would be happier not doing the job, which I was. I never had any regrets.

'I was living in Ireland at the time. I had six children, eldest 14 down to eight, my parents were still alive, and my family were being affected by the criticism. When you become national team manager you become public property. People thought I was a highly paid guy who enjoyed the publicity surrounding it, which I never did. So once the people around me were affected by it, I said I'm not doing it any more, and I never missed it.

'I did the job for professional satisfaction. I was never great with the media and I never promoted myself which I could have done, because I could not be bothered.

'For some reason the idea got around that I was earning a lot of money, and when Jack [Charlton] took the job he was doing it for nothing. The idea persists today. Jack got a lot of money for doing the job and good luck to him. But that is public relations. When you are in the public eye people don't meet you so, if your PR is not good, they can get the wrong impression.'

The first thing Giles had tried to establish was an expectancy that the Republic would qualify for the major competitions.

'I think I was successful in that and it was part of my own undoing because they said he's had two gos at the World Cup and the European Championship and he hasn't qualified for anything yet. We never looked like qualifying for anything before. But it was right for the players and the public to expect to qualify because if you don't, you are never going to do it.'

There are plenty of heroes in the history of the Republic of Ireland team, but none shines so brightly as John Giles, both as a player who initiated change, and as a manager who brought the team to hitherto undreamt of levels. At their best, Giles' team played as sweet a tune as any Irish team before or since, yet, sadly, his critics, even today, choose instead to focus on the days when things did not go right or the opposition was too strong and stifled the Republic's game.

Giles retained his dignity. He knew he had only a limited squad from which to choose, that one or two injuries could, and often did, wreck his plans, but he never complained. He simply got on with the job, retaining the confidence of his players and preparing them for better days ahead.

There were a couple of factors which worked in Giles's favour. Number one was the aligning of the Republic's competitive dates with those of England, which made it easier to secure the release of players. Number two was the arrival of the talented Arsenal trio of Brady, O'Leary and Stapleton, all of whom enjoyed record-breaking careers in the green jersey.

'We had some very good players and some good hard-working professionals but we did not have great all-round talent,' Giles points out. 'We did not have the selection of players. The change in the eligibility rule, which brought in players like Aldridge and Townsend, made a huge difference. They wouldn't have been eligible in the 1970s.'

With typical modesty, Giles remarked: 'I would like to think I made a contribution.' That, surely, is the understatement of all time for, without Giles and the respectability which he brought to the Republic at international level, it is extremely doubtful whether the country would have enjoyed the success it did under Charlton.

While Tuohy continued his good work with the Republic's youth teams in the 1980s, Giles made a clean break, eventually returning to England where he had a second short spell as manager of West Bromwich Albion before finding his niche as a respected commentator on TV and in newspapers.

13

Referees Spoil the Party

The FAI's hoped-for smooth takeover by assistant Alan Kelly as successor to Giles lasted only one game – an impressive 2–0 home win over Switzerland – before Kelly was forced to step down, due to club commitments.

In his short reign, Kelly handed debuts to Gary Waddock and Kevin Moran and appointed Eoin Hand as his assistant. The latter decision had the most far-reaching consequences. Hand, caretaker manager for a home friendly with world champions Argentina on 16 May, kept faith with Kelly's squad and was rewarded with a performance good enough to earn him the manager's job, even though Argentina won 1–0. In appointing home-based Hand, the FAI ignored the lessons of Giles's departure. When the chickens came home to roost five years later, their principal term of reference for Hand's successor was that he be based in the UK.

Hand, at 34, was two years older than Giles had been on his appointment, but he lacked Giles's standing in the game. This made things more difficult for him, especially in his relations with the FAI hierarchy, while most of the players regarded him as 'one of the lads' rather than the mature manager the position demanded.

The vote of 9–7 for Hand, with Paddy Mulligan the runner-up, was leaked to the media. One of the officials later told Hand he had voted for him 'because he thought Mulligan was the person who had thrown a bun at him on one of the foreign trips'. Such revelations suggested that security of tenure was out of the question.

Hand inherited a young side, Giles having steadily replaced the experienced panel he had started out with. The average age was in the early 20s. The new manager was keen to put his own mark on the team, even though he regarded it as 'one of the best we've ever had'. In his view, 'sometimes skilful players think that skill is enough in international football, but there's a physical side to it also and they've got to come to terms with that.'

His answer was to introduce a 4-4-2 system for his competitive debut against Holland, the 1978 World Cup runners-up. To stiffen his midfield, he included Lawrenson alongside Brady, Daly and Grealish for the Group Two World Cup tie at Lansdowne Road on Wednesday, 10 September, 1980. It was a

147

matchwinning move. Although Lawrenson himself considered that he had a 'nightmare', his presence allowed his fellow midfielders more freedom and this led to a generally more adventurous Irish performance. However, when Tahamata punished a defensive lapse after 57 minutes, it seemed like another case of 'nice play, pity about the finish' for the Irish. The chances had been created but Stapleton, Brady, Daly and Lawrenson failed to put them away until the 79th minute when a fine move featuring Brady, Grealish and Stapleton let Daly through for the equaliser. Responding to the encouragement of the 32,000 fans, the winner duly arrived in the 84th minute when a cute Brady free-kick outflanked the Dutch wall. Lawrenson met it with a diving header which curled past Joop Hiele into the net.

The loss of David O'Leary through injury forced Hand to revert to the 4-3-3 system against Belgium in Dublin on 15 October. While Moran was available again, Hand obviously felt that a novice partnership of Moran and Pierce O'Leary at centre-back was too great a risk. Instead he paired Moran with Lawrenson and recalled Heighway in a bid to give added width against a team noted for its use of the offside trap.

Belgium's offside plan spoiled the game, but there was much to admire in the play of 35-year-old Van Moer, a world-class playmaker who outshone Brady in the midfield battle. It was Van Moer's headed pass which put Cluytens through in the 13th minute to open the scoring. For a while, it seemed the Belgians would overrun the Irish, but then, with three minutes to go to the break, Brady pushed a pass through to Grealish. The linesman raised his flag, but referee Rolles from Luxembourg waved play on and Grealish went around Pfaff before scoring from an acute angle.

Both managers, Hand and Guy Thys, seemed content to share the spoils. They were also in agreement on the poor state of the pitch, stating that the grass was too long, a problem the FAI would have to face for many more years at the Lansdowne Road venue.

Holland, Belgium and 13 days later, France in Paris – it was certainly a case of going in at the deep end for Hand. The French seemed to be the toughest of the three, for their UEFA rating ranked them second only to West Germany. Besides, they had won 7–0 in Cyprus, where the Irish had scraped home 3–2.

The lack of pace and punch up-front was proving a problem but FAI President Dr Brendan Menton was busy trying to solve it. Brighton striker Michael Robinson had expressed an interest in playing for the Republic. Five days before the game in Paris, Dr Menton received a phone call from the Department of Foreign Affairs informing him that, if the necessary documents were not with them the following day, Robinson would be out of the game.

'In order to qualify him I had to get his mother an Irish passport and this involved searching through registries of births, deaths and marriages going back to his great-grandmother, who was a West End beauty in the 1860s,' recalled Dr Menton. Fortunately, the search was successful, and Robinson was able to make his debut on 28 October in Paris.

Apart from David O'Leary and Daly, Hand had a full-strength squad for the game, but only thanks to an appeal to FIFA for the release of a number of players whose clubs were anxious to hold on to them for League Cup ties. Dave Langan was among them. He showed how much playing for Ireland meant to him when he offered to forego his pay if manager Jim Smith would release him. Smith still said no until FIFA overruled him.

Another problem was the late arrival of captain Liam Brady, now playing with Juventus. He had a game on Sunday and only arrived at the Irish camp on Monday, 24 hours before kick-off. It was not the ideal preparation, which became apparent as the game went on. France had detailed Tigana to do a marking job on Brady, which he did extremely well, but the bonus for France was that, in his fatigued condition, Brady was not able to chase Tigana back when an Irish move broke down.

The French put the Irish through the wringer from the start, and it was no surprise when Platini opened the scoring after 10 minutes. He gave Peyton no chance when he was left unmarked at the far post to meet a cross from Tigana. For a time it seemed the French would go to town, but gritty defence kept them at bay, and then the Irish fightback began.

With Robinson proving a lively partner for Stapleton, the chances were created – mainly by Brady – but bad luck and some good goalkeeping by Dropsy denied them. Then, in the 57th minute, Heighway got free down the left and swung over a perfect far-post cross which reached Moran, whose knockdown to Robinson was promptly slammed home. Elation quickly turned to despair when Spanish referee Lamo-Castillo indicated a free-kick out for an offence that still remains a mystery. It was Paris 1976 all over again.

The Irish attacked at every opportunity but, in doing so, they left themselves open to the quick counter and, in the 77th minute, this was their undoing. A pass went astray and allowed Six to set up Zimako to score easily. Pressing to the end, chances fell to Robinson and sub Gerry Ryan, but there was not even a consolation goal for the gallant Irish who were, on this occasion, heroes all. It was one of the best performances away from home for some time, with the Irish equal to the French in everything except finishing.

The Stapleton-Robinson partnership made a big impression when Cyprus visited Lansdowne Road on 19 November. With captain and playmaker Brady well rested following a weekend off, the Republic had no problem running up a 6–0 win. Robinson and Chris Hughton scored their first international goals, with Stapleton, Daly 2 (one penalty) and Grealish the other scorers.

With seven points from five games, the Republic were in a good position, but manager Hand still had his enemies on the home front. As manager of Limerick United, he had informed the League that, due to injuries and illness, he would not be able to field a team to play Athlone Town on Sunday, 7 December. The League ordered that the game go ahead.

When Limerick failed to travel, the League imposed a £1,500 fine on the club and suspended Hand and Chairman Michael Webb. In doing so, they called the international manager's integrity into question. A precedent had been set two years earlier when Giles, as manager of Shamrock Rovers, had found himself in a similar predicament but no action had been taken. Hand's standing obviously made him more vulnerable than his distinguished predecessor.

Despite Limerick's successful appeal, the action of the League's officials, most of whom doubled as FAI officials, was a reminder to Hand of the vultures hovering in the background. It certainly was not a vote of confidence.

With the vital return game against Belgium scheduled for 25 March in Brussels, the FAI arranged a friendly with Wales on 24 February. Although intended as preparation for the big game, only five of the team were available for this first International in Tolka Park. Despite the boost of a 25th minute goal from Grealish, the home side went down 3–1 to a Welsh side that was top of its World Cup group. It proved a fiery baptism for former England Youth goalkeeper Jim 'Seamus' McDonagh who failed to impress, and had to suffer the abuse of some fans. This was unusual treatment as the fickle fans usually reserved their abuse for players they considered over the hill.

Of more significance was the Under-21 game the following night at Anfield. In the Irish team were Packie Bonner, Ronnie Whelan, Kevin Sheedy and John Anderson, all of whom later contributed to the glory days under Jack Charlton. In comparison, none of the England team, which won 1–0, were to make any great impression in the international arena.

In Brussels, with qualification within reach, the Irish played as men possessed on a night which was marked by spectacular thunder and lightning. The centre-back pairing of Moran and Martin, both of whom played magnificently, drew the sting of the Belgian attack and then, in first-half injury time, Brady's free-kick from the edge of the box was flicked in to the net by Stapleton. The celebrations began, only to be cut short by referee Nazare who signalled for a free-kick to the home side for no apparent reason.

Played in a constant downpour, with the addition of celestial fireworks in the second half, the Irish appeared to have earned a hard-fought point until Belgian captain Eric Gerets took a hand in the 87th minute. Gerets, later to be suspended for involvement in a bribe scandal, showed the dark side of his character when he took a deliberate dive with Heighway in attendance. Nazare bought the dummy. Vandereycken's free-kick beat the wall but struck the crossbar, rebounding into the air. Goalkeeper McDonagh slipped as he adjusted his footing and Ceulemans, with the advantage of forward momentum, rose above Martin and Moran to head in to the net.

Hand lost his composure and confronted Nazare as he came off the pitch.

'You are a disgrace and a cheat,' he told him within full hearing of the cameras. Perhaps FIFA agreed, for no reprimand was issued to the Irish manager by the world body.

Brady noted how tears were shed in the dressing-room.

'As Steve Heighway said, the difference between making it and not making it is so slight – but why is it that we never get the breaks that would make the difference?' he asked. Brady also remarked: 'The referee's final controversial decision angered me more than anything. I was beside him when he gave the free and I can tell you there was no way he could have seen a foul from where he was. When Gerets got up off the ground he was laughing – and he was still laughing when the goal was scored. He knew his con job had won the game.'

If the referee was the focus of most fans' ire, commentator Eamon Dunphy honed in on Brady's performance and found it wanting.

'I believe that it is the intensity of Brady's commitment, compounded by the responsibility of captaincy, that drains him of emotional, and consequently, physical resources on major occasions,' he wrote. 'That plus the simple football fact that he doesn't, in any event, possess the stamina to cover the field in the role of midfield general.' Dunphy was on the mark when he questioned Brady's stamina. At Arsenal, under the regime of Don Howe and playing almost 70 games a season, Brady had worked hard to build up his stamina, and was duly acclaimed the best midfielder in the English League and won the PFA Player of the Year award. However, in Italy the demands, in terms of 90 minute activity and the number of games, were no longer as great and, as a result, his fitness level slipped back. Hand was aware of this, but what to do about it was another matter.

'While Liam might disagree, I feel he lost a lot of stamina during his time in Italy,' said Hand. 'He would tire but perhaps he tried to do too much. His contribution was still immense. I compensated for his weakness by picking someone, like Tony Grealish, who was prepared to do the running. It certainly was not a situation where I was putting out a lame duck. I don't think his lack of stamina was a big point because, in the creative sense, he was of such value to the team. He could win a match out of nothing.'

In Brussels, Brady made no contribution for the last 20 minutes, affected by cramp in both legs.

'I just stretched for a ball and both legs seized up,' he reported, adding, 'I think it must have been the tension. I have been very uptight lately about playing for Ireland.'

Hand's dilemma was whether to take off his captain and possibly damage the morale of the side, or leave him on in the hope that he might, as he said, 'win the match out of nothing'. He chose the latter, but it was a gamble which did not come off. And, sad to say, there is not much evidence to support his contention that Brady could win a match – he was too fond of taking the ball from his defenders and did not do enough work around his opponents' penalty area.

Irish footballers were enjoying unprecedented success with the biggest clubs in England – Arsenal, Tottenham, Manchester United and Liverpool – yet Hand found it difficult to get all the pieces of the jigsaw together. He was not helped by the FAI's attitude to friendly games and, especially, foreign tours. In successive years, he was asked to select a squad for games in two of the world's trouble spots. In 1981 it was Poland, then in the midst of the Solidarity uprising which eventually overthrew communist rule, and in 1982 it was Argentina, which was at war with Britain over the Falkland Islands.

'Their attitude was that they had got so many dollars and they had a commitment and they did not put any thought into what sort of team we were going to put out,' recalled Hand. 'They just said, "You're the manager, get a team together, because if you don't someone else will." The South American tour was a ridiculous tour to go on. My part was one of protest but it could not be a strong protest because I would have been disposed of.'

The tour to Poland, which started with a 3–0 defeat by West Germany B in Bremen, was notable for the behaviour of certain FAI officials who, instead of accompanying the team to the match venue, opted for more luxurious surroundings in Warsaw. Perhaps they knew what the journey to Bydgoszcz entailed – a five-hour drive in a vehicle with no springs, no heating and no air-conditioning – and a primitive hotel where the food led to four players going down with food poisoning!

In these less-than-auspicious circumstances, Packie Bonner celebrated his 21st birthday with his first cap. After two minutes, he was picking the ball out of the net, and Poland went on to score a resounding 3–0 win. Bonner was not overly impressive and confirmed Hand in his view that McDonagh was his number one goalkeeper.

Bonner may have been unlucky, as David O'Leary, who put one of the three goals past his own goalkeeper, admitted afterwards: 'I was not fit enough to go on that tour and I made a mistake playing. it is a mistake I won't make again – you learn from your experiences.' Significantly, he missed the debacle in South America the following year, but his bad luck with summer tours was to return with a vengeance when Charlton took over.

Considering the damage to morale that such trips can cause, it was nothing short of amazing that, in the games after Poland, both difficult World Cup assignments, the Republic performed in masterly fashion.

On 9 September 1981, they travelled to Rotterdam with what was, in most respects, a full-strength team. Daly, who was suspended, was the only notable absentee and that let Martin move to midfield to add some bite to that area. When, straight from the kick-off, Brady, Stapleton and Devine combined to give Robinson a chance which he deflected just wide, the Dutch knew they were in for a hard battle.

Irish teams seem to raise their game once they go behind, and this game provided a classic example. Twice they fell behind, and each time they fought back to create excellent goals. Heighway, on his 34th and last appearance in the green jersey, was caught in possession for Holland's opening score, but he made amends with a perfect cross which was volleyed home by Robinson just before the break.

In the second half, Langan took down Rep for Muhren to restore the home side's lead from the penalty spot, but Lawrenson, in a rare foray from defence, beat two defenders to get to the end line and crossed to the far post for Stapleton to equalise with a firm header.

Belgium, with a 2–0 win over France the same night, had secured their World Cup spot, but the chase for the remaining place ensured a sell-out 54,000 crowd at Lansdowne Road on 14 October for the visit of France. It was a game the Republic had to win, and so involved were the fans that one went so far as to steal the French tricolour from its flagpole!

With Daly and Grealish injured, Hand opted for a combination of steel and skill in midfield with Lawrenson, Martin, Brady and Ronnie Whelan, who had recently broken into Liverpool's first team. It was a midfield which fired on only three of its four cylinders, for Brady was strangely out of sorts and was overshadowed by Michel Platini, who was destined to replace him at Juventus the following season.

When Whelan and Robinson combined to stretch the French defence and Mahut, under pressure from Stapleton, turned the resultant cross wide of his goalkeeper after only five minutes, the Irish were on a roll, but three minutes later they were quickly brought back to earth when Bellone struck a sweet equaliser.

France had not come to Dublin to defend, so it was pulsating, nerve-wracking entertainment for the enthralled crowd as goalmouth incidents followed in rapid succession at either end. Eventually, after some sustained Irish pressure, the coolness of O'Leary set up Stapleton to make it 2–1 after 25 minutes. More near misses followed before Robinson profited from a Larios backpass which fell short. That made it 3–1 at the interval and Stapleton almost scored again on the resumption. However, from then on it was practically all France with the Irish performing defensive heroics to keep them at bay. Platini finally found an opening in the 82nd minute to make it 3–2, and it took a superb reflex save by McDonagh from Six in the last minute to secure an historic victory.

Ireland's performance was put into perspective by Brady: 'Ten points from a group containing Holland, Belgium and France is a marvellous achievement for Ireland.' Unfortunately, it was not enough. France won their two remaining games to pip the Republic on goal difference and then went on to greater things, only losing in the semi-final to West Germany after a penalty shoot-out. They staked their claim to be one of the great French teams by winning the European Championship in 1984.

One of the immediate benefits of the Republic's fine showing was the recruitment of Spurs winger Tony Galvin. Like most of the England-born players who make their mark with the Republic, Galvin was a late developer, turning professional at 22. Now 25, he already had an FA Cup medal and international football seemed the logical next step. Hand agreed.

The post mortems concentrated on the controversial refereeing decisions which went against Ireland in crucial games, but a more realistic assessment was made by Stapleton, who came of age as an international striker in this competition.

'We did not have the players, it always comes down to that,' he reasoned. 'France and ourselves were the best teams in the group, but where we were going to get 22 players if we had made the finals is another question. You'll always have the numbers, but it is quality you want. There mightn't have been better quality in Jack Charlton's squad than in '82, but there was more quality.

'Around '82 we always had a good nucleus, maybe eight to 12 players who could compete quite comfortably, but we did not have any more. And when you get players not travelling for one reason or another then you are down to the bare bones and you are playing with a less than full-strength team. We always had players who did not just come up to it and you can't get away with that. You might get away with one, but not with three or four.'

What made the near miss harder to take was the inevitable comparison with Northern Ireland who qualified for the finals in Spain with less impressive statistics. It was a comparison which was destined to haunt Hand during his term in office, and ultimately built up the pressure for his removal.

14

Decline and Fall

Follow that! That was the task facing the Republic of Ireland after the near miss of 1981. Expectations had been raised, belief in the team was high; to the public it seemed only a matter of time before the breakthrough to World Cup or European Championship finals was achieved.

Things might have worked out too if Hand had received a little more help from his masters. However, with interest in the team at an all-time high following the thriller against France, all the FAI could conjure up in the following months was a trip to Algeria and a tour to South America. Not a home game in sight to tap into the goodwill of the fans and to bring the players together to cement their good work.

The games in Algeria and South America were against World Cup finalists rounding off their preparations for Spain, but in neither case had Hand anything like a full squad at his disposal. In Algiers the Republic went down 2-0 while, for the South American tour, it was almost a case of find a player, as clubs refused to release players for a tour which included a visit to Argentina, then at war with Britain over the Falkland Islands.

South American tours, which had been initiated by Louis Kilcoyne in 1972, had been successful up to now in both a financial and a playing sense. But for Hand, South America '82 was a disaster from the start. It was an ill-conceived tour that should never have taken place and one that, in the end, seriously undermined his position as the Republic's football supremo both with the players and, as a direct consequence of the results, with the public.

So who was to blame? In insisting that the tour go ahead and for his lack of sensitivity to objections from English clubs, FAI Secretary Peadar O'Driscoll must shoulder a lot of the blame. He adopted the simplistic 'The war has nothing to do with us, we're neutral' approach when club after club refused to release players. Eventually, the sheer weight of the refusals wore him – and the other officials – down and Argentina was taken off the itinerary. By then, it was too late to be much good to Hand, who had to pick a squad without Arsenal, Tottenham, Liverpool or Manchester United players. He somehow scraped together 15 players which, for a three-match tour, was cutting things fine. Further FAI inefficiency led to Hughton staying at home after he received a message at Heathrow from FAI headquarters that he was not required to travel.

For the first game – against Chile – Mike Walsh, Sean O'Driscoll and Mick Fairclough received their first caps, while Eamonn Deacy received his second and John Anderson his third. In the circumstances, a 1–0 defeat to a first-minute goal was not a bad result. However, Robinson had to return home for treatment, leaving novice internationals Fairclough and Brendan O'Callaghan as the only strikers in the party. In addition, Hand was faced with a players' mutiny before the big game against Brazil. They had been promised a fee of $1,080 but, after a week, had only received $180 and were threatening to return home after the Brazil game. It required all Hand's diplomatic skills to iron out that problem.

It was not the best preparation for a game against a team enjoying a run of 16 games without defeat. What happened that 27 May in Uberlandia remains the biggest blot on the FAI's copybook: a 7–0 trouncing. Only one goal ahead at half-time, Brazil exploited Ireland's lack of height at centre-back and in the second half scored five of their six goals from corners.

'We were shocked afterwards,' recalled Deacy, 'all we wanted was to go home. Brady was really shattered and he more than anyone wanted to go home.' Brady, who relinquished the captaincy to Grealish on this tour, was in tears and inconsolable. Playing for Ireland meant so much to him that he had sacrificed his first wedding anniversary to play against Brazil and the margin of defeat was too much for him to take. When the team moved on to Trinidad, Brady stayed in Rio, adamant that he was returning to Italy. Hand's assistant, Terry Conroy, remained with him and eventually persuaded him to travel to Trinidad where further mortification awaited him.

Two games had been hastily arranged in Trinidad and the first, after a marathon plane journey, was deemed a full international against Trinidad and Tobago. The squad was in almost total disarray at this stage, and the jet lag did not help. Brady opened the scoring, but the Caribbean minnows took over to record a shock 2–1 win.

The confusion which reigned in the Irish camp was symbolised by Deacy lining up with his shorts on back to front. Interviewed a decade later, Deacy admitted that he always thought the second game in Port of Spain – against top club side ASL – was the international match.

'The first game was a farce,' he recalled. However, the 3–1 win over ASL was no consolation and has left no mark on the record books.

Significantly, six of the players involved against Trinidad had no future role with the team. The 1982 tour was remarkable for the fact that, from all the newcomers, not one came through to claim his place in the European Championship campaign. In effect, the advantage to Hand was nil.

To add insult to injury, the FAI failed to secure accreditation for Hand at the World Cup finals in Spain. To gain admission to games featuring Ireland's European Championship opponents Spain, journalist Jimmy Magee and managers Billy Bingham and Ron Greenwood came to his rescue.

Hand had also been the victim of FAI Secretary O'Driscoll's failure to secure accreditation for the European finals in 1980. Epitomising relations between the two was a brief altercation which occurred at Tolka Park. There was a small room under the main stand which the FAI used for hospitality purposes and when Hand put his head around the door, O'Driscoll remarked: 'What are you doing here?' While Hand gave as good as he got, it was a public humiliation for the manager at the hands of the FAI's most powerful official.

It was back to the old reliables for the European Championship, with the addition of Tottenham's Tony Galvin. Kevin Sheedy, whose career at Liverpool had been put on hold by repeated injury, moved to Everton where he became a key member in a successful team, and he was introduced towards the end of the campaign.

The loss of three points at home proved fatal to the Republic's chances in Group Seven, which was dominated by heavyweights Spain and Holland. Spain took a point from Lansdowne Road in a thrilling 3–3 draw, when the Republic came from 3–1 down to equalise with two Stapleton headers. It was the reverse of the same coin at Dalymount against Holland, who came from 2–0 down at half-time to win 3–2, the matchwinning move being the switching of Ruud Gullit from sweeper to a forward role.

The Republic, by recording home and away doubles over Malta and Iceland, showed they were a cut above the minnows of Europe, but their results against Spain and Holland indicated that they had some way to go before they could measure up to the big boys.

Off the field, the big boys showed the way also. With Malta banned from using their home ground, Holland persuaded them to play at the 'neutral' venue of Aachen – the equivalent of playing the Republic in Newry – and rattled up a healthy 6–0 win to boost their goal difference. Spain went one better when, faced with the need to score 12 against Malta to pip Holland on goal difference, they did just that in a game which did nothing for the image of football or the credibility of the European Championship.

If Hand was finding success elusive, one of his predecessors was enjoying a remarkable run. Liam Tuohy, in a voluntary capacity, was putting his considerable knowledge to good effect as manager of the Republic's youths. In three successive seasons they qualified for the UEFA finals and, on one memorable occasion, for the World Cup finals. These successes were a triumph for Tuohy's tactical know-how and a commentary on the great rapport he developed with his players. There was a steady stream of quality talent and all benefitted from their time under Tuohy. Prominent among them were John Sheridan, Denis Irwin, Terry Phelan, Alan Kelly, Niall Quinn and Steve Staunton.

Preparations for World Cup Group Six – in which the Republic were joined by Denmark, the Soviet Union, Switzerland and Norway, with two to qualify – consisted of seven friendlies, home to Mexico and Poland, away to Israel and four games in Japan, These were against China, a Brazilian club side (twice) and a Japanese Universities XI.

It was hardly top-notch opposition, but it pinpointed Hand's major problem. In seven games, the Republic scored twice, one by Eamonn O'Keeffe in the 1–0 win over China and the other by Stapleton against the Brazilians. On the credit side, among the players introduced were classy Liverpool left-back Jim Beglin and gritty Manchester City centre-back Mick McCarthy.

The disappointing preparation was reflected in the attendance at the opening World Cup tie at Lansdowne Road on 12 September 1984. Only 28,000 paid to go in for the visit of the Soviet Union, who were on a 12-game unbeaten run and who had franked their fine form with a 2–0 defeat of England at Wembley. In the event, the faithful fans were treated to a thriller as the Soviets eschewed a defensive game in the belief that they could take both points. After surviving early Irish pressure, they took over and were unlucky when, for once, an offside decision favoured the boys in green, Aleinikov's goal being disallowed.

This measure of good fortune revived Irish hopes and a swift break after 65 minutes, instigated by Whelan and carried on by Robinson in a memorable dash up the right wing, was clinically finished by Mickey Walsh, who seemed to control Robinson's low cross and shoot all in one movement. Soviet goalkeeper Dasaev had not moved by the time the ball nestled in the back of his net.

It was one of the great goals scored at Lansdowne Road and it proved sufficient to win the game, but not before the Soviets came close on a number of occasions. The game was a triumph for centre-back pair Lawrenson and O'Leary – one of their rare outings together at the heart of the defence – and also for Brady, whose teasing, tormenting display in midfield had much to do with the fans singing 'Here We Go, Here We Go' at the final whistle.

The win over the Soviet Union was the perfect answer to the critics, but the Republic faced two difficult away trips: to Norway and Denmark. The trip to Norway appeared to offer the best hope, and Hand recalled Stapleton in place of goalscorer Walsh in the only change from the opening game. Stapleton's recall was a gamble as he had not returned to first-team action since a knee operation, but Walsh was also short of first-team football.

Despite a bright start, during which Stapleton should have scored but displayed his lack of sharpness by placing his header from a Galvin cross too near goalkeeper Thorstvedt, the Irish performed way below par. They were caught by a sucker punch three minutes before the break, Jacobsen breaking through from the centre circle to score the only goal of the game.

The biggest disappointment was the poor showing of the Liverpool trio, Lawrenson, Whelan and Robinson, none of whom showed anything like club form or the form displayed against the Soviet Union. Whelan and Robinson suffered the indignity of being substituted, and there was no place for them in the team to play Denmark in Copenhagen the following month.

Mick McCarthy made his World Cup debut against the Danes.

'I remember being full of optimism,' he said later. 'I looked around and thought, the team is full of good players – why shouldn't we qualify? But then

I did not know much about international football and the strengths and weaknesses of the opposition.'

McCarthy was in for a rude awakening. The Danes, one of the surprise packets of the European Championship finals in 1984, had pace right through their 11 and, with their superior teamwork, put the Republic under pressure for practically the entire 90 minutes. The eventual 3–0 scoreline could have been much more, and their manager, Sepp Piontek, bemoaned missed chances which could have helped their goal difference.

About the only consolation was the display of Jim Beglin. The tall, slim Waterford lad, who had played under Giles at Shamrock Rovers and was Bob Paisley's last signing for Liverpool, rescued his fellow defenders time and again as the speedy Danes continually outpaced and outflanked them. For McCarthy it was an unhappy introduction to World Cup football. His lack of pace suggested that he would never be more than back-up for O'Leary, Lawrenson and Moran.

In three friendlies before the return with Norway on 1 May 1985, Hand introduced three more newcomers – John Byrne, Paul McGrath and Alan Campbell. Of the three, McGrath, who was making a big impression at Old Trafford after a move from St Patrick's Athletic, was the one who oozed class and composure the minute he stepped into the exalted company of world champions Italy at Dalymount Park.

McGrath was a ninth-minute replacement for Lawrenson who injured himself in a reckless tackle on Altobelli which led to Rossi opening the scoring from the penalty spot. In the 2–1 defeat, McGrath played like a man used to matching wits with world champions. His performance was a beacon of hope on a night when the Dalymount capacity was severely tested and chaos reigned until spectators were shepherded on to the touchlines. Unfortunately, McGrath was a centre-back and Hand had four centre-backs already. He resolved his dilemma by playing the elegant McGrath in midfield in the next two friendlies, away to Israel (0–0) and England (1–2).

Hand, under mounting pressure from his critics, might have helped his cause had he taken action on a *Football Monthly* article in its March issue. In it, Fulham's busy midfielder Ray Houghton stated that he was willing to declare for the Republic. A native of Glasgow whose father was from Buncrana, Co Donegal, he had tired of waiting for a call-up from Scotland.

McGrath never liked a midfield role and this dislike must have relayed itself to Hand who did not keep him there for the tie against Norway at Lansdowne Road, the less talented Waddock being preferred. McGrath was on the subs' bench, while Lawrenson and O'Leary resumed their centre-back partnership.

With the return of Langan and Daly, it was as strong a team as Hand was likely to have, yet it produced a strangely inept performance. A goal ruled marginally offside was all the Republic had to show for 90 minutes of uninspired effort. The chief talking point was the 67th minute substitution, with Whelan in for a subdued Brady, who had received a gold medal to mark his 50th cap before the kick-off. The 0–0 draw was a sore blow to qualification hopes.

That such a star-studded team should perform so poorly may have had something to do with the timing of the game, as it came in the middle of a period of top-quality club games. Brady had just suffered the agony of losing out in extra-time in the semi-final of the UEFA Cup with Inter Milan; Manchester United's Stapleton, McGrath and Moran had an FA Cup final date in 10 days' time, while the Liverpool contingent of Beglin, Lawrenson and Whelan had a date with destiny at the Heysel for the European Cup final; and Sheedy was in the Cup-Winners' Cup final with Everton. The Norwegians had no such distractions.

Some of the so-called fans among the small (15,000) attendance vented their displeasure at Hand and his players as they left the pitch. It was a nasty moment, and it persuaded Hand that it was time to resign. He told the players that, as he obviously could no longer motivate them, it would be better if someone else took over. It was the right thing to do. He realised that he had gone as far as he could go with this squad and someone else would probably get a better response. The failure of the squad to build on their near miss in the 1982 World Cup was his failure also, and he was prepared to admit it.

However, the players persuaded him to change his mind. Just how vital this proved to be can be seen in retrospect. Had Hand resigned, it is likely that retired Liverpool manager Bob Paisley would have been chosen to replace him. Charlton was not then available.

Football had been scarred for ever by the tragedy of Heysel, but all the major club games were out of the way by the time the Republic played Switzerland on 2 June. The transformation in the Irish performance was remarkable. The return of Grealish and Sheedy for Waddock and Galvin added workrate, skill and clinical finishing to the midfield. Both were on target in a comprehensive 3–0 win which began with a seventh-minute Stapleton goal following a Sheedy free-kick.

It was the high point of the Republic's campaign as they took over temporarily at the top of the table. With the pressure eased, Hand looked around for talent to strengthen his squad, and gave striker Tony Cascarino his chance in the Jimmy Holmes Testimonial on 7 August at Dalymount. A latecomer to professional football, Cascarino's game had many raw edges, but he did enough to get the nod over Robinson for the return game with Switzerland in September.

Hand again moved Lawrenson to midfield, with McCarthy partnering O'Leary at centre-back, but Lawrenson was not comfortable in his new berth and the service to Stapleton and Cascarino suffered. In a game marred by 52 free-kicks, the Irish had their chances – notably one with which Stapleton failed to connect properly – but the 0–0 draw was a commentary on the lack of quality play from both sides and effectively killed off their chances.

However, while there was still hope, Hand decided to leave no stone unturned to achieve his goal. Once again, though, he found little support from his bosses. It took some time to persuade them that he should attend the Soviet Union–Denmark game in Moscow to check out both the opposition and the hotel arrangements. He eventually received more help from his rivals in the Swiss and Danish FA than he did from the FAI.

Deciding that it was imperative for the game in Moscow on 16 October that the players should have their food brought in and prepared by an Irish chef, Hand's request was initially turned down on the basis of cost. Hand's wife Pat came to the rescue, offering to make the trip and prepare the meals without payment. Not even the cash-strapped FAI could turn down that generous offer, although when Hand went to Merrion Square to discuss arrangements with Treasurer Charlie Walsh and Secretary O'Driscoll, they were more interested in arguing about who would travel with the official party. The argument got so heated that both officials stormed out of headquarters, leaving Hand to turn off the lights and lock up.

Whether it was the food or the importance of the game, the team responded with one of its better away performances. In early exchanges, Beglin was taken down in the penalty area but Italian referee Casarin waved play on. With Lawrenson employed as sweeper behind O'Leary and McCarthy, the Irish defence had a more secure look and it took the Soviets 60 minutes to make the breakthrough, with Cherenkov turning Protasov's cross past McDonagh. The Irish came back strongly but had no luck, a point which was emphasised in the final minute when Protasov's diving header deflected off McCarthy to make the score 2–0.

It was an emotional Hand who announced that he would be stepping down after the final game against Denmark in Dublin the following month. Tears were shed in the dressing-room also by players who had given their all and probably felt that their last chance of World Cup glory had gone.

Hand's fate had been in the balance from the start of the year. The appalling abuse which he and his family suffered from fans who two short years previously had hailed him as a hero, made him glad to be out of the international scene.

'I felt the whole world, the whole nation, was against me,' he recalled. 'It was magnified because all you heard was the criticism; the yobbos screaming and shouting and spitting. Now, the amount of goodwill I experience tells me I did a good job and can be proud of what I did because I worked very hard on a part-time basis for part-time money and spent a lot of time at it, to the detriment of my sports business which went bust.'

One important lesson, which this time was not lost on key members of the FAI, was that, in future, the manager would be better based in England. The drawback was that the Association's finances were in a dreadful state – over £50,000 in the red at the start of the year, and World Cup gates had only broken even.

Hand's last game in charge ended in an ignominious 4–1 defeat by a Danish side so superior that they were able to take off midfielder Lerby after 57 minutes so that he could catch a flight to Germany to play in a Cup match. Yet eight of this Irish team were to form the backbone of Charlton's successful squad. The attendance of just over 15,000 was boosted by 6,000 Danes, many in full Viking regalia, lending the only colour to a grey afternoon. Adding to the FAI's misery was the result later that evening at Wembley. Northern Ireland earned a 0–0 draw with England to secure their place in a second successive World Cup finals.

The Republic had the quality players but the wee North had once again shown that organisation and determination often mean more than class. It also emphasised that football had become more manager-driven than player-driven. To emulate Billy Bingham's success with Northern Ireland, the FAI would have to choose Hand's successor carefully.

One of the more bizarre incidents of Hand's reign occurred before his last match. Like many journalists, John O'Shea of the *Evening Press* wondered at Hand's faith in the less-than-pacy McCarthy ahead of Moran or McGrath. O'Shea bet Hand £50 that he could beat McCarthy in a race. Hand took the bet. McCarthy duly raced O'Shea and beat him – 'not by much but I beat him,' McCarthy recalled. 'Then I said, do you fancy best of three and he said yeah, so we went back and he pulled his hamstring. The legend has it that I got injured in the race but I did not, I got injured training the following morning and it was my hamstring so I missed the game against Denmark. But that race should never have happened.'

The incident reflects Hand's lack of authority.

'My background – second division – was nothing near the background Giles or Charlton had. When I was appointed it was a battle to try and keep the thing professional or improve it – to make sure we travelled as best we could, that we stayed in the best hotels. In that respect I don't think I had enough clout.'

Another area where this lack of standing failed him was in the recruitment of British-born players. Coventry centre-half Brian Kilcline and Liverpool midfielder Steve McMahon said no to Hand's overtures. Both said they would prefer to wait for a call from England. Kilcline never got a call and McMahon's career with England was very limited. Would either of them have refused an approach from Charlton?

It was often suggested that Hand was influenced in selections by Brady and Stapleton. 'That is totally false,' he responded. 'During their stints as captain, I would pull them aside and say this is the way I'm going about this game and then if they wanted to contribute anything fine. Because I did this with Liam and Frank – and Tony Grealish when he was captain – people used to think they influenced team selection but they wouldn't do it because they would be leaving themselves open to huge criticism.' Charlton operated in the same way with his captains, McCarthy and Townsend, but the same allegations were never made against him.

'At times I felt Eoin could have imposed himself a bit more,' Stapleton remarked. 'He was a little over-awed by some of the players he had. Later on when I worked under him at Huddersfield he had changed, he had got a bit harder and when he needed to lift someone out of it he did. I don't think he felt he could do that when he was manager of the Irish side.'

'Yes, I could have imposed myself more,' Hand agreed, 'but in the early days I did not think it was necessary. I had so much respect for the players that my way of going about the job was to find out as much as I could about the opposition and to impart that knowledge to the best 11 I could pick.

'In one or two of our later games I didn't think some of the players were doing what they should have been doing and I gave them a roasting at half-time and told them they were a disgrace. I should have been doing that all the time, but at 34 to change from the guy they knew to the big bully manager was not in my nature.'

Tactically, Hand did many things right, employing strategies which proved successful under Charlton. He was the first to select Lawrenson and McGrath in midfield; the first to recognise McCarthy's competitiveness and leadership and, on taking over from Giles, he insisted on a more direct game to provide the strikers with more opportunities.

However, in the final analysis, his lack of authority was probably his undoing. He had no hope in his battle with FAI officials who were a constant thorn in his side. Hand, like his predecessors Meagan, Tuohy and Giles, was a manager of whom his players spoke well. Perhaps it was time for a change – no more Mr Nice Guy!

15

Charlton Takes Over

In securing Jack Charlton as manager, the FAI struck gold, but it was not immediately apparent. Such was the public's lack of interest initially that the FAI lost over £30,000 in staging the first two games of his reign – friendlies against Wales (0–1) and Uruguay (1–1) – as crowds of only 16,500 and 14,000 attended. Charlton may have been a big name, but he was going to have to prove himself as an international manager before the fans would flock to see his team in action. Besides, many of the genuine fans were more than a little peeved with the manner in which Charlton had treated Liam Tuohy.

Before the Tuohy affair, Charlton had taken on the media, and seemingly beaten them into submission at his initial press conference. In what seemed a planned agenda but probably was not, David O'Leary, one of the most popular of the players, became, after Tuohy, the next to suffer Charlton's wrath. Thus, within three months, the new manager had tackled head-on the media and two icons of Irish soccer. Clearly, he intended to be his own man.

The press conference affair was, despite subsequent claims to the contrary, much ado about nothing. The Irish media are, by and large, a fair lot, prepared to give a man a chance before sticking the knife in. At his first press conference, Charlton initially created a good impression and talked a good game before his deep-rooted tactlessness let him down.

The question asked by Peter Byrne of the *Irish Times* was about the Bob Paisley vote and was addressed to FAI President Des Casey. Casey would have been well able to handle it, but Charlton, sensing a slight where none was intended, jumped in and ruled the question out of order. This led to a rebuff from Eamon Dunphy, whereupon Charlton became belligerent and invited Dunphy outside to sort the matter out.

The upshot of this timid affair was that the media were made aware of Jack's paranoia and tactlessness – and Dunphy became friendly with the new manager. This friendship lasted for about 18 months, ending acrimoniously when Dunphy became more and more critical of some of Charlton's players and tactics.

The fall-out from Charlton's treatment of Tuohy was more far-reaching, affecting as it did the next generation of Irish footballers. Instead of installing

Tuohy as manager of the Under-18 and Under-21 teams, Charlton settled for the mundane talents of his old sidekick, Maurice Setters. Ten years later, the international team was awash with graduates from Tuohy's teams, while Setters had still to prove himself.

The rude manner in which Charlton brushed Tuohy aside to give team-talks at the youths' game with England at Elland Road on Tuesday, 25 February, was all too characteristic of the gruff Englishman. Charlton's harsh words grated with the young players, who were more used to the gentle cajoling and encouragement of Tuohy. When Marcus Tuite had the temerity to ask, 'Are we not to pass the ball anymore?' Charlton's brusque rejoinder was, 'You'll do what I tell you.'

Insensitivity is a particular Charlton trait and it was to let him down on a number of occasions in his relations with the Irish. Tuohy and his youth team were the first victims. Tuohy, in the belief that he had been left with no alternative, resigned his unpaid post on his return home. It was a sad end to one of the most distinguished reigns of any Republic of Ireland manager.

'I didn't make the decision on the spur of the moment,' he said. 'I was asked by Mr Charlton if I would carry on, which I was prepared to do, but I don't believe I was allowed to act as manager and, taking all things into consideration, I had no choice but to resign. You could say Tuesday was the straw that broke the camel's back.

'Out of courtesy to Mr Charlton I asked him if he would like to say a few words to the players before the game. What I wasn't prepared for was that my position would be taken over at half-time and afterwards when I had no role to play. The position I'm in was forced upon me and the stand I took was the only one anyone of integrity could take.'

Charlton had not intended to attend the youth game, only deciding to do so at lunch-time when he discovered that the game he had planned to watch, the Aston Villa–Oxford United Milk Cup tie, had been postponed. He lost a lot of face with the football public for his ill-mannered treatment of Tuohy, and this rankled with him. For someone who claims to bear no grudges, he certainly holds one against Tuohy. In Paul Rowan's book *The Team That Jack Built*,[1] he is quoted as saying, 'The one thing that gives me great pleasure is that I stuffed it up his [Tuohy's] arse. Whatever I've achieved here is with no help from him.'

In fact, what Jack achieved owed quite a lot to Tuohy for, as manager of the youths, he was instrumental in bringing players like Alan Kelly, Denis Irwin, Terry Phelan, John Sheridan and Niall Quinn to the fore, who proved extremely valuable to Charlton. Similarly, Charlton's whinge about being left with all the international teams to look after and no one to help him is a misrepresentation of the facts. Joe McGrath was in charge of the Under-15s, Tuohy's assistants Noel O'Reilly and Brian Kerr took charge of an Under-17 team that played Northern Ireland and Maurice Price took over for a game against the Scottish Schools. Jack's sole concentration was on the international team.

[1] Mainstream, 1994

It had been the hope of certain officials that Tuohy would end up as Jack's assistant but this was a non-runner from day one. Charlton, in his own way, perceived Tuohy as a threat and, besides, their ideas on the ideal pattern of play were poles apart.

Niall Quinn has reason to be grateful to both Tuohy and Charlton for the help they gave him at different times in his career. Reflecting on the fall-out between the two, he said: 'I often feel Liam should have a more prominent role, having done so much for Irish football and now that it's at its peak he's in the background. That's football and it's a terrible game for things like that. Ninety-nine per cent of the country adore Jack; very few realise what Liam Tuohy put into Ireland's success. I like to think of both of them being a big help to me. Obviously they didn't suit each other.'

While the ill-feeling generated by his treatment of Tuohy was still fresh in the public's mind, a new English soccer magazine, *When Saturday Comes*, contained the following hard-hitting comments about Charlton:

> The Republic of Ireland have made one of the worst decisions of the season by appointing Jack Charlton as manager. The numbing dullness of the sides he's managed before doesn't exactly promise to inject the pride and cohesion which have been lacking in Irish football for so long.

However, the FAI were reluctant to reprimand Charlton for his treatment of Tuohy. Officials who had been to European and World Cup youth finals, thanks to Tuohy, were strangely silent as he was being pushed to the margins. This confirmed Charlton as the uncrowned king of the FAI, but also served as a warning that, should his day come, he need not look for support from the back-slappers in the official party.

The intimidation factor has always been part of Charlton's armoury. From his lofty position as a World Cup winner, he commands respect and has no hesitation in exploiting that. Most of the time, this was a decided plus for his team as, for instance, when he made his pre-match visits to the referee's dressing-room. As the match officials sought his autograph, Jack launched into his prepared script: 'Tackling is part of our game, but we're not a dirty team. However, if you have trouble with any of my lads just give me a signal and I'll have him off.' The officials invariably got the message.

There was, of course, a downside to Charlton the intimidator. In the wake of the Tuohy incident, among all the sycophants who attached themselves to Charlton, there was none to pull him up on this issue. No one in power told him, in the straight-talking manner he himself employed, that he was a thundering eejit to alienate Tuohy. To his credit, Dr Tony O'Neill registered his complaint at an executive meeting, but nothing was done about it.

Having got away with this, Charlton's power gradually grew to monstrous proportions, with officialdom bowing to his every wish. This extended to another rebuff for Tuohy. When he was proposed as coach for the League of

Ireland coaching course, Charlton vetoed the appointment and the proposal was withdrawn. It was another black day for Irish soccer.

Charlton's spat with David O'Leary, one of the Republic's truly classy players, showed the manager in his most stubborn mode. It also revealed the contradictions that are a regular feature of his thinking. O'Leary, blamed by Charlton for the goal which gave Wales a 1-0 win on the manager's debut, was omitted from the squad chosen to travel to Iceland at the end of May. He booked his family holiday to coincide with the games, but then the Liverpool players, Whelan, Beglin and Lawrenson, pulled out to go on a club holiday arranged to celebrate their league and Cup double.

One of the first rules Charlton had laid down was that he expected all players to make themselves available when selected, so this action by the Liverpool trio was the first challenge to the new order. The outcome, which saw the Liverpool players restored to the Republic line-up and O'Leary banished for two and a half years, not only speaks volumes for the contradictions in Charlton's make-up but was also the first indication of his abhorrence of confrontation.

With a depleted squad, he turned to O'Leary who politely told him that he was leaving on his family holiday the following day. When Charlton suggested that he cancel, O'Leary declined, and that was the last contact he had with the manager until November 1988, two and a half years later. In contrast, Lawrenson went straight into the Irish team for the opening European Championship game in September and Beglin and Whelan were both introduced as substitutes and remained in favour thereafter.

The disparity in treatment can be traced to a game in Cork in August when a Republic of Ireland XI played Liverpool. Charlton remonstrated with Liverpool manager Kenny Dalglish after the game, complaining about the club taking the players on holiday when they were wanted by the Republic. In Dalglish, Charlton met his match, for he was told in no uncertain terms that if he made a scapegoat of any of the players, he'd get none of them in future.

O'Leary, on the other hand, had no one to speak up for him and, being a centre-back, he was particularly vulnerable. It was the one position in which Charlton had an embarrassment of riches. Making an example of O'Leary was the soft option and Charlton took it. He had no desire for a confrontation with Dalglish.

Charlton's distaste for confrontation became a regular feature of his press conferences. As soon as a question was asked which was not to his liking – in the early days this was usually about the absence of O'Leary – he would respond with a curt, 'That's it. I'm off!' and walk out. For someone renowned as a communicator, he had a strange unwillingness to explain his position in a group situation, yet journalists found on a one-to-one basis he would explain chapter and verse.

Another occasion when Charlton's distaste for confrontation arose was during Italia '90 when Whelan, who had recovered from injury, publicly forced his case for a recall only to find that the more he pursued it the more the manager dug in his heels and stuck by the less talented Andy Townsend. In this regard, Charlton was showing some consistency for, when the crunch came, he tended to place more faith in his English-born players. All the principal rows were with the natives, Tuohy, O'Leary, Brady, Stapleton, Whelan, Moran . . . it sounds like a roll of honour. The benefactor in each case was English-born . . . Setters, McCarthy, Townsend, Cascarino, Townsend again, Kernaghan. Coincidence or part of a plan? The answer to that depends on your view of Charlton but owes something to the fact that the English-born players, owing their status to Jack, were regarded by him as less independent in their attitude than the natives.

If Charlton was trying to make a point by dropping O'Leary, he certainly succeeded, as McCarthy admitted.

'Before Jack came in, the players were the top dogs and there were some who would have played hail, rain, snow or blow, good, bad or indifferent; and Frank, Dave, Liam and Gerry, the big stars, were those players. It turned it around when Dave was all of a sudden left out.

'All new managers have a look at things like that. They do it at every club. It's like walking into a bar and picking on the bully, and sorting him out. Dave's not like that but it was the psychological thing – if you don't do it my way you won't do it at all. The fact that one of the stars of the team can be left out encourages the rest to toe the line – if anyone had any doubts about messing with Jack.'

Psychological it may have been, but was it intended? Frank Stapleton does not believe so.

'Maybe it was for the sake of the young players that he did it, but I don't think he did it to make them toe the line. He might have got that effect but I don't think it was premeditated. I don't think he's that clever a man.'

McCarthy, on the other hand, subscribes to the alternative view.

'If you don't know him, sometimes you think he's not bothering, but it's quite the opposite. He's very astute, he knows what he's doing. It's all premeditated.'

When it came to football, Charlton certainly knew what he wanted and he displayed a singleminded determination to ensure that his vision of the game prevailed. It was an attitude some players found difficult to accept at first.

Charlton's inspiration came from the two most influential managers in his own career – Don Revie and Sir Alf Ramsey. From Revie he learned attention to detail, informing players of what to expect during a game. Ramsey taught him that the manager decides on a pattern of play and the players apply that pattern or they are out. He once asked Ramsey how he picked his team and Ramsey replied that he picked it to fit the pattern he had in his mind, not necessarily picking the best players. In contrast, when asked early on about his selection policy, Charlton made it clear that the public would always know his team because it would be the best available. He pointed out that Ireland did not have that many players and that it would soon become apparent to him and to the public what the best Irish team was.

Tactically, he was a defender's dream – Moran said he never played under a more positive manager – but his limitations in the creative aspects of the game were apparent from early on. From the start, he cut down the number of defensive errors, making the Republic an increasingly difficult team to beat. His problem lay in taking the team that step further. The plan he devised to combat the continental game of playing from the back mainly on the break, was simple and effective. He set out to seal the flanks and to flood midfield, thus restricting the play to areas more suited to the Irish than the opposition.

'We invented a type of game for Ireland that threw a spanner in the works of teams that played from the back,' he said. 'We wouldn't play the ball into them, we'd start behind them; we'd condense areas, we'd mark people tight in their area of the field and we wouldn't give them room and time to move out.

'It worked like a charm. It's very simple. The full-backs knew where to deliver the ball, John [Aldridge] knew where to run even though he was new to the team. International teams have to be seen to be good players not only facing the play but when they've got their backs to the play. But they found that when they tried to play out we weren't sitting on the halfway line waiting for them. They were confronted by virtually the whole 11 of our players in their half of the field, and the more they tried to play out, the more balls we won and the more chances we created.'

Calls for Charlton to play a more expansive game overlooked the fact that his plan was ideally suited to players operating in the English League. Lacking the pace and technique of the continentals, the players found Charlton's method, which put the emphasis on work rate, closing down the danger areas and repeating a set pattern, hard to fault as it made the most of their strengths.

'When Jack turned up with his flat cap, kicking the ball in his shoes and with no memory for names, a lot of players wondered what had happened,' recalled McCarthy. 'It didn't take him long to turn it around. He doesn't browbeat you with facts and figures – he knows what he wants. The players had a few doubts about him until we started to play the way he wanted us to play, and the turning-point was the trip to Iceland when we beat Iceland and Czechoslovakia. That bonded the squad together – two away victories.'

Charlton's method lacked style, especially in the early home games, but the stylist method had been tried under Tuohy, Giles and Hand and had come up short, especially away from home. No wonder the two victories in Iceland made the players sit up and take notice. The Republic's away form had for long been the team's Achilles heel and here was a system which, practically overnight, had corrected that. From now on, those trips abroad were going to be a lot more enjoyable.

16

The Bandwagon Gathers Momentum

Following the success in Iceland, Charlton had a good idea of the side he wanted to play against Belgium in the opening tie of the European Championship campaign in Brussels on 10 September. The one doubt in his mind was playmaker Liam Brady, who had missed the Reykjavik tournament. Brady liked to go deep for the ball, but that was against the Charlton dogma.

'I wanted him to use his ability on the edge of their 18-yard box, not on the edge of ours.'

The day before the game, Charlton put it bluntly to his midfielder: 'You'll be playing tomorrow, but if you don't play as I want you to then you won't play again.' That chat did Brady a favour.

'Before Jack, I had always felt a lot of pressure playing for Ireland – it was like I was the star returning from Italy and I was supposed to lead Ireland to triumph. Jack's attitude forced me to see things differently. Under him it was not certain that I would be in the team and I had to adopt the attitude that if I played, I played; if I did not, I did not and suddenly all the pressure of playing for Ireland vanished.'

While Charlton maintained that Brady was a problem for him right up to the last Euro '88 qualifier against Bulgaria, the truth is that Brady, in splendid form, was a key element in the Republic's success. Charlton might like to think that Brady had to change his style radically in order to keep his place but the reality is that Brady's skilful play was as important to the team as the contribution of any of the manager's favourites such as McCarthy, Houghton or Aldridge. Like them, Brady was never going to be dropped.

'I did have to adapt to play in Jack's team,' Brady conceded, 'but people often overstated this. The difference under Jack was that we looked for the right pass, and if it was not immediately obvious we did not hang around, we played the ball forward.'

On a night when Ireland conceded two goals following corner kicks – something Charlton ensured would never happen again – the manager had reason to be grateful to old campaigners Stapleton and Brady. Stapleton scored with a superb diving header from a Galvin cross in the first half and then, with time running out and Belgium leading 2–1, he manufactured a penalty which Brady slotted home.

To earn a draw away to the team which had just finished fourth in the World Cup was a start beyond the wildest dreams of most fans. And Stapleton admitted the equaliser was a con. There were only two minutes to go when substitute Jim Beglin played the ball down the inside-left channel for Stapleton to chase. Goalkeeper Pfaff, with a rush of blood to the head, ran out of his goal, and Stapleton seized his opportunity.

'When the ball came through I saw him rushing out and I knocked the ball past him. I was never going to get it but he was close enough so I just ran into him. He saw what I was at too late and he was trying to get out of the way, but as soon as he touched me I went down on my back and the referee had to give a penalty.

'It couldn't have happened to a nicer guy. Just before he had been time-wasting. When the ball was played back to him he was flicking it up and playing it on his chest and we were going mad. At the end of the game it was the other Belgian players who were going mad and Pfaff walked off on his own.'

Building on a good away performance was the next test for Charlton – and he found it beyond him and his team. In fact, that would be a recurring theme under his management. Repeatedly he raised expectations with good results away from home only to find that the same tactics employed at Lansdowne Road led to frustration for players and fans alike.

Scotland, on 15 October, were the first obstinate, defence-minded team to upset Charlton's plans in a game which was devoid of any redeeming feature. However, the fact that a team of Scotland's pedigree should feel intimidated on a visit to Dublin was a decided plus for the Republic, if only Charlton and his squad could turn this to their advantage.

Despite the loss of a valuable home point, Charlton was not critical of his players. They had, after all, followed his instructions. It was a different story the following month when a friendly in Warsaw ended in a 1–0 defeat.

'After that game he gave us the biggest bollocking he ever gave us,' recalled McCarthy. 'We took a short free-kick and it got cut out and they went to the other end of the field. He ripped us asunder, not because we lost but because we hadn't stuck to the letter of his instructions.'

Perhaps that explosion of passion was the turning point, for the disciplined display which the Irish gave in their next game, a difficult assignment away to Scotland on 18 February 1987, proved to be the high point of this campaign. With a substantial Green Army in support and millions more following the action live on TV, this game, perhaps more than any other, convinced the fans that Charlton's system was a winning one. If opposition to Charlton was muted ever after, it was not surprising as this game saw the birth of Jack's Jolly Green Giants.

Forced to reconstruct his defence due to career-threatening injuries to full-backs Langan and Beglin, Charlton opted for McGrath and Whelan on the flanks, with Lawrenson taking over McGrath's role as sweeper in front of the back four. The more clearly defined role given him by Charlton helped Lawrenson make a huge success of a position he had previously struggled to fill under Hand. It was Lawrenson's finest hour in the green jersey, and entirely fitting that he should be the matchwinner.

The goal was set up by the cuteness of Stapleton. Running on to a long ball played down the right wing, he managed to trick two Scottish defenders into an aerial challenge which resulted in an Irish free-kick and both Scotsmen receiving attention. Sizing up the situation in a flash, Lawrenson strolled up through midfield, calling out, 'Play it here, John,' to Aldridge who was waiting for referee Van Ettekoven of Holland to re-start the game. Aldridge quickly put the ball down and rolled it into the path of Lawrenson who strode through the centre and held off Richard Gough before shooting low past the advancing Jim Leighton. It was a master stroke by Lawrenson who proceeded to outshine his classy Liverpool team-mate Alan Hansen as the Republic absorbed all the pressure the Scots could bring to bear.

There was a moment in the second half which defined the Irish performance that night, and it involved Hansen. Receiving the ball in his own half, he looked up to see where he might pass it, discovered all his team-mates were marked by a green shirt, and promptly kicked the ball into touch!

The after-match interviews with the managers were also revealing. Andy Roxburgh made the usual perfunctory comments before excusing himself, saying: 'If there are any further questions I'll be at my desk at 10 in the morning.' Charlton, on the other hand, was naturally buoyant, and the Irish contingent knew that any further questions would have to be asked back at the team hotel because, instead of an office and a desk, the Republic's boss would most likely be located on some river bank the following morning.

For the game against Bulgaria in Sofia on 1 April, Charlton had done his homework. He had seen Bulgaria's three games in the World Cup in Mexico and had also taken in their 1–1 draw with Belgium in Brussels in November.

'When I go to a game I take notes on the pattern of play, the players, corner kicks, free-kicks, even the penalties and how they take them. I don't use videos because they only show you what's going on around the ball. They don't show you the pattern of play. Most times you get in trouble it is not what happens on the ball, it is what happens off it.'

Charlton's plans, even without key men Lawrenson and Houghton, were working like a dream in the first half, with the Bulgarians gradually reduced to punting hopeful balls forward. However, in the 40th minute, one such punt led to a highly controversial goal.

McCarthy, having read the situation, was first to the ball with Sirakov behind him but, just as the Irishman was about to despatch the ball to safety, Sirakov pushed him to the ground, gained possession and passed inside to Sadkov who shot past Bonner. Portuguese referee Valente pointed to the centre circle to the disgust of Irishmen everywhere.

After the break the Republic laid siege to the Bulgarian goal and were rewarded with a fine volleyed goal by Stapleton after 51 minutes. In their eagerness to complete the job they pushed forward at every opportunity, and when John Anderson was caught too far upfield a quick ball played in behind him allowed Sirakov to race clear. Moran's sliding tackle was a fraction mistimed and Tanev converted the penalty.

Most of the controversy after the game attached itself to the penalty, but this was missing the point. The offence happened within the area so the penalty was genuine. The real talking point was the decision by Valente to wave play on after Sirakov had pushed McCarthy, a decision which led to the first goal.

A further setback occurred on 29 April, when Belgium came to Dublin and held out for a 0–0 draw. It was now a case of hoping that one of the other teams would do the Republic a favour, a situation previous managers Giles and Hand had experienced but without catching the eye of Lady Luck.

Unimpressive home and away wins over Luxembourg and a thrilling 1–0 friendly victory over Brazil set the scene for the grudge return with Bulgaria on 14 October. A point would practically secure the visitors' place in the finals but the Republic had to win to keep their hopes alive. Despite having all the right ingredients, only 26,000 fans attended, 8,000 more than for the Luxembourg game and 9,000 more than Brazil had attracted. Clearly, the Irish fan was playing hard to get.

The stay-at-homes missed a thriller. Charlton was able to field his first choice 11 – the team that had won in Scotland – for the first time since February, and they responded with another magnificent display.

While Bonner had to make a couple of first-class saves, the traffic was mostly in the other direction. However, the breakthrough did not arrive until the 52nd minute and then it came courtesy of some fancy footwork from McCarthy. He fooled Stoichkov on the right touchline before crossing for Stapleton to put Ananiev under pressure in the air. The goalkeeper palmed the ball down, only as far as McGrath, who volleyed in to the net.

A brief Bulgarian revival was curbed when substitutes Niall Quinn and John Byrne combined for Moran to head a second goal, but the sweet taste of revenge was soured when Brady retaliated after one foul too many by Sadkov and referee Jan Keizer produced the red card. Brady left to a standing ovation, with the comforting arm of his manager around his shoulders, but it was, sadly, the last serious game he played for his country. Suspension and a career-threatening injury denied him further glory but that game on 14 October was a fitting swansong for a great-hearted player whose commitment was never less than total.

The Bulgarian game also proved to be the end, in a competitive sense, for Mark Lawrenson at a time when his talents were being best utilised. An excellent reader of the game, his tackling was suspect but his ability to intercept amply compensated, making him the ideal candidate for Charlton's 'sweeper in front of the back four' role.

Within a 12-month span, the Republic lost three players of international ability to injuries that effectively ended their careers. The loss of Beglin, Lawrenson and Brady would have been a blow to most countries but for a small country like the Republic these players seemed irreplaceable.

Urgency was added to the necessity of finding replacements when, in one of the all-time shock results, Scotland beat Bulgaria 1–0 in Sofia on 11 November, securing the Republic's place in the Euro '88 finals. The winning goal was scored by Hearts part-timer Gary Mackay who subsequently became more famous in Ireland than in his native Scotland. The real hero was referee Kohl of Austria who waved play on after a typically cynical Bulgarian tackle took a Scottish player out of the game. The ball ran on for Steve Clarke to place Mackay who found the net with minutes to go.

Charlton utilised home friendlies against Israel (5–0), Romania (2–0), Yugoslavia (2–0) and Poland (3–1) to blood newcomers Chris Morris, David Kelly and John Sheridan, all of whom came through with flying colours to book their flights to Germany.

With a doubt over Stapleton, Charlton recalled Cascarino, who took his chance with a goal against Poland. Stapleton, who had undergone surgery on his back, proved his fitness in a dreadful 0–0 draw with Norway in Oslo on 1 June, just 11 days before the Republic were due to meet England in their first game of the finals.

An interesting aspect of the pre-Euro '88 friendlies was the apathy of the fans. The game against Poland on 22 May was the best supported and it attracted only 18,000. The team's historic breakthrough had not convinced the fans that it was time to jump on the bandwagon, suggesting a hollow ring to later moans about 'ever- present' fans being denied tickets.

The draw for the finals placed the Republic in a group with England, the Soviet Union and Holland, with the Republic being asked to do most of the travelling.

Most of Charlton's panel of 20 picked itself but the manager made one surprise choice when he included a defender who was not fit enough to play had he been called upon. The player in question was John Anderson, who had played for Charlton at Newcastle United and for whom Jack appeared to retain a sentimental attachment. For a manager not noted for his sentimentality, the choice of an unfit Anderson had all the appearance of self-induced myopia, and represented a massive gamble.

The player who suffered because of Anderson's inclusion was the wholehearted Dave Langan. While his career may have been on the wane, he was upset that Charlton did not inform him that he no longer featured in his plans. Langan's treatment contrasted with that accorded winger Tony Galvin. By the time the finals came along, Sheedy was the form player for the left-wing role, but Charlton stuck with Galvin in gratitude for the part he played in the qualifying games. Sheedy was limited to one game – in which he was outstanding – filling in for McGrath.

The omission of David O'Leary has often been thrown at Charlton as the

Arsenal man would have been in the top 20 Irish players at the time. However, an Achilles tendon injury ruled him out of contention; he missed the last three months of Arsenal's season, including a Littlewoods Cup final.

In the matter of easing tension before a game, Charlton was the master. On the morning of the game against England, Charlton grabbed Aldridge and said, for all to hear: 'John, you haven't scored for Ireland yet, so don't go breaking the habit of a lifetime this afternoon. I want to be out of here next Sunday, I've got a fishing trip booked and I don't want to be stuck in Germany for some bloody European Championship final!' The laughter which greeted those remarks quickly dispelled the tension.

The three games the Republic played in the finals are summarised briefly by Irish observers as follows: England, Stüttgart, 12 June – the game we won and should have lost; Soviet Union, Hanover, 1 June – the game we drew and should have won; Holland, Gelsenkirchen, 18 June – the game we lost and should have drawn.

Beating England was a tremendous achievement, aided by a healthy slice of luck. Houghton, who scored the winner after five minutes when he capitalised on a mistake by Kenny Sansom to register a rare headed goal, was undoubtedly man of the match. He was a constant threat to the England defence with his pacy runs up the right flank; he also helped to keep England dangerman John Barnes, his Liverpool team-mate, very quiet.

Goalkeeper Packie Bonner had an inspired 90 minutes, repeatedly denying hot shot Gary Lineker, right down to the last minute when he made a magnificent twisting save to turn the ball out for a corner.

If the win against Scotland convinced the football fraternity that Jack's tactics were going to bring the Republic out of the twilight zone, the win against England had a similar effect on the rest of the country. Watched by millions at home on TV, it brought home to the public at large that Charlton had put their country on the world stage.

Special one-day trips were organised for the game against the Soviet Union as the soccer bug bit. The Irish brought a whole new meaning to the role of supporter: pride in their team without the foul-mouthed aggression towards the opposition which characterised many football followers in Britain and on the Continent.

With Sheedy deputising for the injured McGrath, the Irish performance against the Soviets was even better than that against England. Playing Charlton's pressure game to perfection against bemused opponents, they dictated the play for practically the entire 90 minutes. Whelan, who was in inspired form, opened the scoring after 38 minutes with a spectacular volley from a long McCarthy throw-in. Further chances fell to Galvin, who should have had a penalty when tackled feet first by Dasaev, and Aldridge, who headed a Galvin cross wide with Dasaev beaten.

The Soviets could not play their normal game of building from the back because the Irish pushed up to mark their opponents once the ball was played back to Dasaev. This left the goalkeeper with no option but to kick the ball out, with the high ball meat and drink to Moran and McCarthy. However, by letting the Soviets off the hook, the Irish were always vulnerable and Protasov duly struck a fortunate 74th minute equaliser, the ball going between Bonner's legs.

To reach the semi-finals, the Republic only required a draw with Holland. With McGrath fit again and Bonner persuaded by Charlton to play despite a back injury which would require surgery later in the summer, it was the manager's first-choice team which faced Holland who seemed to have the entire Dutch nation present in support, as Gelsenkirchen is very close to their border.

'When we got to the stadium,' McCarthy recalled, 'I looked back down the main avenue and it was packed with orange. But there, right in the middle of it all, was a German policeman on a horse – and on the back of the horse was an Irish supporter, proudly waving the tricolour. It was a wonderful moment . . . the Irish were coming.'

Holland needed to win, yet the first chance fell to the Republic when McGrath's header from a Houghton corner hit the post and Aldridge was just beaten to the ball on the line. The Dutch, meanwhile, were forced to try their luck from long range. Ultimately it was tiredness which defeated the Irish. Playing their pressure game in the mid-summer heat took its toll and gradually they were forced further and further back into defence with sorties up field extremely rare.

Disciplined defence kept the Dutch at bay and seemed sure to frustrate their ambitions until fate took a hand. McGrath headed clear but only as far as Ronald Koeman. Renowned for his long-range shots, Koeman tried one from 30 yards but did not connect properly. The ball spun up wildly near the penalty spot where substitute Wim Kieft headed it goalwards. It was heading off target past the far post, but when it hit the ground the ball spun wickedly and bounced past Bonner's despairing dive low into the right-hand corner.

The goal, which enshrined Kieft alongside John Atyeo in Irish soccer's Chamber of Horrors, was an amazing stroke of fortune for the Dutch who breathed a sigh of relief that Marco van Basten's straying into an offside position had not caused the goal to be disallowed.

The Republic lost no respect in defeat. In fact, Holland's subsequent triumph in the final only served to enhance the tremendous impression the Irish had made in their first major finals. Although the game against Holland was not a pretty one, due mainly to the tiredness of the Irish, their great-hearted battle captured the admiration of the nation.

Eamon Dunphy caught the mood of the moment perfectly when he wrote: 'Jack Charlton and his team arrive at Dublin airport at 12.50. Go out and meet them.' What could have been a wake turned into a massive welcome home which clearly stunned Charlton, and reduced some of the players to tears. A crowd estimated at 20,000 paid homage as the players disembarked. That was only the start, as the open-topped bus which brought the players to a civic reception in Parnell Square had to contend with streets so lined with people that, at times, its passage through the crowds was at a snail's pace. RTE relayed pictures of the triumphant homecoming – and suddenly soccer was the most talked-about sport in a country in which it had, up to then, ranked a poor fourth or even fifth.

Nothing would ever be the same again for the FAI, and already there was talk of the World Cup finals in Italy in 1990. As Moran said: 'Right now, any team which plays us will know that we are a force to be reckoned with and they won't relish the prospect of having to take us on.'

Mind you, the response to the players' heroics came a little too late to benefit the first-ever players' pool. The lack of commercial or corporate interest in soccer pre-1988 was reflected in a share-out which struggled to reach £10,000 for ever-presents. By the time Italia '90 accounts were finalised, the share-out was three times that of 1988.

While the main plaudits for the Republic's success naturally went to Charlton, other key factors should not be overlooked. Two of them, Houghton and Aldridge, began their international careers with Charlton and became synonymous with his successes over the following nine years. In fact, it could be said that when they went into decline so did he.

'Aldridge and Houghton made a big difference to the team in terms of quality,' said Stapleton, captain of the 1988 team. 'Those two lads gave us something more. They were both rising stars.'

Houghton brought pace and a 90-minute workrate to a midfield which up to then had been deficient in both qualities, while Aldridge, although he found scoring difficult at first, represented a second threat to opposing defenders alongside Stapleton. Charlton knew the importance of a second striking threat and, while he strayed from this concept in later years, he was always seeking to supplement the striking talent available.

For the FAI, Euro '88 meant an end to the famine years when international fixtures, their main source of income, recorded a loss. The success of Charlton and his team had turned a deficit of £54,000 into a healthy profit, and the sponsors were queueing up. Already the 1990 World Cup campaign was a guaranteed financial success and, with Dr Tony O'Neill taking a more prominent role as assistant to Secretary Peadar O'Driscoll, even the administration of the Association had received a welcome shake-up.

17

Italia '90 and All That

Apart from one slight hiccup, when an understrength team lost to Spain in Seville, the Republic's qualification for Italia '90 from Group Six was a dream campaign. Charlton's approach was entirely vindicated. He wanted the tough away games first, followed by the home games and an away game to minnows Malta as a not very alarming last fixture. The Group consisted of the Republic, Spain, Northern Ireland, Hungary and Malta.

The new-found confidence of the players, in their ability and in their manager's tactics, was clearly evident, although possibly too much of the manager's caution was applied to the games in Belfast and Budapest, where wins rather than draws were there for the taking.

Luck always played a part in Charlton's success, no matter how much he disliked admitting it. Ever since the day he got two players at Oxford – Aldridge and Houghton – instead of the one he had been aware of, other things fell into his lap at the propitious time. The qualifying draw could not have been improved on. Northern Ireland were in transition following two World Cup finals and Hungary were in disarray because of a domestic betting scandal. Malta were thus in a position to take points off Hungary, the first time a minnow had ever done the Republic any favours.

For the game in Seville, McGrath, Whelan, Hughton and Sheedy were unavailable, but the bonuses in defeat were the return to the squad of O'Leary, and the torrid World Cup debut endured by Steve Staunton. Mind you, it took two solid hours of arguing on the part of Maurice Setters before Charlton conceded that the time was right to restore O'Leary to favour.

The surprise in Charlton's selection was his decision to break up the McCarthy– Moran pairing – 'the best in Europe', he had often declared – and place Moran in McGrath's role in front of the back four. O'Leary, with his greater mobility, seemed a more obvious choice for that role but he lined up beside McCarthy and showed he was still as good as ever.

By the time the return game with Spain came around on 26 April 1989, Charlton had added another useful left-footed midfielder to his squad. Andy Townsend had arrived, and Brady's days were numbered. Brady had made a valiant recovery from a cruciate ligament operation but he had lost maybe a half yard of pace and was regarded as substitute material by Charlton.

The fact that the Republic failed to score in its first three World Cup ties did not deter the fans; nor did a 25 per cent hike in the price of tickets. Receipts for the Spanish game were £472,000, against the previous best of £330,000 for the Euro '88 qualifier against Scotland. TV, advertising and sponsorship flowed in to contribute to an income for the year of over £3 million, bringing the FAI into uncharted territory.

After the Hillsborough tragedy, in which 90 Liverpool supporters lost their lives, the City of Liverpool went into mourning. Liverpool had been due to play Arsenal three days before the Spanish game, but that fixture was cancelled. However, Aldridge, who identified so closely with the fans and their families, cried off. Stapleton, then with French second division club Le Havre, stepped into the breach.

History has a habit of repeating itself, and it did so on this occasion, with Michel putting through his own goal to earn the Republic a 1–0 win, just as Iribar had done in the 1966 World Cup qualifiers. There the similarity ended. In 1965 it had been an entirely fortuitous win; this time it was more a case of Spain's finest being thrashed 1–0. Poor finishing saved the Spanish a hiding, as the visitors' main hope, Butragueno, gradually disappeared in the volatile atmosphere before he was taken off in the 69th minute. While the Spanish complained about the state of the pitch and the rough play of the Irish, it was a well deserved win for the boys in green.

Malta and Hungary were despatched on successive Sundays, 28 May and 4 June, and, to all intents and purposes, that was that. The Malta game marked Stapleton's last World Cup appearance. He was injured and replaced by Aldridge. Charlton appeared to write him out of his plans from then on, a decision which many observers felt was premature. He was replaced in the pecking order by Cascarino and Quinn, two players who had none of Stapleton's cuteness, and whose naivety was shown up in the finals in Italy.

A friendly with West Germany on 6 September at Lansdowne Road gave Charlton the chance to experiment. Instead he chose to start three veteran campaigners – Stapleton, Brady and Galvin – as a test to see if they were still able to deliver. Stapleton scored after 10 minutes and Galvin played the 90 minutes, but Charlton dramatically called Brady ashore minutes after the Germans equalised in the 32nd minute. Brady, disgusted by this treatment and surmising that, if he were going to Italy, it would only be as a substitute, decided to announce his retirement from international football.

The team put in a strong finish to Group Six. Apart from a few hairy moments early on when McCarthy had to come to the rescue, Northern Ireland were clinically taken apart for a 3–0 win. The game in Malta turned into a double celebration as it not only ensured qualification but also marked Aldridge's first competitive goals, the second a penalty after Townsend was brought down. The attendance of 25,000 in Valetta was mostly Irish, many of whom were late for the kick-off due to fog in Dublin delaying their flights. It was an historic day for the FAI: they had qualified for the World Cup finals at the 13th attempt.

As the man who had guided the team to its greatest achievements, the accolades rightly showered down on Charlton. 'Big Jack', 'Citizen Jack', even 'St Jack'. The Irish people were anxious to show their appreciation for his part in helping their country to a place among world football's giants. In the midst of this acclaim, Charlton kept his feet firmly on the ground. He confessed to apprehension and fear as the products of his success.

'The more successful you get the more you raise the expectations of the fans and the more difficult it is to keep it going,' he said. 'My big fear and the one thing I'd hate is to have to leave this job because I had made enemies. But, in football, today's hero is tomorrow's bum. The old cliché still applies – you are only as good as your last game'.

Home friendlies against Wales, the Soviet Union and Finland confirmed Charlton's view about the bulk of his 22 man World Cup squad. The only significant newcomer was Middlesbrough striker Bernie Slaven, a Scot of Donegal ancestry. Later, in pre-finals training in Malta, Charlton made one of the hardest decisions of his career when he dropped Gary Waddock from the final 22 in place of Swindon Town midfielder Alan McLoughlin. It was heartbreaking for Waddock, who had overcome a career-threatening injury to fight his way back into the squad, but he accepted the manager's reasoning that he needed cover for Houghton, who was striving to overcome a series of injuries.

Four years at the top had taken their toll on the squad, which was the oldest in Italia '90. A survey of the squad's serious injuries since 1986 showed that only four players had been injury free – Cascarino, Quinn, David Kelly and newcomer Slaven. Of the remainder, Whelan's ankle injury and Houghton's pelvic strain were the most worrying. Whelan's fitness proved to be a bone of contention between player and manager right through the tournament.

Meanwhile, the players took on the FAI in a battle for a share of the profits, and won. When the FAI initially called their bluff, the players went public through their agent, Fintan Drury. The public response was overwhelmingly in favour of the players, and the FAI quickly capitulated. Bonuses of £900 for each qualifying game were awarded retrospectively, and 25 percent of the FAI's gross receipts from the finals also went to the players' pool. With that agreement, the concept of players willing to play for the honour of wearing the jersey was buried for ever. From then on, the players were openly mercenary. Playing for Ireland, as with most other countries, had become a commercial proposition.

Charlton had long since started to reap the commercial benefits. Following Euro '88, his salary and bonuses became the least part of his earnings. Personal appearances and speaking engagements up and down the country brought his message to places which had hitherto shown little interest in soccer, and added to his already healthy bank balance. Yet Charlton somehow managed to give the impression that he was only doing the FAI a favour. Giles, who had done the job for buttons, was regarded by the public as grasping, whereas Charlton, the ultimate grasper, never suffered the public's disapproval

The draw for the finals was not very kind. As in Euro '88, no country was asked to do more travelling than the Republic. Ireland's games took place on the islands of Sardinia and Sicily, the consequence of being drawn with England and Holland, countries whose fans were notorious for their hooliganism. Egypt completed Group F and were regarded as the minnows.

The fans went to great lengths to overcome their travel problems. Those who could afford it, moved from island to island; others based themselves on Sicily, Malta, the Italian mainland, even Yugoslavia, and took ferries and planes to the islands; a few even travelled in luxury on the *Achille Lauro* cruise ship.

The FAI, which had voted a grant of £1,000 to councillors travelling to Italy, increased it to £1,500 when the draw was made; 28 councillors took up the offer, some of them earning their keep by undertaking stewarding and security duties.

England were the first opponents, in the idyllic setting of the Sant' Elia stadium in Cagliari. It was an historic occasion for the Irish, their first time in the finals. Sadly, that moment was spoiled for many thousands of Irish fans as the hooligan element among the English whistled and chanted through the Irish national anthem. It was, in hindsight, a moment which characterised Italia '90; a World Cup finals which failed to live up to expectations.

The Italian media rated the Ireland–England game as the worst of the first-round games, and it was hard to argue the point. While a 1–1 draw satisfied honour on both sides, the game was, like practically all the Irish games in Italy, a war of attrition, with skill making little or no impact. Charlton, aware of the need to combat the heat, had his players programmed to pass back to Bonner at every opportunity. Bonner then took his time kicking out.

However, the biggest single factor in the Republic's unappetising fare was Houghton's inability to perform at his usual high level. Injuries had taken their toll on the dynamic midfielder. He did well to start every game, but he was nothing like the dominant force he had been in Germany and in the qualifiers.

The absence of Whelan was another factor. His composure, passing skills and accurate shooting would have given him the edge over Townsend as McGrath's partner in the centre of midfield, but Charlton preferred Townsend's running ability, and ignored Whelan's pleas that he was fit to resume.

Where every other team in the finals put its faith in skill, Charlton put his faith in workrate. Despite the heat, harrying and hassling remained the order of the day, and what little constructive football there was came from the cultured feet of Sheedy, Houghton and Staunton. It was no coincidence that the two goals scored in five games both stemmed from defensive errors following pitch-length kicks by Bonner.

For stay-at-home fans, the closeness of the scoring, or the lack of it, kept them rivetted to their seats in front of the television. Many of them were new to soccer and for them, each game was a special event regardless of the standard of play. There was, therefore, uproar when TV analyst Eamon Dunphy made some less than flattering remarks about the Irish performance in the 0–0 draw with Egypt, and threw his pen across the studio in disgust. His reward for telling the truth was a bag of hate mail from fans who obviously did not want reality to intrude on their dreams.

When Dunphy travelled to Palermo and asked a question at the press conference the day before the vital game against Holland, Charlton walked out, remarking that he would only answer questions from 'proper journalists'. In this, Charlton was out of order, for Dunphy had official FIFA accreditation and was entitled to attend any press conference and ask any question he liked. The upshot of this minor drama was a split among the Irish journalists into pro and anti Dunphy factions. The reporters from the daily and evening papers, who were expected to churn out pages every day no matter how inconsequential the material, were upset because Charlton, one of their major sources, had done a bunk; they were inclined to blame Dunphy.

Charlton, meanwhile, had lost faith in Cascarino, and replaced him with Quinn, a player who had waited patiently for his chance with both Arsenal and the Republic. Things began to turn in Quinn's favour when Howard Kendall brought him to Manchester City and, before travelling to Italy, he had played brilliantly for the B team in a stunning 4–1 defeat of England.

The game against Holland was the nearest thing to a good game of the five Ireland played in Italy; the problem was that it ended in farce. After Gullit had carved open the Irish defence to open the scoring in the 10th minute, it was cut and thrust all the way until Quinn's 71st minute equaliser following a mistake by goalkeeper van Breukelen. Shortly after, word came through that England were leading Egypt 1–0, and a truce was declared for the final 15 minutes, with neither team putting pressure on the other. One of them would have to play West Germany in Milan three days later, so energy conservation was important.

With England topping the group, it was a question of drawing lots to decide who would finish second, as the Republic and Holland had identical records. Once again, Charlton's luck was good, and the Republic were placed second, with a second-round game against Romania in Genoa on Monday, 25 June, while Holland had the much tougher date with West Germany.

As Ireland had been finding goals hard to come by, the Romania game had all the makings of a penalty shoot-out, and so it transpired. Charlton left the penalty decisions to the players, only intervening when he found himself one short.

'Cas didn't want to take one,' recalled McCarthy. 'He didn't fancy it and it showed. I think the keeper went for the sod of grass Cas kicked as the ball bobbled in under him. To be fair to Jack, he said, "If anyone misses, sod it, we've had a good tournament," and I think that helped to take the pressure off.'

It was 4–4 until Bonner saved Timofte's effort. Then the focus of attention shifted to O'Leary. Although he had only ever taken one penalty for Arsenal – and missed – O'Leary was coolness personified as he placed the ball carefully on the spot and, sending goalkeeper Lung to the left, calmly hit it in to the top right-hand corner.

Pandemonium ensued on the pitch and right around the ground as at least 30,000 of the 31,818 spectators were decked out in the Irish colours. This was their moment of triumph, the result which justified the tremendous sacrifices many of them had made to follow their team from Cagliari to Palermo and on to Genoa. In all their travels they had been one of the unexpected delights of the World Cup, embellishing the occasion with their music, their sense of fun, and their welcoming attitude to rival fans. Those fans turned the Luigi Ferraris Stadium into a little colony of Ireland for one beautiful Italian summer afternoon which has gone down in Irish football history.

Sadly, for many of them, Rome was a bridge too far simply because they could not get their hands on tickets, many of which went instead to home-based fans who flew out on one-day specials. There was still a considerable Irish presence, estimated at 20,000, in the Stadio Olimpico in Rome on Saturday, 30 June, when the Republic lined up against the host nation to contest a place in the last four.

With nerves evident on both sides and Portuguese referee Valente awarding 48 free-kicks, the bulk of them to Italy, this was a real test of the Irish team's character. Italy's passing game consigned the Irish to the role of second-class citizens, but they did well to remain in contention right through the 90 minutes, although they never really threatened to score.

The only goal came on 37 minutes when Donadoni's fiercely struck shot from just outside the penalty area was parried by Bonner, but only as far as Schillaci who slipped it into the net. Italy might have had one or two further goals in the second half but the Irish defence, with Moran and McCarthy at their grittiest, kept them at bay. A late Irish onslaught yielded a free-kick just outside the penalty area, but substitute Sheridan struck it poorly and well wide.

For a team that was so limited in attack, the Republic had done wonderfully well and the fans were keen to show their appreciation. Massive crowds greeted the team on its arrival at Dublin airport the following day. The team coach, which normally made the journey in less than an hour, took four hours to get to the civic reception in College Green. However, not everybody was rejoicing in the Republic's performance. In fact, some were rejoicing at their departure from the tournament. As Jeff Powell of the *Daily Mail* put it: 'While Dublin prepared a hero's welcome, it felt here [in Italy] as if a shadow had been lifted.' Taking issue with Charlton's remark that maybe now the Irish team would get some credit for showing the game a different way to go, Powell asked:

'Go where, exactly? And what game is he talking about anyway?' To proclaim caveman attrition and crass long balls as the panacea for Football 2000 betrays how bigoted a convert Charlton has become to a primitive philosophy gaining ground after ground in England for its capacity to destroy rather than delight, stifle not surprise, diminish instead of decorate the greatest game of all.

The irony is that Charlton's miserly style of football is a denial of the spirit of the people behind the team.

Powell's words were harsh – after all, FIFA set the rules of the competition and Ireland had played within those rules – but in many respects he hit the nail on the head. While Ireland rightly celebrated a place in the last eight, there was nothing to celebrate about the style of football used to achieve this feat.

The Republic had been the main beneficiary of FIFA's decision to extend the eligibility rule to players whose grandparents originated from the country they wished to represent, and Ireland's presence in Italia '90 was the first fruits of that decision. However, FIFA must have wondered if they had produced a monster when the Republic's unpleasant style of play earned them a quarter-final spot. It was no surprise that, after the tournament, FIFA organised a think-tank of top officials and players to formulate ideas on how the game could be improved. If Charlton was responsible for a revolution, then this was it. Among the changes which FIFA's think-tank came up with were: (a) goalkeepers would not be allowed to pick up the ball from a pass-back unless it was headed or thrown, and (b) the abolition of the tackle from behind.

Each of these changes had a direct bearing on the way the Republic played under Charlton. While adjustments were relatively easy in regard to the pass-back rule, the abolition of the tackle from behind proved a big blow to the Republic's defenders. McCarthy, the Irish captain and very much the team's leader on the field, had more fouls given against him than any other player in the finals, yet he was not even booked. Had the rule change been made prior to Italia '90 he would not have been as effective as he was. One tackle from behind on Hagi in Genoa would probably have earned him his marching orders, but all Hagi got was a free-kick well out from the Irish goal.

The question for Charlton: could the team retain its effectiveness once the game's predominant emphasis changed from defence to attack? To help him over this potential crisis, two very talented Corkmen, Denis Irwin and Roy Keane, were coming on stream.

18

A Blessing in Disguise

On his return from Italia '90, Charlton's power reached its zenith. Although his team had played better football in the Euro '88 finals, their performance in achieving eighth place in the world carried more weight with the public. Charlton was effectively lord of all he surveyed in Irish football. With the departure of Brady and Stapleton, there were even fewer veteran native players with whom to pick a row, while at FAI headquarters his power was absolute. Having tasted the good life, thanks to Jack, FAI officers bent over backwards to satisfy his every whim.

Unfortunately, in relinquishing their power to Charlton, the FAI took its eye off its principal function – the promotion of football. The international team and its manager were all that mattered. Sure, their success meant that, irrespective of the FAI's efforts, the numbers playing football shot up, but what kind of game were they playing, and what direction was the FAI giving in this important area?

The answer can be gleaned from their treatment of Tuohy, the most successful manager before Charlton. In 1989, Tuohy was proposed as Course Director for the League of Ireland/FAS apprenticeship scheme, but Charlton put a stop to that.

'He won't get in while I'm here,' said the man who claimed never to bear a grudge.

Then, in 1990, when the Football Association of Coaches and Trainers (FACT) was launched, FAI President Michael Hyland stated: 'Jack is our number one man, and any decisions in this area will be made only with his agreement. He has the right of veto.' It was an astonishing abdication of responsibility. In effect, it meant that decisions normally taken by council would have to receive Charlton's approval.

FACT, which aspired to closer liaison with European coaches and their methods – a link that was vital for the future of the game – were thus made subject to the whim of Charlton, a self-confessed dictator when it came to football and the way it should be played. For him, the English way was best, and contempt, rather than openness, marked his attitude to the continental style.

Through his assistant Maurice Setters, Charlton's dictum was put into operation at Under-18 and Under-21 level and, to ensure that the English input was high, every effort was made to recruit English players for these teams through the 'granny' and parentage rules. After some initial interest, Charlton left the Under-15 and Under-16 teams alone, allowing national coach Joe McGrath to take charge of what were essentially the best Irish schoolboys. The tragedy was that these boys inevitably ended up signing for English clubs and disappeared into some mysterious black hole from which few of them surfaced. Between 1975 and 1995, this system brought only one player through to full international honours – and he was released by his first English club. That player was Denis Irwin.

When a team is successful there is, of course, less opportunity for new players to come through other than to replace those with whom age or injury has caught up. So, although Charlton used 58 different players during his nine-year reign, only 34 made their debuts in that period and, significantly, only 13 of that 34 were Irish-born. Five of the 13 established themselves in the team.

The main thrust of Charlton's vision was to qualify as many quality British-born players as possible, and he succeeded to a large degree. Of the 21 non-natives he introduced, 10 established themselves in his team at one time or another, and practically all profited from their association with the Republic through big money transfers.

The past and present of Irish football in monetary terms was put into focus when the Republic played Wales in a friendly in February 1991. Wales, who were like the Ireland of old – a good team but having no luck – were on a £200 match fee. The Irish, while on a £300 fee, had pocketed roughly £70,000 each from their previous year's international endeavours. It was all hard earned. The players had only minimal time off – as little as 10 days in some cases – after their Italian exertions, before resuming with pre-season training at their clubs.

Success had its price, too, for, with the team's higher profile, every aspect of the players' lives now came under intense media scrutiny. The first to suffer from this unwelcome intrusion were Chris Morris and Paul McGrath, when their domestic difficulties were brought to the fore shortly after Italia '90.

McGrath pulled out of the home game with Turkey in October 1990 just hours before kick-off, handing Chris Hughton a surprise call-up, while Morris's difficulties, which involved court proceedings, coincided with his right-back position being usurped by Irwin.

Irwin's promotion was hailed by many as overdue, as they felt he should have been in the team ahead of Morris in Italy. While Morris was better defensively, Irwin was a better passer and crosser, and was deadly accurate from corners and free-kicks. Irwin's problem at the time, was that he played for second division Oldham Athletic. Transferred to Manchester United in the summer of 1990, Charlton immediately promoted him to the international team and he rarely lost his place thereafter.

One player targeted for replacement was left-winger Sheedy. The manager

186

still hankered after the speedier forays of Galvin, and made no secret of his desire to find someone like Galvin to take over from the more cultured left-foot of Sheedy. However, Sheedy had no intention of fading away, and he was one of the big successes of the team in the two years after Italy. In 13 games in that period he scored three goals, and was the architect of five more. He was eventually replaced by Staunton, with Terry Phelan taking over at left-back.

Tactically, during the Euro '92 campaign, Charlton made a minor adjustment which led to a more attractive – and more productive – style of play, especially in away games. The holding role in front of the back four, which had been McGrath's practically since Charlton took over, was bestowed on one of the full-backs when the team broke forward. The idea was to get one of the midfielders in to the opposition's penalty area, with the full-back taking care of any rival breakaway.

This was seen to good effect in a friendly against Wales in Wrexham, where the Republic won 3–0, their first win on Welsh soil. An even better performance followed at Wembley the following month, March 1991, in the European Championship, with England pinned in their own half for long periods. But for bad misses by Sheedy and Houghton and an unfortunate own goal by Staunton, a win rather than a creditable 1–1 draw would have been achieved.

The problem of repeating away form at Lansdowne Road remained, despite a 5–0 win over Turkey. A breakaway goal earned England a 1–1 draw, while the pitiful state of the pitch was blamed for the poor fare served up in a drab 0–0 encounter with Poland on 1 May. With England winning 1–0 in Turkey, qualification hinged on the remaining games: England at home to Turkey and away to Poland; the Republic, away to Poland and Turkey.

In the meantime, an event of some significance occurred on 22 May, when Roy Keane made his debut in a 1–1 draw with Chile at Lansdowne Road. Although Charlton's style of play was the antithesis of that which he enjoyed at Nottingham Forest under Brian Clough, Keane showed enough aggression and workrate to ensure that he would be a key element in Charlton's plans.

That game against Chile was also notable for one of a number of disasters which marred O'Leary's latter days in the green jersey. After 64 seconds he came off worst in a clash of heads with Moran and had to retire. Worse followed in the vital game away to Poland in October. With the Republic cruising at 3–1, O'Leary dithered on the ball near his own corner flag, was dispossessed, and Poland scored from the resultant move.

That incident may well have been seen by Charlton as vindication for his earlier preference of Moran and McCarthy over O'Leary, but he refrained from pointing the finger in his after-match comments, and remained faithful to the Arsenal defender until injury forced him out of the reckoning.

At any rate, O'Leary was not the only defender to blunder in Poznan. Another goal, gifted by an ill-advised shout from Bonner to Moran, meant the Republic settling for one point instead of the two their play deserved. England, meanwhile, beat Turkey 1–0, so they needed only to draw in Poland to qualify.

The Republic duly turned in another stunning away performance to beat Turkey 3–1 in Istanbul, but England got the draw they needed, thanks to Austrian referee Forstinger. He refused to award Poland a penalty 20 minutes from time when goalkeeper Woods seemed to pull down Furtok. At the time Poland were leading 1–0; a minute later Lineker equalised.

For the first time in any qualifying group, World Cup or European Championship, the Republic emerged unbeaten and for only the second time – the other being Euro '76 – they finished with the best goal difference. Neither distinction was any consolation as England headed off to Sweden.

The Irish fans kept faith with their team and travelled in large numbers to the games in England, Poland and Turkey. Sadly, the game in Istanbul, although a triumph on the pitch, was a disaster on the terraces. The Turkish authorities allowed many of their own fans to occupy seats bought by the Irish and, in the chaos which ensued, some Irish fans were denied entrance to the stadium, while others were attacked or had missiles thrown at them by local hooligans. After the game, the fans' buses were a target for attack again, with rocks and flag poles hurled at them. Some fans were hospitalised as a result, but UEFA's findings when the matter was investigated resulted in a derisory £14,000 fine being levied on the Turkish FA. UEFA's observer at the game was well away from the trouble spot and UEFA adopted a three-wise-monkeys attitude. The fine was a token gesture based on 'the amount of fireworks before and during the game and the lack of preparation made by the Turkish Federation in regard to security and safety.'

If UEFA's decision was of no help to the fans hospitalised or injured, the comments of FAI President Michael Hyland added insult to their injuries.

'We are pleased with the decision,' he said. 'It vindicates the stance taken by the FAI in this matter and goes some way towards meeting the justifiable complaints of our fans. I hope too that it helps to ensure that incidents such as this never occur again.'

The FAI's platitudes showed a surprising disregard for the ordeal endured by their loyal supporters. Nothing less than the closure of the Istanbul stadium or the banning of Turkey from the next European Championship should have satisfied the legislators.

Meanwhile, the finances of the FAI rocketed upwards. Revenue from international matches in the 1990–91 season was over £1.5 million, compared to £81,805 in 1985–86, the season Charlton took over. The prospects for the future were even brighter as the World Cup draw had placed the Republic in Group Three alongside Spain, Denmark, Northern Ireland, Albania, Latvia and Lithuania. Given the experience of 1989 when little Malta filled Lansdowne Road, every home game appeared a guaranteed sell-out, so long as the team remained in contention.

As events unfolded, it transpired that the Republic's failure to qualify for Euro '92 was a blessing in disguise. Denmark, called up to replace Yugoslavia at the eleventh hour, went on to win the European Championship, but suffered an inevitable backlash, drawing 0–0 in each of their first three World Cup qualifying games – away to Latvia and Lithuania and home to the Republic. In the end, just one of those results made the difference between qualifying and not qualifying.

19

Jack Loosens His Grip

Towards the end of the Republic's USA '94 qualifying campaign, there were indications that Charlton no longer had a firm grip on team matters. There was the caution he induced at half-time in the home game against Lithuania, the mistaken tactics he acknowledged after the home defeat by Spain and, worst of all, there was the surprising lack of attention to detail in the run-up to the vital decider against Northern Ireland at Windsor Park. The latter omission indicates that Jack's decline started that night in Belfast.

Up to the penultimate game, at home to Spain, the Republic's Group Three campaign was ideal. Most importantly, Charlton's wishes in regard to the fixture schedule had been granted.

A 2–0 victory at home over Albania was an inauspicious start, but one of the principal reasons for the lacklustre display was the fact that Townsend was a spent force by half-time, having played three games in Canada the previous week with Chelsea. In accord with FIFA regulations, he should have been released after the second game, but Chelsea received no request to that effect from the FAI. Charlton's attitude was that he needed to maintain good relations with clubs and managers and so he was not going to quote FIFA regulations to them.

Here again, Charlton had a touch of fortune, for the English FA insisted on blank weekends before their four main internationals, which happily coincided with those of the Republic.

However, Charlton almost pressed the self-destruct button on an innocuous US tour in the summer of 1992. Billed as a dry run for USA '94, the tour was treated lightly, but the manager still managed to take umbrage with Moran when he reported back late to the team hotel following a game of golf. Words were exchanged and Moran was omitted from the next two World Cup squads.

Against Latvia, Moran's absence was unimportant but, with the next game away to European Champions Denmark, Charlton was skating on thin ice. The advent of Keane had enabled the manager to accede to McGrath's request for a move back to his favourite centre-back role, but the question of McGrath's partner was not so readily resolved. Former Northern Ireland schoolboy Alan Kernaghan was selected for his debut against Latvia, but he was very much a novice and, when McGrath had to pull out of the squad for Denmark, Charlton was in a quandary, as McCarthy was also unfit and had, it transpired, played his last game for the Republic.

McCarthy was a big loss to Charlton for whom he had been the 'enforcer' both on and off the field. His lusty voice ensured that the manager's tactics were faithfully observed as long as Mick was on the pitch, while, in the dressing-room, he forcefully reminded his team-mates of their duties. His strict adherence to Charlton's tactics – which, paradoxically, he did not apply when he became a manager – made him an invaluable leader when the going got tough, but it did not always endear him to his team-mates. As a result, his subsequent elevation as Charlton's successor did not meet with the universal approval of the Irish squad.

In Kernaghan, Charlton saw a budding McCarthy, but the Middlesbrough defender lacked McCarthy's presence and he was not as astute a reader of the game. The Northern Ireland authorities were dismayed at Kernaghan's selection by the Republic. They were hamstrung by their own strict adherence to a ruling of the International Football Board which precluded them from selecting players beyond the parentage rule. Kernaghan, born in England, had grandparents who were born in Northern Ireland before 1921 and so qualified for an Irish passport. He had tried in vain for some years to play for Northern Ireland but, in the end, he was grateful to Charlton for the chance of international honours. Subsequently sold to Manchester City for a big fee, he was never less than wholehearted in his efforts for the Republic.

The Kernaghan case led to a re-think on the part of the International Board. Under pressure from Northern Ireland and Wales, the Board decided that their members – the English, Scottish, Welsh and Northern Ireland Football Associations – could, in future, select non-natives on the basis allowed by FIFA.

With McGrath and McCarthy unavailable, Charlton had no option but to recall Moran, and the Dubliner turned in a typically courageous performance alongside Kernaghan to thwart the European Champions.

Denmark had won the European Championship playing the Irish style of game, and now they were finding, at home, the same problems Ireland faced at Lansdowne Road. It was no surprise when the return game in Dublin also ended in stalemate.

The game in Copenhagen marked the emergence of Kernaghan and Phelan as internationals with a future. The rain and soft conditions suited Kernaghan's aggressive style, although he picked up a booking which ruled him out of the game against Spain, while a disciplined Phelan used his pace to curb the speedy Danish attack.

Phelan had only come into the side because of an injury to Staunton, but his assured play convinced Charlton to leave him there and deploy Staunton further upfield. It proved to be a highly productive move as Staunton, with his well-driven, curling crosses from the left wing, proceeded to take over the mantle of Sheedy, tantalising defenders and laying on a string of chances for Quinn, Aldridge and Cascarino.

Staunton's move ultimately proved to be the difference between Ireland qualifying and not qualifying. Quinn was in a position to appreciate the impact he made.

'With the emergence of Steve, who has terrific acceleration – even Terry [Phelan] can't keep up with him half the time and he's the quickest – and Townsend, who attacks straight through the middle, Roy Keane, who can run all day, and Ray Houghton, who gets up and down there as well, we find we're 10 yards further up the pitch.

'We're not trying to win the ball back on the half-way line, we're trying to win it back on the edge of their box so that if they do make a pass, our midfielders are tackling in their half. Therefore when we win it we're nearer the goal and getting into more dangerous positions. That's when we can peel away and find space, because you don't have such a long pass coming to you. We now have one of the most exciting midfields in world football.'

Spain in Seville was the ideal testing ground for Quinn's theory, for it is not a happy hunting ground for visiting teams. But, at full-strength – Bonner, Irwin, McGrath, Moran, Phelan, Houghton, Keane, Townsend, Staunton, Aldridge and Quinn – it was only a combination of poor finishing and a linesman's error which denied Ireland victory. Still, the 0–0 draw meant that a major hurdle had been overcome.

This game served notice that a new Irish star had arrived, for Keane, at 21 and in only his 10th international, displayed all the composure and wiles of a veteran. Strength, workrate, good tackling and heading were the attributes for which the Corkman was already renowned. In Seville, he also demonstrated good close control and a vision and awareness that had not been so noticeable in previous internationals.

Charlton had every reason to be pleased with his team's performances, but there was one nagging doubt that remained to be addressed: had they the killer instinct necessary to win enough games to qualify? Since the successful campaign of 1989, draws rather than wins had been the hallmark of the team's performances in competitive games. There had been four draws in Italia '90, followed by four more in the Euro '92 qualifiers and now two more in the USA '94 qualifiers. The manager had succeeded in stopping other teams playing; could he now transfer territorial superiority into matchwinning scores? Failure to achieve this would put qualification at risk as happened in Euro '92.

The players went some way towards answering this question in their opening World Cup tie of 1993 when, with a breathtaking first-half display, they took Northern Ireland apart at Lansdowne Road on 31 March. Three goals up at the break, they rested on their laurels somewhat in the second half, while a section of supporters aggravated a tense situation by chanting: 'There's only one team in Ireland'. If only it were true!

Northern Ireland, having beaten Albania in Tirana in February, had travelled hopefully, but three goals between the 20th and the 28th minutes dashed their hopes. The Republic, at full strength apart from the inclusion of Tommy Coyne for the injured Aldridge, were an intimidating sight, and their first-half display must have sent chills down the spines of the Danish and Spanish managers.

Especially pleasing was the quality of the goals. The first involved Houghton and Irwin before a Townsend–Quinn one–two let the captain score from inside the penalty area. For the second, Houghton hit a Staunton pass first-time to Quinn, who had stolen a yard on his marker and volleyed in to the net. The third was a Staunton special, a fiercely struck, swirling corner from the right-hand side which flew directly into the net – his second such score in four internationals, having managed the feat against Portugal in the US Cup.

A contributory reason for this good display was the attention the IRFU had given to the preparation of the pitch. A rugby match scheduled for the previous weekend had been moved to the back pitch, which did not go down well with some of the rugby fraternity, but the IRFU, in receipt of vast sums from the FAI, were anxious to avoid a repeat of the criticism which followed the Republic's failure against Poland in 1991.

The FAI were also offering another carrot. FIFA rules required that, in future, international grounds should be equipped with floodlights and the FAI were prepared to pay half the cost of installing the most up-to-date lights, a facility which the IRFU would be glad to have.

Good performances often inspire a backlash, and so it proved when Denmark visited on 28 April. They had beaten Spain to keep their hopes alive and they set out on a mission of containment, targeting midfield as the key area. So successful were they that when Kim Vilfort lobbed Bonner from 40 yards for a spectacular individual effort after 27 minutes, it began to look like the Vikings were once again about to depart with the spoils.

However, relentless Irish pressure eventually led to a sweet equaliser, with Quinn glancing in a Staunton cross following a short corner by Houghton. It was no more than they deserved, but a winner was beyond them, the Danes' five-man midfield blocking the path to goal.

Critics of the team felt a more thoughtful, passing game might have borne fruit, but Townsend made a spirited defence of the Charlton method.

'If we start at a hard pace and go behind we're never going to slow down. That's not our way. All we did was all we know . . . to bash on their door a bit harder. That's the recipe of our success. It is easy to say we should be cleverer, but we like to strangle teams, to choke them to death.'

Besides, the pitch had not been in the same condition as for the Northern Ireland game.

'Our game is to play the ball wide and then deliver good ball to Quinn and Cascarino, and the one area where the ball did not run true was on the wings. It is no coincidence that when we play on a good surface we play well, because we are all good players and can play.'

The point dropped meant that the Republic could afford no slip-ups on their summer safari to Eastern Europe. Charlton, with notable attention to detail, prepared a list of items, a survival kit, which the players were to bring to Albania on 26 May. In a hit-and-run raid, the FAI, bringing their own food, drinks and chefs, flew in the day before the game and flew out straight after the match.

Charlton's plans were dealt a shock blow when, prior to departure, McGrath, who had started the campaign as captain before willingly relinquishing the role to Townsend, went missing. The rumour factory went into overdrive as McGrath was reported to have left Cork, where he had a coaching engagement, with a mystery blonde. The girl was later identified as Caroline Lamb, who subsequently became Paul's wife.

McGrath was suffering a double crisis, with problems domestically and injury-wise. On 9 May, he had injured his knee in a tackle on QPR's Les Ferdinand. Five days later he left for Mauritius with Aston Villa and played against Everton. When the knee swelled up, he returned home for treatment and also to handle the problems caused by the break-up of his marriage. A very private man, who, despite immense talent, suffered from an inferiority complex except while on the pitch, McGrath could not stop the doubts about his fitness and his marriage from overwhelming him. Instead of making a plea for his release, which would have been granted, he chose to hide, thus drawing greater attention to himself.

With all the fuss, Charlton did well to keep his squad focused on the job in hand. Moran came in for McGrath and, although Albania took the lead after seven minutes when Kushta outpaced Kernaghan, the Republic stuck to their task and were rewarded with a 2–1 win, thanks to two set-piece goals.

The first came five minutes after Albania's score, with Staunton scoring direct from a free-kick, but the winner was delayed until the 77th minute, Staunton again being involved. His corner was headed in to the net at the far post by Cascarino, who had replaced Aldridge three minutes earlier.

After a short break, the squad assembled in June for the trips to the Baltic States of Latvia (9 June) and Lithuania (16 June). The good news was that McGrath was fit again. He apologised for his failure to make contact before the Albania game and Charlton, always very understanding where McGrath was concerned, was delighted to slot him into his team again.

McGrath quickly repaid the manager with the second goal in the 2–0 defeat of Latvia. He headed in a Houghton cross just before half-time. Aldridge opened the scoring after 14 minutes with a header from an Irwin cross. It was shooting practice in the second half, but poor finishing by Townsend, Aldridge, Staunton and Keane meant the score stayed as it was.

After a quick break in Ireland, it was on to Vilnius for the final game of a long season. Lithuania were the strongest of the three minnows in Group Three, and the Republic struggled to impose themselves. It took a slightly fortuitous goal to break the deadlock and it once again underlined Staunton's importance. His free-kick from outside the penalty area was deflected past his own goalkeeper by Baltusnikas in the 40th minute for the only goal of the game.

It was a relieved Irish squad which departed Vilnius, the only sour note being a booking for Houghton for taking a free-kick too quickly in the opinion of the Luxembourg referee. As this had also occurred to Staunton in Albania, Charlton was not amused. A second card could mean either player missing out on one of the last two vital games, home to Spain or away to Northern Ireland.

'You can't legislate for referees' interpretations,' claimed an incensed Charlton. 'The referee said to Ray, "The moment you take the free I'm going to blow for time," but because he did not signal – which we debate – he gave him a card. He was applying a rule which is not a rule at all. His attitude was that we were taking the free quickly so that he'd have to call us back and that would waste time. Work that one out.

'I get annoyed at some of the bookings we've had because you get cards for anything now. There's no way that we do anything nasty, but we still get booked, and that hurts us more than other countries who have greater player resources.

'The one that dismays me is Paul's bookings. When you think of all the times he makes a tackle and then the only time he mistimes one he gets a card. I don't think that's right. You should earn a card before you get one.'

Vilnius offered another indication of the remarkable upsurge in the Republic's fortunes. A total of 54 Irish journalists travelled, a far cry from pre-Charlton days when the reporting was left to a handful of scribes.

McGrath, with two bookings, was out of the return game with Lithuania on 8 September, and Charlton was also worried about six other players who had a booking each – Staunton, Keane, Moran, Houghton, McGoldrick and Quinn.

'A good result, but a poor performance' was Charlton's succinct and accurate after-match summing-up of the 2–0 defeat of Lithuania. Two goals up after 25 minutes, courtesy of headers from Aldridge and Kernaghan (who found it hard to contain his delight), the team once again eased up after the break, but this time it was the manager's fault. The risk of four of his starting line-up missing the vital game against Spain was pointed out by Charlton.

'The emphasis I put on yellow cards may have inhibited the lads in the way they approached the game,' he admitted. 'I feel I've got to take responsibility because I made a point of drawing their attention to the situation.'

However, the win kept Ireland on top of Group Three and, with Spain doing a 5–1 demolition job on an Albanian side minus some of their best players, the stage was set for another of those 'most important game in the history of Irish soccer' scenarios. Victory would guarantee a place in the finals, and anything else would mean that the trip to Belfast in November would have more importance than Charlton considered desirable. The game was another sell-out, earning the FAI £1.4 million in gate receipts, TV rights and perimeter advertising, making it the biggest single money-spinner in Irish sport.

Spain's manager, Javier Clemente stoked the flames with his declaration: 'It will be hell in Dublin; I'm preparing my boys to go to war,' while Charlton had to plan without Townsend and Aldridge, both injured. It was a crisis and, in crises, Charlton did not have a good record. Fortunately, they were few and far between during his years in charge. For this crisis, he took his biggest tactical gamble, opting for a five-man midfield, with Quinn as a lone striker. It handed the initiative to Spain, who had travelled with a draw in mind, lining up with only Salinas up-front. Charlton also made the cardinal error of not giving his players enough notice of his change of plan. He confirmed his game plan only hours before kick-off and even then he was vague about what he wanted from the new formation.

Charlton's gamble quickly came unstuck, with Spain scoring three goals within the 11th and 25th minutes, through Caminero and Salinas (2). The first goal, following a long throw-in, was a rare slip by the defence to a set-piece, while the third goal had an element of luck, with the ball looping off substitute Sheridan's heel to put Salinas in the clear. By then, hundreds of fans were streaming out of the exits.

Confused by the sudden collapse of his game plan, Charlton had introduced Sheridan when Moran was forced to retire injured after 23 minutes. McGrath, who had started in midfield, moved back to his true position. The problems increased with injuries to Irwin and Staunton, the latter not resuming after the break. He was replaced by Cascarino, with the team reverting to its more familiar 4-4-2 shape.

Benefiting from the change, a spell of pressure was rewarded with a Sheridan goal in the 78th minute. It was only a consolation score, as the Republic's 29 match unbeaten run at Lansdowne Road ended, but it was to prove vital when the Group Three tallies were finally totted up.

While fans of the Republic, Spain and Denmark concentrated on the matches which would decide their destiny on 17 November, the people of Northern Ireland were being fed a diet of terrorist tit-for-tat atrocities. This led to speculation that the game with Northern Ireland would be moved from Windsor Park, which is in the heart of a loyalist, anti-Republic area, to an English venue. FIFA at first seemed to indicate a change of venue, but then left the decision to the IFA authorities. In due course, the IFA confirmed Windsor Park as the venue, and informed FIFA and the FAI that they would guarantee the security and safety arrangements.

The uncertainty added to the tension surrounding the fixture, and Northern Ireland manager Billy Bingham, who was bowing out afterwards, added fuel to the fire when he labelled some of the Republic's players as mercenaries compared to his all-native team.

Charlton based his squad in the Nuremore Hotel in County Monaghan, near the Northern Ireland border. With Aldridge and Townsend fit again, his only absentee was Staunton, whom he replaced with utility player McGoldrick.

Security forces were everywhere on the approaches to the ground, leaving the Republic's players in no doubt that they were in a war zone. While this added to the tension, there is no history of terrorist attacks on sporting occasions in the North.

The Republic stepped into a veritable lion's den that night with a noisy, hostile crowd present. The six British-born players were treated to chants of 'English rejects', while Phelan and McGrath were abused because of their colour, Cascarino and Bonner because of their association with Celtic, and Kernaghan had to listen to taunts of 'Judas'. Much has been made of this hostility, with some reporters searching for extremes to describe the intimidation. Considering the crowd was limited to approximately 11,000, this was laughable, and the players afterwards dismissed the notion of fear by pointing out that the hostility never came near that which they regularly experienced in Glasgow, Manchester or North London derbies.

Without Staunton, the Republic were like a bird with one wing. McGoldrick was a fine kicker, but he was not a natural left-footer and, although he was instructed to take the corners on the left, no time was spent in practising them in the run-up to the game. As the Republic's game plan depended on taking advantage of set-pieces, a good understanding between kicker and target men was essential, so this oversight on Charlton's part was extremely damaging. At no time did McGoldrick's kicks look dangerous, and Irwin eventually took over his role.

The Republic had the best chances, and failed to take them, before Jimmy Quinn capitalised on a poor clearance to shoot the North into the lead after 73 minutes. As he raced over to celebrate with the fans, there was a strange irony at play, for Quinn's family had originally been victims of the same bigotry which was rife that night in Windsor Park. They had been burned out of their home in Rathcoole many years previously, forcing them to emigrate to England, where Quinn, a late developer, went on to become one of the most prolific goalscorers in the lower divisions of the English League.

Charlton replaced the luckless Houghton with Alan McLoughlin and, four minutes after the North's goal, the move paid dividends. An Irwin free-kick, beautifully flighted from the right, was knocked down by a defender to where McLoughlin was loitering just outside the penalty area. Chesting it down, he struck the ball left-footed into the bottom left-hand corner well out of goalkeeper Tommy Wright's reach.

It proved to be a golden goal, as the point it earned was enough to clinch a place in USA '94. The agony lingered on for the players and the fans after the final whistle when TV coverage showed that the game in Seville was not yet over. Spain, down to 10 men, were leading 1–0, there were four minutes still to play and Denmark needed only to draw to qualify at Ireland's expense. Those four minutes seemed interminable and Jack Charlton, waiting to be interviewed as soon as the result became known, looked haggard and drawn. At 58, he certainly expended a lot of nervous energy that night, and an altercation with his old friend Billy Bingham had also left its mark.

When someone on the North's bench had given the Republic bench the two fingers after Jimmy Quinn's goal, this was relayed to Jack as coming from Bingham. So incensed was Charlton that, when Bingham offered the traditional end-of-match handshake, he spurned it, giving him a belligerent 'Up yours too' instead. Later, when he had calmed down, Charlton apologised to Bingham. Bingham, however, was making no apologies for his 'mercenaries' remark. When asked if he would be supporting the 'mercenaries' in America, he grudgingly replied, 'Some of them'.

A lot was made of Bingham's incitement of the crowd from the touchline after the half-time break. Some writers considered it offensive, but he had nothing to apologise for as he was merely appealing to the fans to increase the volume of their support. It was similar to Charlie Hurley's gesture to the Dalymount crowd during a famous win over Scotland in 1963, and nobody complained about that.

Before leaving Northern Ireland, Charlton made the short journey to the Linfield Social Club to present an award, and was greeted with rapturous applause. He found it strange that these people who had wanted so much to beat his team could turn around and signal their appreciation of his, and the Republic's, achievement. But that is the way it is in Ireland, for fans in the Republic had followed avidly the North's exploits in the 1982 and 1986 finals.

In fact, the Northern Ireland players and officials were glad for all but one of the Republic's players. The exception was Roy Keane, whose verbal abuse of the Northern Ireland players during the game was not appreciated, and marred an otherwise sporting contest.

The evening ended on a happier note and was recorded for posterity by the makers of the *Road to America* video. Travelling by car from Windsor Park they managed to get to Dublin airport to film the team's arrival from Belfast, and what a heartwarming sight that was. Even though it was after midnight, the fans were there lining the arrivals area, singing and applauding as the players walked past. The players, taken by surprise, were rendered speechless by a homecoming they were unlikely to forget.

Charlton had little time to celebrate a second World Cup qualification for, on 29 November came the devastating news that Niall Quinn, who had been such a tower of strength through the campaign, was out of the finals. Ruptured cruciate ligaments meant a long period of rehabilitation for the Dubliner, with a return to action timed for the following September.

It was a bitter blow, but it was not unprecedented. For Euro '88, Charlton had to plan without Beglin, Lawrenson and Brady, while Whelan had been a casualty before Italia '90. The manager had overcome those problems; now he had to devise a plan to minimise the loss of Quinn.

20

USA '94: The End in Sight

In January 1992, before the start of the USA '94 campaign, Charlton stated: 'My changes in this World Cup will be imperceptible. You will hardly notice them. I found three players of real quality in the European Championship in Denis Irwin, Roy Keane and Terry Phelan; if three more of their class emerge over the next 18 months, I will be more than happy.'

By January 1994, with qualification in the bag, his prayers had been answered. Waiting in the wings, ready to play a major role in Charlton's plans, were Gary Kelly, Phil Babb and Jason McAteer. Add the arrival of the two Alans, Kernaghan and Kelly, and the manager had gone nap in a very short span of time.

The Three Amigos – as Gary Kelly, Babb and McAteer became known – fitted the Republic of Ireland stereotype, in that none of them was a boy wonder. All had suffered rejection of one sort or another. Kelly was a forward going nowhere at Leeds United until manager Howard Wilkinson switched him to right-back in a crisis. Using his pace to good effect, he made the position his own at Elland Road, and provided Charlton with a strong alternative to the dependable Irwin.

Babb had been let go by his first club, Millwall, where he had played centre-forward. Frank Stapleton switched him to centre-back at Bradford City and he became a target for Premiership clubs. Coventry City won the race to sign him but, with the Charlton imprint on him, he was transferred to Liverpool after the finals for £3.7 million.

McAteer graduated from non-league football, becoming a professional in his 20s with Bolton Wanderers, and playing a prominent part in their rise to Premiership status. With Bolton, he was an exciting central midfielder, with the ability to go past opponents and make exciting runs. As far as Charlton was concerned, he was the logical successor to Houghton on the right wing. Convincing McAteer of this did not prove so easy.

The draw for the finals did the Republic no favours. Group E, with Italy, Mexico, Norway and the Republic, was quickly labelled the Group of Death, but the Republic, rated 10th in the world by FIFA, were expected to advance. Italy were the other favourites and the draw paired the two of them in the first game in New Jersey on 18 June.

Charlton, suffering a reaction to all the demands on his time, was ordered into hospital for a check-up. Although he was given a clean bill of health, he was warned to cut back on his busy schedule. One of the casualties of this cutback was the pre-finals meeting of World Cup managers in New York in February. The FAI had made arrangements for him to travel, but he decided to stay at home, stating that he had nothing to learn from what, he claimed, was essentially a talk-shop.

It was bad judgement on his part, as subsequent events proved. When Charlton later led a chorus of Irish whingeing about the heat, the humidity, the need for water for the players and the delay in permitting substitutes to take part, FIFA Press Officer Guido Tognoni reminded him forcefully that, had he attended the February meeting, he would have been clear about all these matters and he would have had an opportunity to discuss them with officials.

It was another own goal on Charlton's part, one of many as he adopted an attitude of one who has 'been there, done that', and had nothing to learn. Ultimately this inability to adapt to new situations and apply the necessary solutions contributed to his downfall.There was no hint of this in the run-up to the USA, as Charlton's preparations went even better than he had dared hope. Lining up friendlies with other qualifiers was a calculated gamble, but it paid off.

The Three Amigos got their chance against Russia at Lansdowne Road in March and helped light up an otherwise tame 0–0 draw. In Tilburg in April against Holland, Gary Kelly and Babb came of age, coached and coaxed by the veteran Moran. With Quinn and Cascarino injured, Charlton had to plan without a tall target man. He opted for a 4-5-1 system, which also spared him the need to make a decision about which two of three central midfielders to use; in this system he could use all three – Keane, Sheridan and Townsend. It was a system which failed badly against Spain, but it worked like a dream in Tilburg and produced a surprise 1–0 win.

The goal was scored by Tommy Coyne, and there could not have been a more popular goalscorer. Nine months previously he had suffered a terrible tragedy with the loss of his wife Alison shortly after the birth of their third child. He had been forced to drop out of football for a while to look after his children. A move to Motherwell in November saw him make a belated start to the season, but he quickly showed that he had not lost his touch. While he lacked pace, Coyne had a brilliant positional sense and, being four years younger than Aldridge, was reckoned by Charlton to be a better bet when it came to playing in the heat of New Jersey and Orlando.

Cascarino proved himself in the more difficult game against Germany in Hanover in May, booking his seat to the USA with his 12th goal for Ireland in a shock 2–0 win. Gary Kelly scored the other goal on a day when Alan Kelly, Babb and McAteer also showed up well. It began to look like Charlton had, for once, an embarrassment of riches.

The bubble was burst, to a degree, by the Czech Republic, who won 3–1 at

Lansdowne Road and spoiled what was intended to be a farewell party on 5 June. However, it was impossible to learn anything from a game in which the main priority of the Irish players was to avoid injury.

On arrival in Florida on 6 June, the players had 12 days to acclimatise. This was when Charlton earned his pay, driving home to players how they should play, and what they could expect from their rivals. The manager had been offered a wide range of advice about playing systems to combat the heat, with the emphasis on a passing game, but he did not agree. He told *Observer* writer Patrick Barclay: 'I want us playing the way we played before. We've been playing too much of the football the pundits say we should play. We can do that, as well as most, but we're better at our own way than anybody.' The re-instatement of Sheridan was his only concession to the more thoughtful game advocated by the pundits.

One person offering Charlton advice was his old adversary, Billy Bingham: 'I believe Jack needs to make a few bold decisions. He needs to gamble. Jack tends to play backs out wide instead of wingers. That's great defensively but, offensively, it isn't good for you. They can't beat people. When you beat a defender it opens up Pandora's Box. If two are beaten, it opens up the world.'

Bingham also pointed out that, with three points for a win, containment would not be enough in the US.

'What got him through the first phase four years back, probably won't do this time. He's got to gamble. He's got to be brave.'

However, caution is Charlton's watchword and, having a healthy respect for the Italians, containment was still the order of the day when he named his team for the 18 June clash in the Giants Stadium: Bonner; Irwin, McGrath, Babb, Phelan; Houghton, Keane, Sheridan, Townsend, Staunton; Coyne. This 4-5-1 line-up placed a heavy onus on Coyne to cause problems on whatever scraps he was fed. It was typical Charlton philosophy – stop the other team playing and you never know what might happen; you will certainly get a chance or two yourself and, if you take one of them, well, it could be your day. It was a philosophy ideally suited to Ireland, a country which produced defenders by the score but seldom a forward of note. And, on 18 June 1994, Charlton's luck was in evidence again.

In an enthralling 90 minutes, the Irish gave as good as they got. There were green-shirted heroes all over the pitch. Bonner made an important save, Irwin, McGrath, Babb and Phelan made the vital tackles, while the five men in midfield and lone attacker Coyne ran themselves into the ground harrying their opponents and getting forward as often as possible.

The only goal of the game had that element of good fortune which characterised Charlton's era. Sheridan played a long ball forward; Costacurta headed it up in the air; Baresi, under pressure from Coyne, could only head it down as far as Houghton. He took it on his weaker left foot and, with no other option available, had a shot at goal. Pagliuca, off his line, could only watch in dismay as the ball dipped under his bar and into the net. One–nil and only twelve minutes played; Irish fans braced themselves for another 80 minutes of siege.

It was not as bad as that. This time, the boys in green had all the answers. In fact, the best chance fell to Sheridan following a tremendous Keane run to the end line and a neat dummy by Coyne, but the shot from 12 yards struck the crossbar and bounced to safety. It was a bad miss.

The introduction of McAteer (on his 23rd birthday) gave a fresh impetus to the attack, but the delay in replacing Coyne was a costly oversight on Charlton's part. Having run himself into the ground, Coyne suffered badly from dehydration after the game and was in agony on the journey back to Florida. So bad, in fact, that his chances of playing against Mexico on 24 June were regarded as slim.

In every other respect, this was Charlton's finest hour. His team had humbled one of the favourites. It was also the first time Ireland had defeated Italy – the last bogey team had succumbed to the Charlton method.

A contributory factor to this success was the presence of so many Irish fans. The Italian players, on emerging from the tunnel into the stadium, asked 'Where are the Italians?' so bewildered were they by the sea of green, white and orange banners around the ground. Officially, the Irish were entitled to 8,000 of the 71,000 seats. Somehow they had secured well over 30,000, and they knew how to make themselves seen and heard. At the game against Norway, an American writer counted the banners and gave his verdict as 137 to 5. For Ireland, of course! It later emerged, during the FAI crisis in 1996, that deals had been done with touts to secure seats for the US games. The cost to the Association was £250,000, and this was one of the revelations which led to the resignations of President Louis Kilcoyne and Treasurer Joe Delaney.

The victory over Italy struck a chord with Irishmen everywhere. A Dublin priest greeted his congregation on the Sunday morning with a dissertation on 'the greatest victory Ireland ever achieved,' and then added: 'I don't think the Lord will mind if we sing a chorus of Olé Olé,' which he duly led in his booming baritone!

Sadly, the match was marked by an incident of a different sort all together in the small, mainly Catholic, County Down village of Loughinisland. The locals had crowded into the Heights Bar to watch the match, but before the 90 minutes were up six of them had been killed and many more injured as loyalist terrorists raked the bar with machine-gun fire in a cowardly attack. News of the massacre put a damper on the euphoria which the victory over Italy had engendered.

Having negotiated Italy successfully, the Republic had to tackle their most difficult hurdle – the heat and humidity of Orlando. Making it worse, the game against Mexico was scheduled for noon – a crazy notion, dictated solely by the demands of television, which was largely geared to the European market.

As soon as the players went on the pitch they started sweating and the biggest difficulty was sucking air back into the system after making any effort.

Babb discovered another drawback, which he described in the *Irish Times*.

'One thing that really sticks out is how still it was. Every time there was a roar from the crowd, just a couple of seconds later on the pitch there would be an unbelievable smell of stale lager. Nothing was getting carried away. The smell was unbelievable after the goals.'

Charlton, who had been waging war against FIFA on the matter of getting water to the players during games, achieved an important victory when FIFA conceded that waterbags could be thrown on to the pitch. Before this, the players had to step off the pitch for a drink, which made it extremely difficult for those in the central corridor of play.

While Charlton's campaign was applauded and even seen by some as deflecting the pressure of the games themselves from the players, it could be equally said that, putting such emphasis on the issue only served to accentuate whatever doubts his own players had in regard to their ability to cope with unfamiliar conditions. In fact, the Irish coped admirably, with one or two notable exceptions. Townsend suffered from an allergy and his knee swelled up, limiting his effectiveness, while the fair-haired Staunton never came to terms with the heat, and was only a pale shadow of his earlier self.

Charlton stuck with the team that beat Italy but, not surprisingly, Coyne was unable to repeat his New Jersey form and was eventually replaced by Aldridge.

In a pointer to what lay ahead, Ireland controlled the game early on, but when they failed to score Mexico grew in confidence and began to undermine the Irish defence on the wings. Irwin and Phelan were both in difficulty, which led to two well-taken goals by Luis Garcia. The full-backs were also booked for a second time, Irwin unfairly, which meant they were out of the game against Norway.

Two goals down, Charlton decided on a double substitution – McAteer and Aldridge for Staunton and Coyne. McAteer got on straightaway, but an official held up Aldridge's entrance. This led to a shouting match, in which Aldridge told the official he was 'a f***ing cheat', words that carried clearly into homes worldwide via TV. When he was eventually allowed on, a fired-up Aldridge scored a superb headed goal from a McAteer cross to bring Ireland back into the game, and it took a diving save by Campos from Townsend to deny the Irish a draw in the closing minutes.

After two games, Ireland were second in Group E, on goals scored, with all four teams on three points. But, following the touchline row in Orlando, Charlton was banned from the dug-out for the Group decider against Norway in New Jersey. He was also fined £7,000 by FIFA, while the more culpable Aldridge was fined £1,250. Understandably, Charlton was convinced that this was FIFA's heavy-handed way of getting even for the hassle he had given them.

With Gary Kelly and McAteer in for the suspended Irwin and Phelan, the Three Amigos started against Norway. Staunton switched to left-back, while Aldridge was rewarded for his goal with selection ahead of Coyne, who was due a rest.

If Ireland v Egypt was the worst game of Italia '90, then Ireland v Norway was a candidate for the same dubious honour in USA '94. Knowing that a draw was enough to qualify for the second phase, the ever-cautious Charlton planned accordingly, while Norway, who needed a win, lacked the inspiration to make a game of it. The result was a boring 0–0 draw which saw the Republic through and Norway eliminated. The downside was that the Republic had to return to Orlando to play Holland for a place in the quarter-finals.

To say that the game against Holland on Monday, 4 July, was an anti-climax would be an understatement. Having defeated the Dutch less than three months previously, hopes were high, but it was Holland's coaching staff who had learned most from that encounter in Tilburg.

As against Mexico, it was Ireland's full-backs who proved vulnerable, undermining what had been a bright opening. Apart from the torrid time they gave Kelly and Phelan, there was nothing exceptional about the Dutch, and the game was decided by two unforced errors by established members of the team.

Phelan was the first to press the self-destruct button when, instead of heading a relatively simple ball into touch, he headed it behind him, allowing Overmars to sprint on to it and cross from the end line. Bergkamp swooped to hit the ball into the net despite McGrath's best efforts to retrieve the situation.

Coming up to half-time, Ireland appeared to have weathered the storm, but then Bonner boobed and put the game out of reach. Wim Jonk, allowed surprising latitude, sauntered through the centre before essaying a shot straight at Bonner from 25 yards. The big Donegalman, weighing up his options on where to despatch the ball, inexplicably allowed it to bounce off his chest and over his shoulder into the net.

In the cruel heat there was no way any team could hope to claw back such a deficit. The spirit was willing, but the flesh, and more importantly the imagination, was weak. Babb, from a knock-down by substitute Cascarino, had the best chance, but he did not even find the target.

It was a sad end to what had promised to be a glorious tournament, and it is to Charlton's credit that there were no recriminations in the wake of the self-inflicted exit. He simply went round the dressing-room, shook the hand of each member of the squad, and thanked them for all the hard work they had put in, not just in the USA, but in the qualification games as well.

As Townsend explained: 'With Jack, the time you know you'll get a bollocking is when you err and get away with it. I admire him for that. When you make a cock-up and they run through and score, you don't have to be reminded that you should have cleared it into the stand, do you?'

Jack the dressing-room bully did not exist – it was merely a figment of certain writers' imaginations. Like any manager, he laid down the method of play he thought best suited his players, and he expected them to follow his instructions; but, in the aftermath of defeat caused by a player's error, he retained his dignity and made things as easy as possible for the offending player.

The big winners of USA '94 were the Irish fans. Win or lose, they partied through the night, evoking admiration from all quarters. England striker Teddy Sheringham, visiting former team-mate Cascarino, could not get over the good cheer of the fans and how they mingled on the best of terms with the players.

'This is special all right,' he told Townsend. 'Can you imagine standing here amongst England fans after we had just gone out of the World Cup? They would probably want to have a go.'

The other side of the coin was evident in Dublin, where defeat turned to dejection which in turn fuelled violence. Dozens were arrested and several were hospitalised with serious injuries, mostly the result of drunken brawls as fans spilled out of pubs. Women's Aid reported that an increase in domestic violence was noted whenever Ireland lost.

No sooner was the team eliminated than plans were set in motion for a welcome-home party. Charlton was committed to ITV for the remainder of the tournament, but he allowed himself to be persuaded to return to Dublin. After all, he had been made a Freeman of the City prior to departure on 26 May.

Compared to the scenes in 1988 and 1990, the Phoenix Park party was a lukewarm effort, with less than 10,000 attending, including numbers of young girls who were clamouring for a look at the Three Amigos.

In the aftermath of defeat, there were some calls for Jack to resign, and pass on the baton to a younger man. Even Jack, then 59, seemed to be having doubts, as he wrote in his *Sunday Press* column: 'I don't know if I want to go through all this again. Maybe I'm getting a little bit weary over the whole business, maybe my thoughts are not as clear as they should be, maybe I'm not as sharp as I was.'

However, the carrot of bringing the Republic to his native country for the finals of Euro '96 convinced him to stay in the hot seat.

'If we go to England,' he said, 'we'll have bigger gates than them. Oh, I'd bloody love that.'

21

Jack Bites the Bullet

In December 1994, Charlton was on top of the world. His team was unbeaten after three games of the European Championship, had yet to concede a goal, and were regarded as firm favourites to qualify for the finals. Yet, 12 months later, Charlton had stepped down from the position he had elevated to such a high profile, and the future of Irish football was in disarray.

What went wrong in that time to bring to an end one of the greatest success stories of Irish sport? Surprisingly, he made no attempt to answer this question in his autobiography, but a solution may be found in Jack's own admission after USA '94 that he was no longer as sharp as he had been. There were signs in the US that such was the case. For example, in the second-round game with Holland, Townsend had to give the half-time team talk such was Jack's state of weariness and consequent lack of motivation.

The influx of new blood had created problems for the manager. McAteer and Babb had gone straight into the team, without what Charlton considered the necessary 'schooling' in the Under-21s or the B team. With these players, and with Gary Kelly, Jack became aware for the first time of a generation gap which prompted doubts about his ability to get his message across to the Three Amigos.

He was also having doubts about the effectiveness of his message after eight years. There was a danger that the players might be taking him for granted after hearing the same thing so often.

Unfortunately, in harbouring doubts, Charlton's hitherto clear focus became blurred. Throughout 1995, he made a number of bad decisions, all of which affected the team, and it was the culmination of these, plus a breakdown in team discipline, which ultimately cost him his job.

There was no hint of these problems in September 1994 when the return of Niall Quinn provided a huge boost for the opening European Championship game away to Latvia. Charlton opted for a 4-4-2 formation, with Aldridge as Quinn's striking partner and Alan Kelly taking over in goal from Bonner. Gary Kelly and Irwin manned the full-back berths.

The competition for places in midfield was eased by a succession of injuries to Keane and the relegation of Houghton to the subs' bench. McAteer was

Charlton's choice for Houghton's role, with Sheridan, Townsend and Staunton retaining the other midfield places.

An impressive 3–0 win over Latvia in Riga and the less impressive 4–0 defeat of Liechtenstein at Lansdowne Road, were overshadowed by the 4–0 trouncing of Northern Ireland in Belfast, the first time the Republic had won there. Significantly, Keane was back for the game in Belfast and was placed on the right wing at the expense of McAteer who hadn't impressed in the first two games. Keane scored his first goal for Ireland before limping off with hamstring trouble just before half-time, at which stage the Republic were 3–0 up. It was a display which revealed the Republic in all their might, and Northern Ireland as a team going nowhere. Yet later results indicate that it was the North's manager, Bryan Hamilton, who learned most that night as he re-shaped his team into contenders by the end of the campaign.

Apart from the Republic, the top teams in Group Six were Portugal and Austria but, for once, Charlton did not get his way at the fixtures meeting. Instead of getting the tough games in Austria and Portugal out of the way early in the campaign, they were scheduled for September and November 1995, respectively, while the home game against Austria was ominously listed for June – 25 years after their previous visit, which had ended in an ignominious 4-1 defeat and had had repercussions at managerial level.

After a B international at Anfield on 13 December 1994, which England won 2–0, Charlton and England manager Terry Venables came up with what seemed a good idea. England would visit Dublin on 15 February 1995. It would be ideal preparation for the Republic's return game with Northern Ireland in March, and would also be a good test of England's travelling fans in the run-up to the Euro finals. Only 2,000 tickets were made available to the English FA, to be distributed to members of their travel club. The FAI, in acknowledgement of the peace process and confident there would be no repeat of the aggro displayed on England's last visit, decided on a scaled-down security presence.

The FAI's optimism proved sadly unfounded as 300 or so thugs, who had somehow secured seats in the West Stand upper deck, proceeded to wreak havoc when, after a bright opening, Ireland took the lead with a well-worked David Kelly goal. As the thugs went to work, tearing the wooden seats from their mountings and throwing them down on top of helpless fans in the lower deck, the Garda response was slow to materialise. As the Irish fans watched in bewilderment before filing out quietly when referee Jol of Holland abandoned the game after 27 minutes, the thugs revelled in their new status as the centre of attention.

It was not until the ground was cleared of all but English fans, a handful of pressmen and the camera crews of Sky News and RTE, that the Gardai moved in, beating the thugs into submission and making a number of arrests. It was over so quickly one wondered why it had not been done much earlier.

It was a sad and sorry start to 1995 for Charlton, seeing his fellow countrymen disgrace themselves on a visit to his adopted country where he had always been treated royally. For him, football had always been a game to be enjoyed; unfortunately, some Englishmen preferred to see it as an occasion to do battle.

For the FAI, it was a case of heads down and hope the flak stops flying, as the board left it to Chief Executive Sean Connolly to face the media. Fortunately, in Connolly they had someone who was camera friendly, and whose utterances were given with a sincerity which could not be matched by any of his masters. The irony of this was not revealed until 12 months later when Connolly, the saviour of the FAI's tattered reputation following the riots, was dismissed in an upheaval which saw Bernard O'Byrne, Head of Security that infamous day, elevated into his place. Not one FAI head rolled for the incompetence displayed over the England game when fans' lives were put at risk, yet 12 months later, allegations of monetary losses over ticket sales at the 1990 and 1994 World Cup finals led to the removal of the President Louis Kilcoyne and Treasurer Joe Delaney.

Security was once again an issue with the visit of Northern Ireland in March but this time the FAI got it right. Unfortunately, the players – or more particularly McGrath – got it wrong, his crossfield pass being intercepted by Keith Gillespie who set up an equaliser for Iain Dowie.

McGrath's error was a replica of the many giveaway goals which scuppered Giles' and Hand's hopes in the past but which had been eliminated up to then by Charlton. It was all the more unnecessary as Northern Ireland's only ambition was to avoid another trouncing. Even when they went a goal down they still defended *en masse* and the clearance which reached McGrath was typical of the many aimless kicks which their harassed defenders booted out straight to the home side.

Parity induced another bout of caution in Charlton and, instead of going for the win, he replaced striker David Kelly with winger McAteer, moving Keane into the centre, to make sure of the point. With three points for a win, it did not make sense. Neither did Charlton's rudeness to RTE's Ger Canning when approached for the usual after-match interview. Charlton, usually dignified in the face of setbacks, was fraying at the edges.

There was no Keane for the home game with Portugal in April, but Charlton, who recalled Houghton and Aldridge, had done his homework on the visitors. His instructions were spot on and helped the defence weather a stormy opening 20 minutes.

The game was one of the more enjoyable at Lansdowne Road during Charlton's reign, because the Portuguese came for a win. The score could have been 3–3 but, in the end, it was decided by a freak goal. Staunton, proving his value yet again, crossed low from the left and goalkeeper Vitor Baia, unsettled by the presence of Aldridge, allowed the ball to twist under his body and over the line.

Gary Kelly's display at right-back was particularly eye-catching in an all-star show. He used his pace to devastating effect in attack and defence and gave a performance *par excellence*. Above all, the game was a triumph for the Charlton system but, even as he basked in the glow of victory, the manager warned: 'It's up to us now not to let our standards drop [for the games against Liechtenstein and Austria]. If we keep up our commitment, then the fact that we have better players will show and we can win both games.'

Some people are prescient. While the media were talking about the 3 June game with Liechtenstein in terms of a goal feast, McGrath spoke about how, for a footballer, a 'dream' tie is often a nightmare waiting to happen!

It was three weeks after the end of the season and midfield dynamos Keane and Townsend were injured – not the ideal situation, but then Liechtenstein were amateurs, everyone else had taken them to the cleaners, so the result had to be a formality. It might have been if Quinn and Aldridge had been on their game, but they missed early chances and home goalkeeper Martin Heeb had an inspired day. To compound matters, Charlton was in an uninspired mood.

'There's nothing I can do for you,' he told the players at half-time. 'You'll have to work this one out for yourselves.'

Charlton, whose leadership had brought Ireland to unprecedented heights in the previous nine years, had abdicated once again in the face of a crisis, but in Liechtenstein of all places! It was the low point of his reign and the beginning of the end. Regaining the players' confidence would not be easy.

Left to themselves, the players kept firing in high balls to the off-form Quinn and Aldridge, and even the introduction of Cascarino for Quinn did nothing to improve matters. Tactically, it was a disaster for Charlton, but why pass-masters Sheridan and Whelan did not display more initiative is also astonishing. After the high of the Portugal game, this was one time when no one in the Irish camp could take any credit.

History was waiting to repeat itself when the Republic prepared for the visit of Austria on 11 June. Charlton's blunders continued. For a start, he ignored the advice of the FAI and insisted on taking a party of 24 players to Limerick for a week-long preparation. The choice of venue was Charlton's way of saying 'thank you' for the honorary doctorate conferred on him by the University of Limerick, but it was a decision which had no merit in footballing terms.

With almost half of the 24 players aware that they would not figure against Austria, the seeds were sown for disruption. When Charlton went to Belfast to see Northern Ireland's game with Latvia and was missing for two to three days, the party really took off. Charlton had written in his *World Cup Diary*: 'I've been long enough in this business to know that when the No 1 is away, the players are tempted to take things a little easier than they would normally do.' He was referring to training but, in Limerick, it was the discipline which broke down, with late-night drinking and visits to nightclubs.

With Charlton away and Setters on Under-21 business in Dublin, the ludicrous situation arose where Charlton's son John was in charge for a friendly with a local XI. Irwin probably expressed the feelings of his team-mates when he said that he should be lying on a beach rather than playing football. Charlton had his own doubts about the wisdom of the Austrian fixture and confided to journalists that if ever he could call a game off, this would be it. Unfortunately, despite being aware of the pitfalls, he did nothing to lessen the damage.

The original plan was for the players to move to the upmarket Kilkea Castle Hotel the night before the game, but Charlton changed that plan. Instead, the players were brought to the Harry Ramsden fish and chip shop on the Naas Road – in which Charlton had taken a stake – before spending the night in the Airport Hotel. It was a farcical ending to the most shambolic week's preparation the team had endured under Charlton.

In light of the disciplinary infractions in Limerick, it was hardly surprising that a breakdown of discipline on the pitch should contribute to the shock 3–1 defeat by Austria. After much huffing and puffing, Houghton finally opened the scoring in the 65th minute. Then, asked to defend the lead, the hitherto impregnable Irish defence fell apart. With German referee Merk a central figure, goals were conceded through hesitancy on the part of Irwin and Whelan and poor man-marking of a free-kick, with 5ft 9in Gary Kelly the nearest defender to 6ft plus scorer Toni Polster.

Charlton had contributed to his own problems by his insistence on starting Staunton. The Aston Villa player, nursing a thigh strain, did not want to play but allowed Charlton to change his mind. He lasted only 45 minutes, being replaced by Jeff Kenna, who was asked to play out of position.

The return of Keane and Townsend offered hope for the visit to Vienna in September. Unfortunately, the breakdown of discipline continued unabated on the pitch and led to the first back-to-back defeats under Charlton. Despite the manager's warning to the players against attacking like headless chickens, that is precisely what they proceeded to do. Central to this was Keane, who had been delegated to play the defensive role in front of the back four. Instead of following orders, he was seen more often in the Austrian half than shoring up the Irish defence.

The defensive limitations of full-backs Irwin and Gary Kelly were once again revealed. The first goal stemmed from a ball played in behind Irwin, with the subsequent cross finished off by Stoger, the winger Kelly was delegated to mark. Stoger's hat-trick settled the game in Austria's favour, with the Republic's response confined to a McGrath header.

Now playing for the runner-up spot, the home game with Latvia in October assumed critical importance, yet the message had not got through to some of the players. The night before the game, an FAI official returned from the Under-21 game in Galway to be greeted by the sight of Gary Kelly and one or two others sailing into the team hotel at one o'clock in the morning. Charlton was away and once again discipline had broken down.

It was just as well Latvia were providing the opposition. Even so they were a difficult nut to crack. The recalled Aldridge eventually proved to be their nemesis with goals from the penalty spot and following a free-kick, both laid on by Staunton's impeccable left foot.

The trip to Portugal in November with an understrength team was essentially a damage limitation exercise, with the hope that Northern Ireland would do the Republic a favour by beating Austria. Northern Ireland obliged with an impressive 5–3 win, while the Republic held out for an hour before collapsing to a 3–0 defeat in extremely wet conditions. The upshot was a play-off with old rivals Holland at Anfield on 13 December to secure the last place in the finals.

When it came to naming his team for the play-off, Charlton was beset with problems. Quinn was suspended, Keane and Staunton were injured, while Sheridan was only just back from injury. On the plus side, Anfield conferred a distinct advantage as it was the nearest thing to a home game. However, in weighing up the pros and cons, Charlton again came down heavily on the side of caution. He later admitted that he had given the Dutch 'too much respect', but by then it was too late. Holland were preparing for the finals and Charlton's final team – a lopsided affair featuring four full-backs – had been consigned to history.

In many respects, the play-off game proved a fitting end to the Charlton era. The players displayed tremendous character in keeping the game alive for so long, despite being 'beaten for pace in every position' as Cascarino admitted. In the end, it was the individual brilliance of 19-year-old Patrick Kluivert which separated the sides. He scored after 30 and 88 minutes while, in between, the Irish fought a gallant rearguard action.

Once again, thanks to the fans, it was a wonderful night. The atmosphere of cordiality and good humour which united both sets of supporters had Euro '96 officials purring with delight, for they regarded this game as a trial run for the finals. The warmth of the crowd's applause for Charlton when he took a post-match standing ovation was also very moving and showed how appreciative the fans were of all the big Englishman had done for Irish football.

In contrast, Charlton, normally dignified in defeat, acted churlishly at the press conference, leaving abruptly when questioned on tactics, Derek Dougan, the former Northern Ireland player, who was present, was taken aback by the Irish manager's action. 'He was like a big child,' he commented.

The FAI, who had expected Charlton to confirm his retirement after the game, as agreed beforehand, were taken aback when there was no word from the manager. The day before the Anfield game the draw for the '98 World Cup qualifiers had been made and the Republic had been dealt a very favourable hand. Charlton had noted this with interest, and was now hedging his bets.

However, while speculation linked a variety of top names with the job, the FAI finally lost patience with Charlton. In a dramatic intervention on Sunday, 17 December, Treasurer Joe Delaney informed Network 2, prior to the screening of a documentary on 'The Charlton Years', that if the manager did not make an announcement about his future before 1 January, then the FAI would have to make one for him. From that moment on, the game was up.

Charlton's prevaricating, which had begun at Anfield and appeared to have a closing date of late January, was well and truly scuttled. A phone call from President Louis Kilcoyne followed, insisting that the manager travel to Dublin. The FAI Officer Board of Kilcoyne, Delaney, Pat Quigley, Des Casey and Michael Hyland were unanimous in their view that the Charlton era had run its course and that the manager should retire.

Charlton's original intention had been to announce his plans as soon as Ireland qualified for Euro '96. He would have travelled to England and quit after the finals. When hopes of qualification faded, he agreed to make his announcement after the Portugal or Anfield games. The favourable '98 World Cup draw had caused him to have second thoughts; and the fans' acclaim after the Anfield defeat must have convinced him that he had many faithful allies if he chose to remain.

However, by the time he arrived in Dublin on Thursday, 21 December, for his meeting with the FAI, it appears he had already made up his mind to resign. The meeting was a little emotional – for both sides. At one stage Charlton asked each of the four officers present – Casey was missing – if they wanted him to go. The answer in each case was yes, it is time for a change. Once this had been settled, the relief on both sides was palpable. For Charlton the stress which he had felt in the job over the previous six months was lifted and life could return to normal. For the FAI, it was a relief to know that they could now go about appointing a successor.

Charlton had not made it easy for the officers, but they had held their nerve. In Paul Rowan's book *The Team That Jack Built*[1], Charlton had spoken about the Irish attitude to heroes: 'With Ireland, you see, they don't give up their f***ing heroes easily, so you've got to show them.' He was referring to Brady and Stapleton, but now the boot was on the other foot and, fair play to the FAI, they showed them!

In the wake of his resignation, tributes flooded in from high and low, from the President Mary Robinson and members of the government to the ordinary supporter. One of the most interesting was that penned by Charlton's former team-mate, Giles.

'Irish international football needed the drive and single-mindedness of a Jack Charlton', he wrote. 'It needed his cussed determination to get results. But in the pursuit of success something eroded.

'Jack's Ireland did a superb, indeed unprecedented job in reaching the big stages of international football, but there has to be some question marks about the football they displayed when they actually trod those exclusive boards.

'There were times I would like to have seen a brand of football that could have been more easily identified as Irish, football catering for the individual strengths of players, football which lived comfortably with the kind of flair which the likes of Carey and Brady brought to the international field.'

Giles's was a common complaint about the Charlton era usually articulated

[1] Mainstream, 1994

212

by people who were steeped in Irish football from birth. However, it did not pay enough attention to the facts. It appeared to draw its inspiration from a mythical 'beautiful game' (prototype Brazil 1970) which has never been part of Irish football and which, when attempted, has inevitably ended in failure.

Charlton, being a pragmatist, adopted a style of play which made the most of the players he inherited. He qualified for three finals from five campaigns and it is interesting to note that the best football – from a purist's point of view – was played in the two campaigns in which he failed: Euro '92 and Euro '96. Mind you, they also included some of the worst football of his era. To say that, on reaching the finals stage, the team displayed no flair is to ignore two of the finest displays ever given by an Irish team – against the Soviet Union in 1988 and against Italy in 1994. Italia '90 was a different kettle of fish.

However, Charlton's main success was in raising the profile of the game within the Republic of Ireland. The numbers of children playing football rocketed; international games became sell-outs; sponsors, who before had ignored the sport, flocked to the FAI which, as a result, enjoyed hitherto undreamed of wealth.

Charlton's legacy, apart from being a hard act to follow, was a new respect on the international stage for the Republic of Ireland, and a wider net of home-based talent for future Irish teams. Where before Dublin boys dominated Under-15 to Under-18 selections, now there are boys from Wexford, Kerry, Donegal, Galway and Meath, apart from the other traditional strongholds of Cork, Waterford, Limerick, Sligo and Dundalk.

The purists may argue all they like about the negative aspects of the Charlton era, but the positives far outweigh them, as time will undoubtedly tell.

22

McCarthy Learns the Ropes

The difficult task of succeeding the legend that Jack Charlton had become fell to Mick McCarthy – and the first 18 months of his tenure in office were marked by farce, frustration and some fine football.

McCarthy had made no secret of his desire to succeed Charlton but, when the opportunity arose, his career as Millwall manager, which had been full of promise, was in a tailspin (a long run without a win ultimately saw them relegated after his departure). His rivals for the position were Kevin Moran, Joe Kinnear, who was enjoying success with Wimbledon, Dave Bassett and Mike Walker.

Once Kinnear opted out – he had unfinished business with the Dons and wasn't prepared to be a full-time international manager – the job rested between McCarthy and Moran, with McCarthy getting it on a 3–2 vote, but not before the farcical situation arose where the interview location was leaked to the media and the applicants had to run the gauntlet of TV crews before and after their interviews.

Moran's lack of managerial experience didn't help his cause, while McCarthy's early days in the job weren't helped by the frank admission of FAI President Louis Kilcoyne that McCarthy hadn't been his choice. However, the new manager had little to fear from that direction as Kilcoyne and Treasurer Joe Delaney were ousted from office shortly after.

Apart from the circumstances of his appointment and the difficulty of replacing a legend, McCarthy inherited a squad, which included some of those who had let their country down during the Euro '96 qualifiers with their lack of discipline. He also brought some of his own past to the job in the form of his previous incarnation as Charlton's enforcer. He had a bridge to heal with Roy Keane whom he had taken to task in Boston in the summer of 1992 when Keane and Moran delayed the team bus on its departure for the airport. While Charlton had tackled Moran, McCarthy had laid into Keane – and the young Corkman wasn't impressed with the verbal tongue-lashing he had to endure.

As evidence of his goodwill, McCarthy installed Keane as captain for his first game in charge – against Russia in March 1996 – but Keane spoiled the occasion by being sent off minutes before the end of a 2–0 defeat for aiming a kick at a defender in retaliation.

With a difficult series of friendlies lined up before the World Cup campaign began on 31 August, McCarthy's belief in his preferred 3-5-2 formation was sorely tested as one defeat followed another. However, a 2–0 defeat in Prague to European finalists Czech Republic offered hope, the first half display being particularly eye-catching.

Frustratingly, the lessons learned were not easy to apply, as many of the senior members were unavailable for the close season US Cup tournament. As a result, young players like Ken Cunningham, Ian Harte, Keith O'Neill and David Connolly were given the chance to make their mark, while Alan McLoughlin, often overlooked by Charlton, was the star of the show in midfield in the absence of Keane, Townsend and Houghton. Keane's absence was another farcical situation which McCarthy could have done without. Appointed captain for the US trip, he failed to make contact with the manager, thus precipitating a summer-long saga in which his commitment to the Irish cause was widely questioned in the media and among the fans.

McCarthy, minus Keane, got a gentle introduction to the World Cup with a 5–0 win in Liechtenstein and a 3–0 home win over Macedonia. On Keane's return, for the home game with Iceland, McCarthy played into the visitors' hands by including the Manchester United midfielder in defence. It was one of a number of self-inflicted wounds on the part of the manager. The result against Iceland, a 0–0 draw, effectively left the Republic battling for second place in a group which was proving easy meat for Romania.

By using Denis Irwin and Steve Staunton as centre-backs, McCarthy not only picked them out of position but also weakened his hand when it came to set–piece situations around the opposing goal. For frees and corner kicks, Irwin and Staunton had proved their worth but, in McCarthy's line up, they remained isolated at the back when these opportunities arose. That was all right when games were being won without difficulty, but it didn't make sense for the bigger tests ahead.

A friendly against Wales in Cardiff proved Paul McGrath's swansong in the green jersey. He was his usual masterful self in a 0–0 draw, but less encouraging were the performances of players like wing-backs Jason McAteer and Terry Phelan, and midfielder Roy Keane, three players in whom McCarthy put great faith. McAteer lacked the defensive qualities necessary for this role – as Kiriakov amply illustrated in the Russian game – and, being almost totally right–footed, he didn't have enough tricks in his bag to cause problems for international defenders. Phelan was all right as a man–marker but he lacked the ability to pass or cross the ball with any great degree of accuracy. Keane's play-safe game added nothing creative to the Irish attacking effort. McCarthy paid a terrible price for his misguided faith in McAteer and Phelan when the World Cup resumed with the return game against Macedonia in Skopje. The wing–backs were a disaster, each of them conceded a penalty and, in the dying minutes of the game, McAteer was sent off for 'violent conduct'. FIFA subsequently banned him for three World Cup games.

The 3–2 defeat by Macedonia, after a bright start which had yielded an eighth minute goal by McLoughlin, was a bitter blow to McCarthy, who decided to re-shape his team to a 4-5-1 formation for the 30 April trip to Romania. Cunningham and Harte took over at centre–back, with Irwin and Staunton restored to full-back duties, while Gary Kelly returned to favour on the right wing in place of the suspended McAteer. Mark Kennedy got his chance on the left wing, but the most significant changes involved two players returning from injury – Ray Houghton, who took over from the suspended McLoughlin, and David Connolly, whose inclusion after a season of injuries and mainly reserve football was a gamble by McCarthy.

In a fighting display of great promise and some slick football, Ireland, after going a goal down after 33 minutes, had a chance to save the game when Connolly released Houghton through the middle. He was taken down by goalkeeper Stelea who then redeemed himself by saving Keane's penalty kick. Romania held on to win 1–0 and confirm their status as the top team in Group Eight.

By a strange twist of fate, McCarthy's problems were then very similar to those encountered by Charlton ten years earlier. There was a need for a right–sided attacker and another striker. In Connolly, McCarthy had unearthed a little gem – provided he could stay clear of injury – but he needed someone alongside him and Cascarino and Quinn were not getting any younger.

The right wing has been a perennial problem for Ireland because English clubs tend to target left-sided players when they scout in the Republic. As a result, there was no shortage of candidates for the left-wing role. The right-footed players were generally full-backs who were uncomfortable receiving the ball with their backs to goal and didn't possess the pace or inventiveness necessary to open up defences.

Although the jury was still out on McCarthy, the FAI decided to give him a vote of confidence. After the facile 5–0 home win over Liechtenstein on 21 May, which restored the Republic to second place in Group Eight, it was announced that agreement had been reached on an extension of the manager's contract to the year 2000.

As an international manager, McCarthy still has a lot to learn, but he has shown a refreshing willingness to place his trust in young players. Along with the appointments of Ian Evans as Under–21 manager and Brian Kerr as Under-16 and Under-18 boss, the future of the Republic of Ireland gives promise of exciting days ahead.

The Games

1926
21 March Turin v Italy (0-3)

1927
23 April Dublin v Italy (1-2)

1928
12 February Liege v Belgium (4-2)

1929
20 April Dublin v Belgium (4-0)

1930
11 May Brussels v Belgium (3-1)

1931
26 April Barcelona v Spain (1-1)
13 December Dublin v Spain (0-5)

1932
8 May Amsterdam v Holland (2-0)

1934
25 February Dublin v Belgium (4-4), WC
8 April Amsterdam v Holland (2-5), WC
16 December Dublin v Hungary (2-4)

1935
5 May Basle v Switzerland (0-1)
8 May Dortmund v Germany (1-3)
8 December Dublin v Holland (3-5)

1936
17 March Dublin v Switzerland (1-0)
3 May Budapest v Hungary (3-3)
9 May Luxembourg v Luxembourg (5-1)
17 October Dublin v Germany (5-2)
6 December Dublin v Hungary (2-3)

1937
17 May Berne v Swtizerland (1-0)
23 May Paris v France (2-0)
10 October Oslo v Norway (2-3), WC
7 November Dublin v Norway (3-3), WC

1938
18 May Prague v Czechoslovakia (2-2)
22 May Warsaw v Poland (0-6)
18 September Dublin v Switzerland (4-0)
13 November Dublin v Poland (3-2)

1939
19 March Cork v Hungary (2-2)

18 May Budapest v Hungary (2-2)
23 May Bremen v Germany (1-1)

1946
16 June Lisbon v Portugal (1-3)
23 June Madrid v Spain (1-0)
30 September Dublin v England (0-1)

1947
2 March Dublin v Spain (3-2)
4 May Dublin v Portugal (0-2)

1948
23 May Lisbon v Portugal (0-2)
30 May Barcelona v Spain (1-2)
5 December Dublin v Switzerland (0-1)

1949
24 April Dublin v Belgium (0-2)
22 May Dublin v Portugal (1-0)
2 June Stockholm v Sweden (1-3), WC
12 June Dublin v Spain (1-4)
8 September Dublin v Finland (3-0), WC
21 September Liverpool v England (2-0)
9 October Helsinki v Finland (1-1), WC
13 November Dublin v Sweden (1-3), WC

1950
10 May Brussels v Belgium (1-5)
26 November Dublin v Norway (2-2)

1951
13 May Dublin v Argentina (0-1)
30 May Oslo v Norway (3-2)
17 October Dublin v West Germany (3-2)

1952
4 May Cologne v West Germany (0-3)
7 May Vienna v Austria (0-6)
1 June Madrid v Spain (0-6)
16 November Dublin v France (1-1)

1953
25 March Dublin v Austria (4-0)
4 October Dublin v France (3-5), WC
28 October Dublin v Luxembourg (4-0), WC
25 November Paris v France (0-1), WC

1954
7 March Luxembourg v Luxembourg (1-0), WC
7 November Dublin v Norway (2-1)

217

1955
1 May Dublin v Holland (1-0)
25 May Oslo v Norway (3-1)
28 May Hamburg v West Germany (1-2)
19 October Dublin v Yugoslavia (1-4)
27 November Dublin v Spain (2-2)

1956
10 May Rotterdam v Holland (4-1)
3 October Dublin v Denmark (2-1), WC
25 November Dublin v West Germany (3-0)

1957
8 May London v England (1-5), WC
19 May Dublin v England (1-1), WC
2 October Copenhagen v Denmark (2-0), WC

1958
11 May Katowice v Poland (2-2)
14 May Vienna v Austria (1-3)
5 October Dublin v Poland (2-2)

1959
5 April Dublin v Czechoslovakia (2-0), EC
10 May Bratislava v Czechoslovakia (0-4), EC
1 November Dublin v Sweden (3-2)

1960
30 March Dublin v Chile (2-0)
11 May Dusseldorf v West Germany (1-0)
18 May Malmo v Sweden (1-4)
28 September Dublin v Wales (2-3)
6 November Dublin v Norway (3-1)

1961
3 May Glasgow v Scotland (1-4), WC
7 May Dublin v Scotland (0-1), WC
8 October Dublin v Czechoslovakia (1-3), WC
29 October Prague v Czechoslovakia (1-7), WC

1962
8 April Dublin v Austria (2-3)
12 August Dublin v Iceland (4-2), EC
2 September Reykjavik v Iceland (1-1), EC

1963
9 June Dublin v Scotland (1-0)
25 September Vienna v Austria (0-0), EC
13 October Dublin v Austria (3-2), EC

1964
11 March Seville v Spain (1-5), EC
8 April Dublin v Spain (0-2), EC
10 May Kracow v Poland (1-3)
13 May Oslo v Norway (4-1)
24 May Dublin v England (1-3)
25 October Dublin v Poland (3-2)

1965
24 March Dublin v Belgium (0-2)
5 May Dublin v Spain (1-0), WC
27 October Seville v Spain (1-4), WC

10 November Paris v Spain (0-1), WC

1966
4 May Dublin v West Germany (0-4)
22 May Vienna v Austria (0-1)
25 May Liege v Belgium (3-2)
23 October Dublin v Spain (0-0), EC
16 November Dublin v Turkey (2-1), EC
7 December Valencia v Spain (0-2), EC

1967
22 February Ankara v Turkey (1-2), EC
21 May Dublin v Czechoslovakia (0-2), EC
22 November Prague v Czechoslovakia (2-1), EC

1968
15 May Dublin v Poland (2-2)
30 October Katowice v Poland (0-1)
10 November Dublin v Austria (2-2)
4 December Dublin v Denmark (1-1, abandoned
51 mins), WC

1969
4 May Dublin v Czechoslovakia (1-2), WC
27 May Copenhagen v Denmark (0-2), WC
8 June Dublin v Hungary (0-2), WC
21 September Dublin v Scotland (1-0)
7 October Prague v Czechoslovakia (0-3), WC
15 October Dublin v Denmark (1-1), WC
5 November Budapest v Hungary (0-4), WC

1970
6 May Poznan v Poland (1-2)
9 May Berlin v West Germany (1-2)
23 September Dublin v Poland (0-2)
14 October Dublin v Sweden (1-1), EC
28 October Malmo v Sweden (0-1), EC
8 December Florence v Italy (0-3), EC

1971
10 May Dublin v Italy (1-2), EC
30 May Dublin v Austria (1-4), EC
10 October Linz v Austria (0-6), EC

1972
11 June Recife v Iran (2-1)
18 June Natal v Ecuador (3-2)
21 June Recife v Chile (1-2)
25 June Recife v Portugal (1-2)
18 October Dublin v Soviet Union (1-2), WC
15 November Dublin v France (2-1), WC

1973
13 May Moscow v Soviet Union (0-1), WC
16 May Wroclaw v Poland (0-2)
19 May Paris v France (1-1), WC
6 June Oslo v Norway (1-1)
21 October Dublin v Poland (1-0)

1974
5 May Rio de Janeiro v Brazil (1-2)
8 May Montevideo v Uruguay (0-2)

12 May Santiago v Chile (2-1)
30 October Dublin v Soviet Union (3-0), EC
20 November Izmir v Turkey (1-1), EC

1975
11 March Dublin v West Germany B (1-0)
10 May Dublin v Switzerland (2-1), EC
18 May Kiev v Soviet Union (1-2), EC
21 May Berne v Switzerland (0-1), EC
29 October Dublin v Turkey (4-0), EC

1976
24 March Dublin v Norway (3-0)
26 May Poznan v Poland (2-0)
8 September London v England (1-1)
13 October Ankara v Turkey (3-3)
17 November Paris v France (0-2), WC

1977
9 February Dublin v Spain (0-1)
30 March Dublin v France (1-0), WC
24 April Dublin v Poland (0-0)
1 June Sofia v Bulgaria (1-2), WC
12 October Dublin v Bulgaria (0-0), WC

1978
5 April Dublin v Turkey (4-2)
12 April Lodz v Poland (0-3)
21 May Oslo v Norway (0-0)
24 May Copenhagen v Denmark (3-3), EC
20 September Dublin v Northern Ireland (0-0), EC
25 October Dublin v England (1-1), EC

1979
2 May Dublin v Denmark (2-0), EC
19 May Sofia v Bulgaria (0-1), EC
22 May Dublin v West Germany (1-3)
11 September Swansea v Wales (1-2)
26 September Prague v Czechoslovakia (1-4)
17 October Dublin v Bulgaria (3-0), EC
29 October Dublin v USA (3-2)
21 November Belfast v Northern Ireland (0-1), EC

1980
6 February London v England (0-2), EC
26 March Nicosia v Cyprus (3-2), WC
30 April Dublin v Switzerland (2-0)
16 May Dublin v Argentina (0-1)
10 September Dublin v Holland (2-1), WC
15 October Dublin v Belgium (1-1), WC
28 October Paris v France (0-2), WC
19 November Dublin v Cyprus (6-0), WC

1981
24 February Dublin v Wales (1-3)
25 March Brussels v Belgium (0-1), WC
29 April Dublin v Czechoslovakia (3-1)
21 May Bremen v West Germany B (0-3)
24 May Bydgoszcz v Poland (0-3)
9 September Rotterdam v Holland (2-2), WC
14 October Dublin v France (3-2), WC

1982
28 April Algiers v Algeria (0-2)
21 May Santiago v Chile (0-1)
27 May Uberlandia v Brazil (0-7)
30 May Port of Spain v Trinidad & Tobago (1-2)
22 September Rotterdam v Holland (1-2), EC
17 November Dublin v Spain (3-3), EC

1983
30 March Valetta v Malta (1-0), EC
27 April Zaragoza v Spain (0-2), EC
21 September Reykjavik v Iceland (3-0), EC
12 October Dublin v Holland (2-3), EC
16 November Dublin v Malta (8-0), EC

1984
4 April Tel Aviv v Israel (0-3)
23 May Dublin v Poland (0-0)
3 June Sapporo v China (1-0)
8 August Dublin v Mexico (0-0)
12 September Dublin v Soviet Union (1-0), WC
17 October Oslo v Norway (0-1), WC
14 November Copenhagen v Denmark (0-3), WC

1985
5 February Dublin v Italy (1-2)
27 February Tel Aviv v Israel (0-0)
26 March London v England (1-2)
1 May Dublin v Norway (0-0), WC
26 May Cork v Spain (0-0)
2 June Dublin v Switzerland (3-0), WC
11 September Berne v Switzerland (0-0), WC
16 October Moscow v Soviet Union (0-2), WC
13 November Dublin v Denmark (1-4), WC

1986
26 March Dublin v Wales (0-1)
23 April Dublin v Uruguay (1-1)
25 May Reykjavik v Iceland (2-1)
27 May Reykjavik v Czechoslovakia (1-0)
10 September Brussels v Belgium (2-2), EC
15 October Dublin v Scotland (0-0), EC
12 November Warsaw v Poland (0-1)

1987
18 February Glasgow v Scotland (1-0), EC
1 April Sofia v Bulgaria (1-2), EC
29 April Dublin v Belgium (0-0), EC
23 May Dublin v Brazil (1-0)
28 May Luxembourg v Luxembourg (2-0), EC
9 September Dublin v Luxembourg (2-1), EC
14 October Dublin v Bulgaria (2-0), EC
10 November Dublin v Israel (5-0)

1988
23 March Dublin v Romania (2-0)
27 April Dublin v Yugoslavia (2-0)
22 May Dublin v Poland (3-1)
1 June Oslo v Norway (0-0)
12 June Stuttgart v England (1-0), ECF
15 June Hanover v Soviet Union (1-1), ECF
18 June Gelsenkirchen v Holland (0-1), ECF

14 September Belfast v Northern Ireland (0-0), WC
19 October Dublin v Tunisia (4-0)
16 November Seville v Spain (0-2), WC

1989
 7 February Dublin v France (0-0)
 8 March Budapest v Hungary (0-0), WC
26 April Dublin v Spain (1-0), WC
28 May Dublin v Malta (2-0), WC
 4 June Dublin v Hungary (2-0), WC
 6 September Dublin v West Germany (1-1)
11 October Dublin v Northern Ireland (3-0), WC
15 November Valetta v Malta (2-0), WC

1990
28 March Dublin v Wales (1-0)
25 April Dublin v Soviet Union (1-0)
16 May Dublin v Finland (1-1)
27 May Izmir v Turkey (0-0)
 2 June Valetta v Malta (3-0)
11 June Cagliari v England (1-1), WCF
17 June Palermo v Egypt (0-0), WCF
21 June Palermo v Holland (1-1), WCF
25 June Genoa v Romania (0-0, 5-4 pens), WCF
30 June Rome v Italy (0-1), WCF
12 September Dublin v Morocco (1-0)
17 October Dublin v Turkey (5-0), EC
14 November Dublin v England (1-1), EC

1991
 6 February Wrexham v Wales (3-0)
27 March London v England (1-1), EC
 1 May Dublin v Poland (0-0), EC
22 May Dublin v Chile (1-1)
 1 June Boston v USA (1-1)
11 September Gyor v Hungary (2-1)
16 October Poznan v Poland (3-3), EC
13 November Istanbul v Turkey (3-1), EC

1992
19 February Dublin v Wales (0-1)
25 March Dublin v Switzerland (2-1)
29 April Dublin v USA (4-1)
26 May Dublin v Albania (2-0), WC
30 May Washington v USA (1-3)
 4 June Boston v Italy (0-2)
 7 June Boston v Portugal (2-0)
 9 September Dublin v Latvia (4-0), WC
14 October Copenhagen v Denmark (0-0), WC
18 November Seville v Spain (0-0), WC

1993
17 February Dublin v Wales (2-1)
31 March Dublin v Northern Ireland (3-0), WC
28 April Dublin v Denmark (1-1), WC
26 May Tirana v Albania (2-1), WC
 9 June Riga v Latvia (2-0), WC
16 June Vilnius v Lithuania (1-0), WC
 8 September Dublin v Lithuania (2-0), WC
13 October Dublin v Spain (1-3), WC
17 November Belfast v Northern Ireland (1-1), WC

1994
23 March Dublin v Russia (0-0)
20 April Tilburg v Holland (1-0)
24 May Dublin v Bolivia (1-0)
29 May Hanover v Germany (2-0)
 5 June Dublin v Czech Republic (1-3)
18 June New Jersey v Italy (1-0), WCF
24 June Orlando v Mexico (1-2), WCF
28 June New Jersey v Norway (0-0), WCF
 4 July Orlando v Holland (0-2), WCF
 7 September Riga v Latvia (3-0), EC
12 October Dublin v Liechtenstein (4-0), EC
16 November Belfast v Northern Ireland (4-0), EC

1995
15 February Dublin v England (1-0, abandoned 27 mins)
29 March Dublin v Northern Ireland (1-1), EC
26 April Dublin v Portugal (1-0), EC
 3 June Eschen v Liechtenstein (0-0), EC
11 June Dublin v Austria (1-3), EC
 6 September Vienna v Austria (1-3), EC
11 October Dublin v Latvia (2-0), EC
15 November Lisbon v Portugal (0-3), EC
13 December Liverpool v Holland (0-2), EC

1996
27 March Dublin v Russia (0-2)
24 April Prague v Czech Republic (0-2)
29 May Dublin v Portugal (0-1)
 2 June Dublin v Croatia (2-2)
 4 June Rotterdam v Holland (1-3)
 9 June Boston v USA (1-2)
12 June New Jersey v Mexico (2-2)
15 June New Jersey v Bolivia (3-0)
31 August Eschen v Liechtenstein (5-0), WC
 9 October Dublin v FYR Macedonia (3-0), WC
10 November Dublin v Iceland (0-0), WC

1997
11 February Cardiff v Wales (0-0)
 2 April Skopje v FYR Macedonia (2-3), WC
30 April Bucharest v Romania (0-1), WC
21 May Dublin v Liechtenstein (5-0), WC

Abbreviations: WC World Cup; WCF World Cup Finals; EC European Championship; ECF European Championship Finals

Summary of Results
(up to and including 21 May 1997)

	P	W	D	L	F	A
Totals:	329	122	78	129	455	472

SOURCES

INDIVIDUALS
Brian O'Brien, Diarmuid O'Luanaigh, Billy Behan (RIP), Matt Giles, John Kelly, Cathal Dervan, Willie Cotter, Roman Hurkowski (Warsaw), Tamas Denes (Budapest), Jan Buitenga (Holland), Stig Forsingdal (Luxembourg), Cara Computers

NEWSPAPERS
Irish Independent, Evening Herald, Sunday Independent, Irish Press, Evening Press, Sunday Press, Irish Times, Cork Examiner, Evening Echo, Belfast Telegraph, Irish News, Football Pivot, Sport, Football Sports Weekly, Magill, Los Angeles Times, Gazzetta Dello Sport, Corriere Dela Sera

AUTOBIOGRAPHIES
Liam Brady, Mark Lawrenson, John Giles, Frank Stapleton, Eoin Hand, Mick McCarthy, Jack Charlton, Paul McGrath

TESTIMONIAL BROCHURES
Jimmy Holmes, Liam Brady, Kevin Moran

BOOKS
The Team That Jack Built (Paul Rowan, Mainstream); *Jack Charlton's World Cup Diary*; *Jack Charlton's American World Cup Diary*; *The Book of Irish Goalscorers* (Irish Soccer Co-op); *Gillette Book of the FAI Cup* (Irish Soccer Co-op); *Ireland on the Ball* (Donal Cullen, Elo); *Con Martin Annual*; *Irish Football Handbook* (Red Card, Cork); *Rothman's Football Yearbook*; *Sunday Chronicle Football Annual*; *News of the World Football Annual*

MANAGERS INTERVIEWED
Mick Meagan, Liam Tuohy, Sean Thomas, John Giles, Eoin Hand, Jack Charlton, Mick McCarthy

PLAYERS INTERVIEWED
Tom 'Bud' Aherne, John Aldridge, Paddy Ambrose, Eric Barber, Jim Beglin, Packie Bonner, Liam Brady, Shay Brennan, Willie Browne, David 'Babby' Byrne, Pat Byrne, Noel Cantwell, Tony Cascarino, Paddy Coad, Martin Colfer, Terry Conroy, Jimmy Conway, Dermot Curtis, Eamon Dealy, Miah Dennehy, John

Devine, Joey Donnelly, Charlie Dowdall, Christy Doyle, Denis Doyle, Tommy Dunne, Tony Dunne, Tommy Eglington, Sean Fallon, Paddy Farrell, Al Finucane, Jack Fitzgerald, Peter Fitzgerald, Arthur Fitzsimons, Mattie Geoghegan, Shay Gibbons, Don Givens, William 'Sacky' Glen, Dessie Glynn, Tony Grealish, Alfie Hale, Billy Harrington, Joe Haverty, Charlie Hurley, Denis Irwin, Roy Keane, Alan Kelly Jr., John Keogh, Alan Kernaghan, Joe Kinnear, Dave Langan, John 'Kit' Lawlor, Mick Leech, Charlie Lennon, Andy McEvoy, Paul McGee, Eddie McGoldrick, Paul McGrath, Gerry Mackey, Owen Madden, Con Martin, Paddy Mulligan, Ronnie Nolan, Tony O'Connell, Turlough O'Connor, Kevin O'Flanagan, Mick O'Flanagan, David O'Leary, Joe O'Reilly, Niall Quinn, Charlie Reid, Frank Stapleton, Steve Staunton, Alex Stevenson, Tommy Taylor, Peter Thomas, Andy Townsend, Ray Treacy, Liam Tuohy, Johnny Walsh, Mickey Walsh, Ronnie Whelan Sr., Joe Williams